Data  and Data
Analy... Research

Data Construction and Data Analysis for Survey Research

RAYMOND KENT

palgrave

First published 2001 by
PALGRAVE
Houndmills, Basingstoke, Hampshire RG21 6XS and
175 Fifth Avenue, New York, N.Y. 10010
Companies and representatives throughout the world

PALGRAVE is the new global academic imprint of
St. Martin's Press LLC
Scholarly and Reference Division and
Palgrave Publishers Ltd (formerly
Macmillan Press Ltd).

ISBN 0-333-76306-8

This book is printed on paper suitable for recycling and
made from fully managed and sustained forest sources.

A catalogue record for this book is available
from the British Library.

Library of Congress Cataloging-in-Publication Data
Kent, Raymond A.
   Data construction and data analysis for survey research / Raymond Kent.
      p. cm
   Includes bibliographical references and index.
   ISBN 0-333-76306-8
   1. Sociology—Statistical methods. 2. Sociology—Data processing. 3. Social
sciences—Research. 4. Social surveys—Statistical methods. 5. Market surveys—Statistical
methods. I. Title.
HM535.K45 2001
301'.07'27—dc21   2001036165

10   9   8   7   6   5   4   3   2   1
10   09   08   07   06   05   04   03   02   01

Copy-edited and typeset by Povey–Edmondson
Tavistock and Rochdale, England

Printed and bound in Great Britain by
Antony Rowe Ltd, Chippenham, Wiltshire

Contents

part II
ANALYSING SURVEY DATA:
CHOOSING THE RIGHT DATA ANALYSIS TECHNIQUES

part III

ANALYSING SURVEY DATA: KNOWING HOW TO HANDLE YOUR DATA

List of Tables

List of Figures

Preface

The idea for this book was occasioned by an uncounted, but certainly large, number of students (and in some cases colleagues) who over the years have come to see me and asked, 'OK, so now I've collected all my data, what do I do next?' or 'I've looked at a lot of statistics books, but I don't know which statistics to use to analyse my data' or 'I've used a set of 5-point rating scales, but how do I analyse the results?' or 'I've run off all these tables, but I've no idea how to make sense of them' or 'Do I add the neutral category to the agree or to the disagree group?' or 'What do I do with the don't knows?' or 'My sample is not really a random one, do I have to calculate tests of significance?' or 'Can I use a spreadsheet to analyse my survey data?'

This book is addressed to all these students – and to their tutors and supervisors who will no doubt appreciate having some literature that they can recommend. It should assist tutors and lecturers to give students some good advice. It might also help market and social researchers who have sought in vain for help on the 'nitty gritty' of analysing data from surveys they have undertaken.

The present structure of the book owes a lot to six anonymous reviewers who made many useful suggestions (although one of them did wonder whether I had recently had a disagreement with a statistician, given some of the jibes I had made at their expense in earlier drafts). Although I have toned down some of the comments, I could not bring myself to expunge them all, so I expect some flak from that quarter. If any of the reviewers read the final version of this book, I hope they will recognise that many of their comments have been taken on board. Needless to say, the reviewers did not all express the same viewpoint, so it was not possible to incorporate all their suggestions.

University of Stirling   RAYMOND KENT

The author and publishers are grateful for permission given by SPSS, St Andrews House, West Street, Surrey, to produce screen shots of a range of SPSS windows. This book is not sponsored or approved by SPSS and any errors are in no way the responsibility of SPSS.

Introduction

THE SCOPE OF THIS BOOK

This book focuses on showing you how researchers construct and analyse data derived from survey research, for example, in social or market research surveys, rather than how they analyse data from experimental studies or qualitative data arising from depth interviews, focus groups or participant observation. Survey data are usually mostly quantitative in nature, but qualitative data may arise from open-ended questions. The survey analyst must be able to tackle these data along with the more quantitative elements. While the focus is primarily on market and social surveys, the contents of this book would be of considerable help to those undertaking surveys in other areas such as politics, education, health care, leisure and tourism, sports studies and so on.

Despite providing the essentials of statistical operations, it is worth emphasising that this is *not* a statistics book in the conventional sense. Such books tell you how to calculate lots of 'gee-whiz' statistics, but not usually when, where and how to use them. Calculating statistics is, in fact, only a very small part of the survey data analysis process. Researchers need to begin by being clear about why they are using a survey in the first place, and how this relates to the objectives that the research is designed to achieve. They also need to understand what they can or should do with the data *before* they design their research, and then utilise that design in such a way that good quality data are entered into the analysis.

In order to be able to use survey analysis computer software packages effectively, researchers must appreciate (a) what sorts of data there are, (b) how they arise from the twin processes of measurement and scaling, (c) how to create a data matrix, and (d) what data transformations may be required before they even think about appropriate statistical calculations. The statistics themselves are pointless unless the data on which they are performed are of good or at least acceptable quality. 'Garbage in, garbage out' (GIGO) is a phrase that is commonly heard, but whose implications are seldom given the attention or credence they deserve. If the data going into the analysis are of dubious quality, then no degree of statistical sophistication can prevent the ensuing analysis being similarly suspect.

Many statistics texts assume that the data on which operations are to be performed involve some kind of unit of measurement – Pounds Sterling (£), tonnes, litres, number of vehicles and so on. Such data we will be calling 'interval' data. For a lot of survey research, however, many data arise as sets of categories – what we will be calling 'categorical' data. These require different kinds of statistics, sometimes called 'non-parametric' statistics, which tend to receive insufficient attention in most statistics books. In addition, most statistics books place great emphasis on what they refer to as 'statistical inference', that is, using probability theory to estimate the probable sizes of random errors when we take random samples. It is argued later in this book that such an emphasis is almost certainly misplaced when, for example, (a) the research is non-experimental, (b) there are many observations, but few controls, (c) there are several sources of error apart from random error, and (d) randomness is in any case difficult to achieve. The idea that researchers have 'tested' an hypothesis by conducting a significance test on it is a dangerous one, yet statistical inference is generally regarded as the only viable procedure for establishing scientific knowledge.

All or nearly all of the processes involved in data analysis are illustrated in this book using what is now almost certainly the most widely-used survey analysis computer package, the *Statistical Package for the Social Sciences* (SPSS). The initial design dates back to 1965 when some 7000 separate computer programs were integrated into a 'batch/command' data analysis system for use on a large mainframe computer. SPSS was later adapted for personal computers (PCs) when these became widely available.

After the introduction of Windows 95, a new release of SPSS (Release 7) was designed to run on this operating system with considerably enhanced graphics and tabular output. SPSS has been revised three times since with Releases 8, 9 and 10. This book uses Release 9 on the basis that Release 10 may not yet be widely available. If you have Release 7, 7.5 or 8 then there will be few differences between these and Release 9. However, Appendix 3 explains the key differences between Release 9 and Release 10. If you still have Release 6, the output will look rather different, but the menu structure will be broadly similar.

The illustrations of SPSS screens and output from Chapter 3 onwards are derived from a dataset arising from a survey which is described at the end of Chapter 3. The data are available on the Palgrave website. The address is given on the back cover of this book. They are saved as SPSS Version 7.0. If you have versions 7.5 or later, you should have no problem accessing these.

There are now many excellent texts on how to use SPSS such as by Kinnear and Gray (1999 and 2000), Foster (2000), Babbie and Halley (1998), and Bryman and Cramer (1999). However, this book is *not* an introduction to using SPSS. There is, for example, nothing on setting up the program, on file structures or operating the program. It does not take you through all the procedures available on SPSS. It only shows you how to use those procedures that, in the author's experience, are essential for those who are analysing the results of survey research.

There are, of course, statistics books that include sections on how to get SPSS, or Minitab or spreadsheets to calculate them for you. This book does not compete with these either. Rather it takes you through the stages you will need to analyse survey data, showing how SPSS can help you on the way, but also using SPSS output to help to explain the nature and role of selected data transformations and statistical operations. Each chapter introduces you to the general principles first and then explains how to use SPSS to produce your own results. The focus is on explaining the meaning and interpretation of the outputs from SPSS rather than going through the sometimes complex formulae on which the statistics are based. SPSS will do all the calculations in a few seconds, so there is no need to detail the laborious routines involved in calculating by hand. However, an attempt has been made to explain the principles or thinking behind various procedures so that you can see why they may or may not be appropriate to your purposes or research objectives.

This text will be of great help to undergraduate students of business, marketing and sociology who are undertaking class projects or dissertations that involve surveys. It will be vital for postgraduates who depend on being able to demonstrate that they can carry out an independent piece of research that ties marketing or social theory to empirical findings. Postgraduates, however, may need to supplement what is here by looking for more detailed explanations of factor analysis, cluster analysis, multiple regression or multi-dimensional scaling, but at least they should have the basics right. There are many excellent books on multivariate analysis, such as by Hair *et al.* (1998), which they can use for this purpose.

For a more general coverage of marketing research have a look at the author's recently published, *Marketing Research: Measurement, Method and Application* (Kent, 1999). Some teachers of statistics to students of marketing or sociology may take a little persuading that the approach adopted here should *replace* existing statistics courses, but students will benefit more by knowing how to handle their data rather than being baffled by the finer points of analysis of variance or multiple regression. I hope that, in time, this book will become a core text for courses in data analysis.

THE STRUCTURE OF THE BOOK

The book is structured into three parts. The first part deals with the process of constructing survey data in such a way that good quality data emerge. No amount of statistical sophistication can overcome the deficiencies in analysis caused by poor data. Data construction entails the two key processes of designing and then filling a data matrix. Chapter 2 considers what data are and outlines the general format of the data matrix. The remainder of the chapter explains in detail the key tasks to be performed in the design of a data matrix. This includes specifying the number and selection of respondents who are to constitute the rows of the matrix, deciding which variables are to form the columns, formulating the processes by which variables are to be measured, and specifying how responses are to be mapped onto a scale of values.

Chapter 3 explains how to fill the data matrix with good quality data. It essentially involves designing and executing the survey in a way that avoids some of the more common pitfalls. The data can then be entered into the matrix. This chapter concludes by introducing the dataset that accompanies this book. If, however, you have already collected your data and are wondering how to proceed, then you can skip Part I before becoming depressed about all the potential sources of error your data might already contain! While it may not be possible, at this stage, to 'turn sows' ears into silk purses', it will still be possible to salvage the maximum value that can be derived from the data you have by studying Parts II and III.

Part II turns to the process of analysing survey data and choosing the right data analysis techniques. This entails being clear about three things. First, what the researcher wants to do with the data, for example, display them, summarise them or draw conclusions from them. Second, on what type of scale the data are recorded; and third, how many variables are to be used in any particular analysis. Chapters 4 and 5 review what can be done by way of data display first for categorical and then for interval variables. Chapters 6 and 7 consider the process of data summary, again, first for categorical and then for interval variables.

Chapter 8 turns to the topic of sampling and explains how sampling error relates to other kinds of error that can arise in surveys. Chapters 9 and 10 show you how to make statistical inferences first for categorical and then for interval variables. Finally, Chapter 11 argues that testing hypotheses for statistical significance is only one way of evaluating hypotheses, and that discovered relationships still need to be explained using one or more of the three main forms of explanation outlined.

Part III is all about knowing how to handle your data in practice. Chapter 12 draws the threads of the whole book together by reviewing a range of strategies for things you may actually need to do with your data. Finally, Chapter 13 turns to the analysis of qualitative data from open-ended questions.

HOW TO STUDY THIS BOOK

The best point at which to study the contents of this book is *before* you begin your project. If you collect your data first, then ask 'OK, so now what do I do?', it is probably already too late to do a first class piece of work. Turning to this book at this point becomes more a salvage operation of making the best of what you have done so far. Ideally, you need to think about how you are going to analyse the data before you collect them.

For those of you with little experience of data analysis or statistical knowledge, I would recommend that you go through the pages that follow chapter by chapter. The book is structured in such a way that you are introduced to more complex material in a gradual manner. Do try (or at least think about) the exercises and points for discussion at the end of the chapters. Your tutor should have access to a teachers' manual that includes answers to the exercises and offers suggestions about the points for discussion. A good strategy for approaching each chapter will be to glance through the learning objectives at the beginning, then turn to the chapter summary at the end. After studying the chapter contents, read these again.

If you have already covered some of the statistics, then obviously you can skip the pages concerned or use them to refresh your memory. For those who have completed a statistics course, focus on Parts I and III, dipping into the other chapters in Part II on an 'as required' basis. You may in addition find it helpful to review the sections on using SPSS at the ends of the chapters and to have a look at some of the *Warnings* and *Suggestions* boxes. Even if you have completed a full statistics course, it is unlikely that you will have covered much of the material in Chapters 4, 6 and 9, which deal with categorical variables. However, the material in Chapters 5, 7 and 10 should be familiar. Chapter 11 focuses on evaluating hypotheses and explaining relationships and should not be overlooked. If you have already collected your data and feel confident about their quality and the basic procedures for analysing them, go straight to Part III, where you will find suggestions about how to handle missing data, how to analyse summated rating scales, what to do if you end up with too small a sample, and so on.

Every attempt has been made to produce a user-friendly text. I have tried to avoid the use of jargon, and technical material is explained in plain, ordinary language. However, where I have felt it necessary, I mention what the appropriate technical terms are in case you come across them in other contexts. Scattered throughout all the chapters are boxes giving either suggestions that should make life easier, or warnings that, if heeded, may avoid problems. At the end of each chapter you will find:

- a detailed summary of the chapter,
- a set of exercises that you should attempt,
- some points for discussion that could be used in class or might at least prompt you to think about some of the issues that arise in the analysis of survey data,
- some suggestions for further reading, which are briefly annotated,
- a list of references made during the chapter.

You can study this book and look at the illustrations without needing access to SPSS, although you will not be able to do some of the exercises. However, if you can try out the various procedures on SPSS as you go along and attempt the exercises, you will find it much more interesting and you will probably find it easier to understand some of the statistical operations.

THE SURVEY IN MARKET AND SOCIAL RESEARCH

Most of us in industrialised societies are familiar with social and market research surveys of one type or another. Few of us would be surprised to find an interviewer on our doorstep asking us to spare a few moments to answer a few questions on travel, television watching, or which brands of a product we have recently bought. Most people, then, will have an intuitive grasp of what surveys are all about: finding out what we think about given issues, what images we hold of organisations, how satisfied we are with their services, what we do in our leisure time, or other information about us. But what exactly *is* a 'survey', how did the notion of conducting social and market surveys begin, and what kinds of survey are there?

A survey in a general sense is any form of systematic data collection undertaken with a view to providing a detailed description and analysis of a particular topic. Social surveys and market research surveys possess the additional characteristic that they entail the systematic collection of data based on addressing questions to respondents in a formal manner and making a record of their replies.

Social surveys have a long history in Britain. They can be traced back as far as the year 1085 when William the Conqueror initiated an inquiry into the extent and value both of the royal demesne and of the land held by the tenants-in-chief. Commissioners were sent into every shire and the information, extracted on oath from the inhabitants, was written down and returned to the Royal Treasury at Winchester. The permanent record of this vast undertaking survives today in the two volumes of the Domesday Book. This survey, however, dealt mainly with economic matters. The earliest survey of social conditions was probably that conducted at the end of the eighteenth century by John Sinclair, an energetic and reform-minded Scottish agriculturist. He sent to the ministers of religion in every parish in Scotland a questionnaire of over 160 items covering the age, sex, occupation and religion of its inhabitants, and the number of births, deaths, suicides, murders, unemployed, paupers and habitual drunkards. (It all sounds very familiar!) The result was *The Statistical Account of Scotland,* which appeared in 21 volumes between 1791 and 1799. In the 1830s middle class members of the numerous statistical societies that sprung up all over Britain conducted house-to-house inquiries asking about and noting down the conditions and circumstances under which people lived. Some 50 years later Charles Booth conducted surveys of poverty on London. He recorded the economic and social conditions of some 4 million people in an attempt to discover the causes of poverty.

Market research came somewhat later than social research and began in the USA in the 1920s. The first independent market survey organisation was set up in 1919 by Percival White, whose book *Market Analysis: Its Principles and Methods* (first published in 1921), stressed the idea that markets were measurable and encouraged the use of surveys to research customers, distribution, sales competition, products and the company. The advertising world took up the practice of market surveying. The J. Walter Thompson Company (JWT) conducted surveys from 1922 onwards. There is evidence of survey research also being used in Britain in the 1920s, but it was not until the 1930s that the practice of research became established. The British Market Research Bureau (BMRB) was set up by JWT in 1933. In 1946 the Market Research Society was founded and over the next 50 years market research in Britain was to become a major success story. For a full account, see *Sampling the Universe* (McDonald and King, 1996).

Survey research involves bringing together three separate, but interrelated, roles:

- the client or principal on whose behalf the research is undertaken,
- the researcher who undertakes the research,
- the respondent to whom questions or information-giving tasks are addressed.

The role of researcher can in turn be subdivided into designer, information extractor and data collector. Together these roles entail the performance of a series of tasks that result in the construction of data. The roles may be performed by the same or by different individuals. In fact for student projects, the student often performs the role of both client and researcher.

SURVEY OBJECTIVES

Many surveys are occasioned simply by the need for administrative facts on some aspect of social, public or commercial life. A government department may, for example, wish to know how much people spend on food; a charity may have to document the living conditions of pensioners; a business may need to know how consumers switch between brands of toothpaste. Such surveys, as we have seen, were the first serious form of survey to emerge. The efforts of these early social surveyors have provided the basis for surveying large numbers of people at minimum cost, including the use of probability sampling techniques.

Other surveys aim at providing an accurate picture of the attitudes and opinions people hold as a guide to their likely behaviour. This kind of survey began in the USA where there was an overriding concern for public opinion and how that would translate into political and economic behaviour. The opinion poll and the market survey arose out of this tradition, which has bequeathed to us the techniques of quota sampling and public opinion surveys. Social psychological surveys use survey design and questionnaires to investigate personality by way of various kinds of attitude measurement techniques. Techniques developed by social psychologists such as Guttman, Thurstone and Likert are still used extensively today.

The main aim of both factual surveys and attitude surveys was accurate description. By contrast some surveys were more concerned with establishing cause-and-effect relationships and testing sociological or marketing theory. Mention has already been made of the attempt by Charles Booth to establish the causes of poverty in London. Others surveys might, for example, seek to assess the factors that relate to criminal activity and to determine which of these factors may be influenced by government intervention.

The above account of different survey analysis objectives obscures three different components that ideally should be clarified at the outset of any project.

The research problem, issue area or topic

This is usually spelled out in terms of one or more key concepts within a specific context. It is usually encapsulated in the title of the research, for example:

Does Culture Matter? A Cross-Cultural Study of Executives' Choice, Decisiveness, and Risk Adjustment in International Marketing
(Tse *et al.*, 1998).

Local Franchising Development in Singapore
(Goh, 1996).

Routes of Success: Influences on the Occupational Attainment of Young British Male
(Bond and Saunders, 1999).

Class Voting, Social Change, and the Left in Australia, 1943–96
(Weakliem and Western, 1999).

The research orientation

This outlines what the research is designed to achieve by way of an overall goal. Thus the research may be exploratory, descriptive, investigative, causal or some combination of these. Exploratory research is aimed at generating ideas, insights or hypotheses rather than measuring, evaluating or testing them. The survey, however, is not an ideal vehicle for such research and although researchers may refer to 'exploratory surveys' it is unlikely that they are genuinely exploratory in this sense. They may be exploratory in the sense that data are analysed without any prior notion of what the researcher is looking for. This approach to analysis is sometimes called 'data dredging' and is explained later on p. 200.

Descriptive research is concerned with measuring or estimating the sizes, quantities or frequencies of characteristics, but not investigating the relationships between them. In such research it is unlikely that hypotheses will be spelled out in advance of undertaking the data collection (Chapter 11 discusses when hypotheses should be formulated). Investigative research focuses on the extent of association or correlation between two or more variables, but does not consider the manner in which one or more variables may influence others. Causal research, by contrast, makes a distinction between dependent and independent variables and looks at the degree of influence of one or more independent variables upon one or more dependent variables.

The research content

This specifies the key variables that will form the focus of the research. These will often be contained within a series of research questions that the research is meant to answer or within hypotheses that it is designed to test, for example, 'Do general cultural differences significantly affect marketing decision making in terms of choice, decisiveness and adjustment of decision environment?' or, 'What are the experiences faced by local franchisors while trying to implement the franchise system?' The orientation of the first of these is clearly causal, while the second is exploratory. For investigative or causal research orientations, it is possible – if the researcher thinks he or she knows the answer to the question – to formulate hypotheses; for example, that general cultural differences *do* significantly affect marketing decision-making.

'Good' research questions or hypotheses should have the following characteristics. They should be:

- clear,
- understandable,
- unambiguous,
- specific,
- answerable/testable,
- interconnected,
- relevant to the research problem and the research orientation.

Spelling out survey analysis objectives in this way helps the researcher to do a number of things:

- delimit the scope of the project,
- give the project a direction and coherence,

- keep the researcher focused,
- indicate the data required,
- focus the analysis on those procedures that are relevant to the stated objectives,
- ensure that the analysis is comprehensive, making full use of the potential in the data,
- make the research efficient by being parsimonious and avoiding duplication of redundancy.

TYPES OF SURVEY

There are several bases on which we can classify different types of survey. We have seen in the previous section how surveys may be classified on the basis of their key analysis objectives and we can make a rough distinction between exploratory, descriptive, investigative and causal research, although in practice many surveys will combine various elements. Other bases on which surveys may be distinguished include:

- duration,
- topic,
- type of researcher,
- method of data capture administration.

In terms of duration it is helpful to distinguish between ad hoc surveys and continuous surveys. Ad hoc surveys are 'one-off' pieces of research that have a beginning point and come to a conclusion after a period of time with the presentation of research findings. The data that arise from such surveys usually relate to a single point of time or to a period of time that is regarded as a single period. Such data may be referred to as 'cross-sectional' data.

In contrast, continuous research takes measurements on a regular basis with no envisaged end of the research process. Its purpose is to monitor change over time. Some of this research actually is continuous in the sense that data collection takes place every day of the year every year. Other research, which may still be called 'continuous' is undertaken at periodic intervals. Most of the surveys run by the Office of National Statistics (ONS) like the *General Household Survey* and the *Family Expenditure Survey* are continuous in this sense. In the marketing field there is continuous monitoring of television viewing, radio listening, newspaper and magazine readership, cinema attendance and traffic past posters and billboards. A market research agency, the British Market Research Bureau, has since 1969 run the Target Group Index (TGI). This is a survey carried out at regular intervals and asks people about their use of about 500 different products covering over 4000 brands, their use of the media and their lifestyles.

Continuous surveys may produce two rather different kinds of data. Panel data refer to repeated measurements from the *same* respondents relating to different time periods; trend data, by contrast, refer to repeated measurements from *different* respondents relating to a number of time periods. Both types of data enable the researcher to talk about change, but only panel data allow conclusions to be drawn about change at the individual level. Trend data allow conclusions about change only at the aggregate level.

Alternatively, it is always possible to describe surveys in terms of the topic they are covering. Thus we could talk about consumer surveys, business surveys, household surveys, surveys of poverty or unemployment. In terms of type of researcher we can distinguish governmental surveys, academic surveys, surveys carried out by private organisations, market research agencies or surveys conducted in-house.

The most common way of distinguishing between different types of survey, however, is by way of method of questionnaire administration, so there are interview surveys, telephone surveys, postal surveys and surveys carried out over the Internet. Each method has its strengths and weaknesses. These types of survey are covered in most of the texts on market or social research.

Any one particular survey can be characterised in terms of various combinations of these dimensions. Thus one survey may be a factual survey that is an *ad hoc*, governmental, postal survey of business preparations for the single currency, while another is a continuous survey of attitudes to environmental protection undertaken by academics at a university using face-to-face interviews.

WHEN TO USE (AND WHEN NOT TO USE) SURVEYS

Not every piece of research in marketing, sociology or in related areas needs a survey. Many questions can be answered quite satisfactorily by means of desk research or by using some form of qualitative research. Part of the skill of the researcher is knowing when to use and when not to use surveys. To help you make your own decision, here are a few pointers to the strengths and weaknesses of survey research.

The main strengths are:

■ Substantial information from many respondents can be gathered over a fairly short space of time. For student projects this would normally be a maximum of about three weeks of data collection, but can be shorter, particularly for telephone surveys.
■ The results can be summarised fairly easily, particularly using a survey analysis package like SPSS.
■ The results can normally be generalised to the population from which the sample of cases was drawn, provided it is reasonably representative.
■ The search for patterns of relationships between variables is facilitated by the design of survey research.

On the downside:

■ While surveys are good for variable analysis they are less effective for generating understanding of the phenomena being researched.
■ The results may well reflect factors other than those being researched, for example, the time of day when it was carried out or the sensitivity of some of the questions.
■ The results can be fairly superficial and can be manipulated relatively easily.
■ There is considerable potential for error in the design and execution of surveys (see Chapter 3).

■ Some (or even many) of the respondents may not take the completion of questionnaires very seriously and while some of the misleading answers may cancel one another out in a large survey, others may not so there is considerable scope for bias.

On the whole a survey is a good idea if a considerable amount of work has already been done on a topic and it is possible to formulate hypotheses that the research can test before the data are collected. For exploratory research, surveys can be too trivial or too unfocused and qualitative research may be better. Always check that the data you are looking for do not already exist, otherwise the conduct of a survey may be a waste of time. Bear in mind that the results of surveys are seldom definitive or conclusive. They are more likely to provide just another body of evidence or a set of indications.

SUMMARY

The main focus of this book is on how researchers construct and analyse data from market and social surveys. The calculation of statistics is only a very small part of this process; more important is being clear what the analysis is trying to achieve and ensuring that good quality data go into the analysis. All the procedures used in this book are illustrated using SPSS Version 9.0, although the book is not a manual on how to use SPSS. Nor is it a statistics book in the conventional sense. The book is structured around the idea of a data matrix, and is organised into parts that deal with getting good quality data to put into the matrix, choosing the right techniques for analysing the data in the matrix, and knowing how to handle a number of practical issues that arise from survey data. Ideally, the book should be studied before the project is started, but it can still be used to considerable advantage if the data have already been collected.

Social and market research surveys have a long history and have been, and continue to be, used for a wide range of purposes and to achieve a considerable variety of objectives. There are many different types of survey, and it is important for the researcher to be clear both why he or she is using a survey in the first place, and what sort of survey would be appropriate to the research objectives.

Further reading

Diamantopoulos, A. and Schlegelmilch, B. (1997) *Taking the Fear Out of Data Analysis: A Step-by Step Approach*, London, The Dryden Press.
Besides having the two longest names in the business, these authors come closest to what is attempted in this book, but they do not explain the use of SPSS and they place rather more emphasis on statistical inference than I do. Nevertheless, to paraphrase a well-known advertisement, the book does exactly what it says in the title.
Kent, R. (1981) *A History of British Empirical Sociology*, London, Gower Press.
Sounds like a plug for me, but if you are interested in following up on the early history of social research in Britain, then have a browse through this one.

Kent, R. (1999) *Marketing Research: Measurement, Method and Application*, London, International Thomson Business Press.

Another plug for me. However, if you want to read about the different types of survey in more detail or you want to look at what is involved in the processes of data capture using questionnaires, diaries or recording devices and data collection using personal interviews the telephone or the post, then I recommend this one.

McDonald, C. and King, S. (1996) *Sampling the Universe: The Growth, Development and Influence of Market Research in Britain Since 1945*, Henley-on-Thames, NTC Publications.

A very readable account of how various types of market research developed in Britain.

In addition, these new texts on the conduct of survey research are valuable.

Fink, A. and Kosecoff, J. (1998) *How to Conduct Surveys: A Step-by-Step Guide*, 2nd edn, London, Sage.

Sapsford, R. (1999) *Survey Research*, London, Sage.

Thomas, S. (1999) *Designing Surveys That Work: A Step-by-Step Guide*, London, Sage.

References

Babbie, E. and Halley, F. (1998) *Adventures in Social Research: Data Analysis Using SPSS for Windows 95*, Thousand Oaks, California, Pine Forge Press.

Bond, R. and Saunders, P. (1999) 'Routes of success: influences on the occupational attainment of young British males', *British Journal of Sociology*, Vol. 50, No. 2, pp. 217–49.

Bryman, A. and Cramer, D. (1999) *Quantitative Data Analysis with SPSS Release 8 for Windows*, London, Routledge.

Foster, J. (2000) *Data Analysis Using SPSS for Windows, Versions 8.0–10.0*, 2nd edn, London, Sage.

Goh, M. and Lee, H. (1996) 'Local Franchising Development in Singapore', *Franchising Research: An International Journal*, Vol. 1, No. 3, pp. 8–20.

Hair, J., Anderson, R., Tatham, R. and Black, W. (1998) *Multivariate Data Analysis*, 5th edn, London, Prentice Hall International.

Kinnear, P. and Gray, C. (1999) *SPSS for Windows Made Simple*, 3rd edn, Hove, Psychology Press.

Kinnear, P. and Gray, C. (2000) *SPSS for Windows Made Simple: Release 10*, Hove, Psychology Press.

McDonald, C. and King, S. (1996) *Sampling the Universe: The Growth, Development and Influence of Market Research in Britain Since 1945*, Henley-on-Thames, NTC Publications Ltd.

Tse, D., Lee, K., Vertinsky, I. and Wehrung, D. (1998) 'Does Culture Matter? A Cross-Cultural Study of Executives' Choice, Decisiveness, and Risk Adjustment in International Marketing', *Journal of Marketing*, October, pp. 81–92.

Weakliem, D. and Western, M. (1999) 'Class voting, social change, and the left in Australia, 1943–96', *British Journal of Sociology*, Vol. 50, No. 4, pp. 609–30.

Constructing Survey Data

Getting Good Quality Data

Introduction to Part I

Before data can be effectively analysed, the researcher needs to be clear about how they were constructed in the first place. He or she must, furthermore, be satisfied that their quality is at least of an acceptable standard for the purposes of the research, otherwise the analysis will be of limited value. If garbage data go into the data matrix, garbage analyses will come out. Part I is about constructing survey data in such a way that good quality data emerge. Data construction in market and social surveys entails two key tasks:

- designing a data matrix,
- filling it with data.

Chapter 2 explains how researchers design a data matrix. It begins by considering what 'data' are in the first place and suggests that surveys in marketing or sociology produce mainly quantitative data. The key elements of all such data are outlined and the general format of the data matrix is described. The main thesis of Chapter 2 is that quantitative data are not 'collected' or 'discovered', but are constructed by individuals. Each individual will be pursuing his or her own goals, will operate in a particular social structure of competing interests and will manifest different levels of sophistication or competence. The key tasks to be performed in designing the data matrix are then explained in detail. The chapter concludes with a background discussion of the limitations of the way in which the so-called 'theory or measurement' is usually explained. This section can be left out if you wish to concentrate on the bare essentials.

Chapter 3 outlines what is entailed in filling the data matrix with good quality data. Essentially, it involves designing and carrying out the survey in ways that avoid various pitfalls, which are carefully explained, and then entering the data into the matrix. This is usually undertaken using a survey analysis package. The package used in this book – SPSS – is introduced along with the dataset that accompanies it.

chapter 2

Designing the Data Matrix

INTRODUCTION

We saw in Chapter 1 that market and social surveys entail the systematic collection of data based on addressing questions to respondents in a formal manner and making a record of their responses. But what are 'data', what different types of data are there, and how do they arise? This chapter shows how quantitative data are constructed by pursuing a number of tasks to be followed in the design of a data matrix. These tasks include selecting the respondents who are to provide data for the matrix, and deciding on the variables to be measured and then scaled. The chapter concludes with a background discussion of how the topic of measurement is normally approached.

WHAT ARE 'DATA'?

People tend to think of 'data' as things known to be true – as hard facts that are somehow beyond challenge. A dictionary will tell us that the word is a plural noun (although commonly treated as singular) and derives from the Latin word that translates literally as 'things given'. As far as researchers in the social sciences are concerned, the 'things' in question may be words, text, images or quantitative values that are 'given' in the sense of having been recorded. Table 2.1 presents what most people would accept as 'data'. However, if we ask how these data were produced, we might, for example, have to explain that they were generated from a survey undertaken by a market research agency with its clients'

Table 2.1   *Adult press readership by title*

Morning Dailies	Readership (000s)	Percentage of adults
The Sun	9717	21.4
Daily Mirror	7780	17.2
Daily Mail	4478	9.9
Daily Express	3777	8.3
The Daily Telegraph	2534	5.6
Daily Star	2448	5.4
Daily Record	1880	4.2
Today	1529	3.4
The Guardian	1285	2.8
The Independent	1064	2.3
The Times	1027	2.3
Financial Times	637	1.4
Total	38156	84.2

interests in mind. Furthermore, we might need to admit that the figures are based on a sample of 38 000 individuals interviewed over the course of a year and chosen to represent the entire adult population of the UK (all 38.2 million). The figures, therefore, are *estimates* generated from the sample. We would further have to admit that measuring newspaper readership is notoriously difficult and quite complex. Box 2.1, for example, outlines some of the difficulties and explains how newspaper readership is currently measured.

Box 2.1 Measuring newspaper readership

There have been major international symposia and many specialised seminars on the measurement of newspaper readership; scores of conference papers and journal articles have been written. Yet, for all this activity, experts and consultants around the world continue to debate the merits and drawbacks of alternative approaches and techniques. At the same time, advertisers depend on readership research to determine the allocation of their spend between the many different titles available. Readership estimates have become the currency in which advertising space is traded. Such data are also of relevance to editorial and circulation departments.

Measuring readership, however, is quite possibly more difficult even than measuring either television viewing or radio listening. Reading, for example, can mean anything from a cursory glance to a thorough study. Usually, it means that the reader has 'read' only those sections of interest and skipped or glanced at others.

Most readership research takes a complete issue of a publication as its focus of measurement rather than a section, a page or an advertisement. Personal interviews remain the favoured method of data collection since the number of questions that need to be asked is inevitably very large. In addition it is usually necessary to show visuals of mastheads or logos to help respondents to correctly identify publications. Since readership tends to be highly seasonal and subject to atypical events and circumstances, most readership research will be continuous, and as the use of panels tends to be too expensive, it will often be based on independent samples.

cont.

Box 2.1 continued

Readerships are usually measured in terms of what is called average issue readership (AIR) – the number of different people who read a single issue, averaged across issues. This measure has attracted some criticism – that it is a very bland measure, or that it seriously inflates estimates. It is based on asking respondents when they last saw a copy of a publication. If they claim to have done so in the last publishing interval, they are added to the AIR. The problem is that if the reader looks at the copy again outside the publishing period, then the reading event may be counted twice. This phenomenon of 'replication' can seriously inflate the apparent AIR estimate. The AIR estimate assumes that the number of people reading *any* issue of a publication – within a period of time equal in length to the interval between successive issues – provides an unbiased estimate of the number reading any specific issue, averaged over issues and measured across an issue's life. It has been argued, for example, by Brown (1994) that this is true only if it is the *first* time an issue is read, otherwise there will be biases from both replication and parallel reading. The latter arises if somebody sees two or more issues within a publishing period. Under AIR this will count only once and will underestimate the amount of reading. Replication and parallel reading will, argues Brown, tend to cancel one another out since they work in opposite directions and the overall model bias is very limited. The matter could be solved by adding another question (to each newspaper or magazine seen) concerning whether it was the first occasion and discounting it if it were not. That, of course, would mean considerably lengthening the existing questionnaire. It would also undermine trend data, since the new measure would not be comparable with the old one.

AIR identifies respondents as either readers or non-readers, but it is also necessary to estimate the frequency of reading. Again, this is very difficult to measure. It is usual to ask respondents about their claimed regularity of reading and to take their answers at face value. But, should we ask about actual past reading behaviour or what people 'usually' do? Should the alternative answers between which respondents must choose be couched in numbers, in verbal terms or in a mixture of the two? An example of a mixture would be: 'About how often do you see *The Economist* these days – frequently (three or four issues out of every four), sometimes (one or two issues out of four) or only occasionally (fewer than one issue out of four)?' There is a tendency, however, for regular readers to overclaim their frequency of reading and for low-frequency readers to underclaim (Brown, 1994). Consequently, it is better, argues Brown, to use the answers only to categorise readers into groups and no more (that is, to restrict the scale to an ordinal one).

At its simplest, data are systematic records. Such records, however, may come in very different forms. The historian likes to think of parish registers, diaries of famous people, or transcripts of what was said in the House of Commons as 'data'. A sociologist with a tape recorder studying women's emotional reactions to domestic violence, or participating in 'street corner society' and making notes of his or her experiences, likes to think that he or she is collecting 'data'. An anthropologist looking at some unusual, remote tribe of people, considers that he or she is generating 'data' by making records of experiences and observations. The archaeologist uses physical traces or remains as evidence or data on past events, conditions or social behaviour. The manager of a business organisation may think more in terms of sales data or information on balance sheets and profit-and-loss statements. The market researcher is more likely to see the results of a telephone survey or the record of a focus group discussion as 'data'.

Data may, in fact, consist of three rather different kinds of record:

- **words or text** – for example in audio tape recordings, interview transcripts, minutes of meetings, reports, historical or literary documents, personnel records, field notes, newspaper clippings,
- **images** – for example, paintings, sketches, drawings, photographic stills, computer-generated images, posters, advertisements,
- **the numerical results of the processes of measurement and scaling** – for example the number of males and females in a group or the size of a supermarket in square metres of floorspace.

Some records may be combinations of these, for example, video and film recordings. Even posters and advertisements normally have some text added. Words, text and visual images are usually regarded as 'qualitative' data while the numerical results of the processes of measurement and scaling are usually seen as 'quantitative'.

Market and social researchers spend a great deal of their time collecting *qualitative data*. These may be isolated words or statements made by respondents and captured by the researcher in response to a series of open-ended questions in a survey, as illustrated in Figure 2.1. Alternatively, qualitative research, which includes depth interviews, group discussions or participant observation, produces qualitative data as text or narrative that has been noted or captured on tape or video. Qualitative data may also arise from unstructured observation carried out by researchers, again provided the observations or experiences have been captured.

Since this book is concerned only with survey data, we will be considering only those kinds of qualitative data that arise in surveys. Chapter 13 deals specifically with this topic. Analysing qualitative data from qualitative research is very different and is a specialised topic on which there are already many excellent books, for example by Miles and Huberman (1994).

Quantitative data, by contrast, consist of numerical records. Sometimes these numbers refer to magnitudes or calibrations recorded in respect of an individual, a group of individuals, or an organisation. Thus a person may be 56 years old, earn £31 000 a year gross and be 5'11" tall. Sometimes the numbers are a result of counting the frequency of things, so a company may have 267 employees, own 6 factories and make 37 different products. Sometimes the numbers are just frequencies with which categories occur, for example, the number of males and females in a group, or they may be labels like your PIN number, your Social Security number or your room number.

Figure 2.1   *An open-ended question*

What is your opinion of the radio services offered by the hospital?

_____

_____

_____

Data arising from market and social research surveys will, for the most part, be quantitative, and, in addition, will have the following characteristics:

- they are derived by addressing questions, or information-giving tasks, to respondents and making a systematic record of their responses,
- they consist of sets of *values* recorded for a specific and identifiable number of *respondents*, each value relating to a particular characteristic or *variable*,
- the data are laid out as a *data matrix*, which records all the values for all the variables for all the respondents, as illustrated in Figure 2.2, which shows a screen-shot of the data with which you will be working from Chapter 3 onwards.

All quantitative survey data consist of the three components indicated above: respondents, variables and values. The respondent in a market or social survey is always an individual to whom questions have been successfully addressed (or who has been asked to perform certain information-giving tasks) and whose responses have been recorded in a questionnaire in a manner and to a degree of completeness that is acceptable to the researcher for the purpose of analysis. In short, respondents provide usable returns, which can then be entered as rows into the data matrix. Variables are the characteristics that respondents are responding about; they need to be measured and scaled in ways that are described later in this chapter so that they can be entered as columns into the data matrix. Values are what the researcher actually records and usually appear as numbers in the data matrix, as in Figure 2.2. They are selected from a scale of such values in a way that reflects the responses given by the respondent. The different kinds of scale are also explained in some detail later in this chapter.

Figure 2.2 *A data matrix on SPSS*

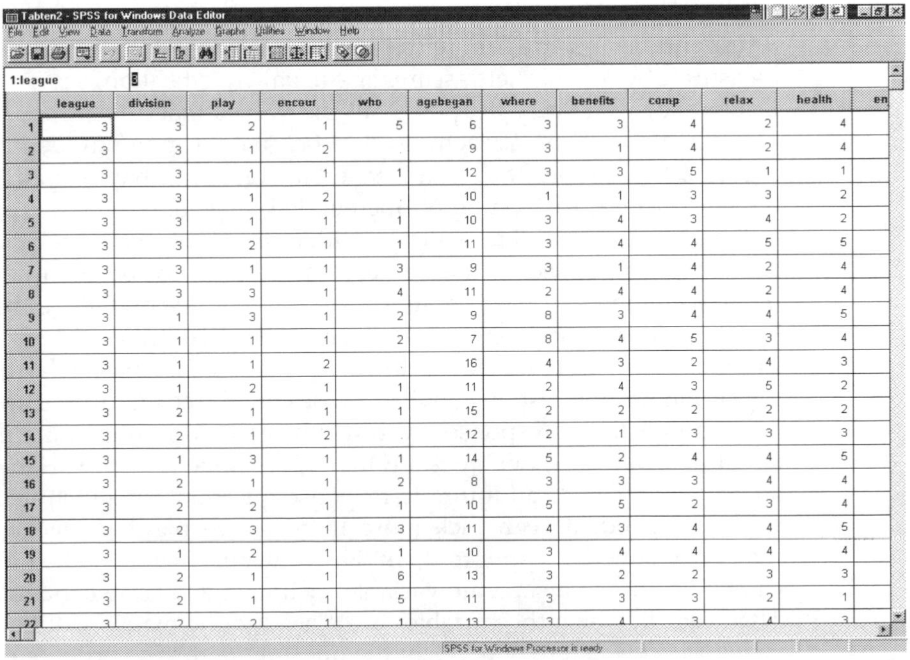

	league	division	play	encour	who	agebegan	where	benefits	comp	relax	health	en
1	3	3	2	1	5	6	3	3	4	2	4	
2	3	3	1	2	.	9	3	1	4	2	4	
3	3	3	1	1	1	12	3	3	5	1	1	
4	3	3	1	2	.	10	1	1	3	3	2	
5	3	3	1	1	1	10	3	4	3	4	2	
6	3	3	2	1	1	11	3	4	4	5	5	
7	3	3	1	1	3	9	3	1	4	2	4	
8	3	3	3	1	4	11	2	4	4	2	4	
9	3	1	3	1	2	9	8	3	4	4	5	
10	3	1	1	1	2	7	8	4	5	3	4	
11	3	1	1	2	.	16	4	3	2	4	3	
12	3	1	2	1	1	11	2	4	3	5	2	
13	3	2	1	1	1	15	2	2	2	2	2	
14	3	2	1	2	.	12	2	1	3	3	3	
15	3	1	3	1	1	14	5	2	4	4	5	
16	3	2	1	1	2	8	3	3	3	4	4	
17	3	2	2	1	1	10	5	5	2	3	4	
18	3	2	3	1	3	11	4	3	4	4	5	
19	3	1	2	1	1	10	3	4	4	4	4	
20	3	2	1	1	6	13	3	2	2	3	3	
21	3	2	1	1	5	11	3	3	3	2	1	
22	3	2	2	1	1	13	3	4	3	4	3	

THE PROCESS OF DATA CONSTRUCTION

All data, then, consist of records – but records that have been created, built, manufactured, in short, constructed by individuals. Data do not exist 'out there' independently of this human activity, waiting to be discovered like lizards under a stone or collected like so many butterflies in a jam-jar. The process of data construction, in fact, involves the performance of a range of different tasks often carried out by different individuals. These tasks can be grouped into three main kinds of activity:

■ deciding when, where and how the construction process is to take place,
■ actually capturing the data by creating a record,
■ assembling the data into their 'raw data' format.

Ideally the whole process of data construction should be logical, rational and systematic – a bit like building a house, brick by brick, following a careful design. To say that we 'construct' data does not, however, imply any kind of 'manipulation', 'fiddling', 'lies' or 'media spin'. Above all, the process needs to be transparent, so it is important to be clear about exactly what each activity involves.

For survey research, these tasks boil down to two main kinds of activity: designing a data matrix and then filling it with data. The next two sections look first at the format of the data matrix and then at the specific task of data matrix design. Chapter 3 takes up the tasks involved in filling the data matrix.

THE FORMAT OF THE DATA MATRIX

A data matrix interlaces each respondent with each variable to produce a 'cell' containing the appropriate value, as illustrated in Figure 2.3, which shows the age, sex, social class and nationality of the first three respondents of a set of *n* respondents, so the first respondent is male, aged 26, is in social class C2 (as measured by the market researcher's usual classification, see pp. 229–30) and is British. For data entry purposes, all the values that appear as words or letters, like 'female', 'C1' or 'French' need to be given a code number, as illustrated in Figure 2.4. The topic of coding is taken up again in Chapter 3 and in Chapter 13, which considers the coding of open-ended questions.

The columns in a data matrix are identified with the variables that are being measured and coded in the survey, one column for each variable. Each value down a column will have come from a different respondent, and in an interview survey different interviewers are likely to have contributed to each column. For the most part, each variable will correspond with a particular question on the questionnaire: the responses will each be coded (see Figure 2.5) and the code that corresponds to the response given will be entered into the data matrix. In some situations, however, one question may give rise to several variables. This will be so, for example, for all multiple-response questions, as illustrated in Figure 2.6, where respondents can pick more than one response category or, indeed, as many categories as apply to them. Each category will be ticked or not ticked, so each gives rise to a separate variable each having a scale containing two values. The order in which the variables are placed in the matrix will tend to follow the sequence in which they occur in the questionnaire. The order is unimportant for

Figure 2.3   *A survey data matrix*

	Sex	Age	Social class	Nationality
1	Male	26	C2	British
2	Female	32	C1	French
3	Male	19	B	Spanish
⋮	⋮	⋮	⋮	⋮
n	Female	33	C1	British

Variables (columns) / Respondents (rows)

Figure 2.4   *A coded data matrix*

	Sex	Age	Social class	Nationality
1	1	26	4	1
2	2	32	3	2
3	1	19	2	3
⋮	⋮	⋮	⋮	⋮
n	2	33	3	1

Variables (columns) / Respondents (rows)

Figure 2.5   *A coded single-answer question*

How important is it to you that the leisure centre has
up-to-date equipment?

Very important   ☐ 1
Fairly important   ☐ 2
Not important   ☐ 3

Figure 2.6   *A multiple-response question*

In which of the following countries have you been on
holiday in the last five years?
(Please tick as many as apply to you)

UK   ☐ 1
France   ☐ 2
Spain   ☐ 3
Greece   ☐ 4
Turkey   ☐ 5
Italy   ☐ 6
Other   ☐ 7

analysis purposes, but such a sequence usually makes sense for data entry, otherwise it will be necessary to move about the questionnaire to find each variable.

The rows in the data matrix are identified with the respondents, one row for each respondent, which usually means one row per questionnaire. A row consists of a series of values that have been entered for each respondent. In an interview survey, each row will be the work of a single interviewer. Again the order of the rows does not matter for analysis purposes. Questionnaires are often entered in the order in which they are received. They will usually be given a number that will correspond with the row number. This means that if there are any queries about a particular questionnaire, it can be traced.

Suggestion

There may be some occasions when the researcher is interested almost totally in entities that are not respondents, for example, companies, organisations, societies. The information on such entities – in a survey – will nevertheless come from individual respondents. So, the rows in the matrix may be identified for example with companies, one row for each company. Provided there is one respondent for each company it does not matter too much whether we call each row a company or a respondent. If, however, there are several respondents in each company then it will be better to keep one row for each respondent and which company they come from will become one of the variables.

The size of a data matrix is a product of the number of respondents and the number of variables. Where there are many respondents and many variables such as in a large-scale survey, the data matrix will be very large. Thus an inquiry that has 200 respondents to a questionnaire survey with 100 questions will produce a matrix that contains (200 × 100) or 20 000 cells. Data matrices will have different shapes depending on the nature of the research. Intensive research will have relatively few respondents but many variables, whereas extensive research will have many respondents and few variables. An opinion poll is a good example of the latter where a large sample (of 1000 or so) are asked a few questions about voting intentions and party support. Usually, data matrices are rectangular – all the rows are of the same length and all the columns are of the same length. Some cells may be empty where data are missing for a variety of reasons which will be explored in Chapter 3.

The data matrix in effect chops up the complex social world of respondents into variables and recorded values. It takes the respondent's multi-faceted experiences, cleanses them of the looseness and 'fuzziness' that characterises everyday knowledge, and refines and classifies them into standard form. It involves translating complex information, views, knowledge, beliefs or attitudes of the respondent into something that is conceptually simple, that may appear as ticks in boxes and that can be subsequently entered into the matrix as a single item of value. Survey knowledge is produced by entering the responses as a row of values that profile a single respondent and then interpreting these entries in columns across respondents to produce distributions. To achieve this, the data matrix needs first to be designed. Exactly how this is done is a topic to which we now turn.

THE DESIGN OF THE DATA MATRIX

In designing a data matrix, the researcher needs to perform a number of tasks. He or she must:

- have a plan for the specification, number and selection of respondents to constitute the rows of the matrix,
- decide which variables are to constitute the columns of the matrix,
- determine how the variables are to be measured,
- be clear how responses are to be mapped onto a scale so that values can be entered into the matrix.

The specification, number and selection of respondents

The specification of the type of respondent may be undertaken either conceptually or pragmatically. Conceptually, the survey population may be defined in fairly general terms like 'all adults' or 'all adults aged 16 or over currently resident in the UK'. Alternatively, the definition might be much more specific, for example, 'motorists' or 'mothers with babies', or even 'motorists with a driving conviction who have held a licence for over 15 years'. All respondents must be a member of the survey population as defined and will have in common those characteristics that are used to define it. Pragmatically, the specification of respondents may refer to a current list like all members of a club or all telephone subscribers in a given area.

Warning

The respondents to a survey when they are being entered into a data matrix are frequently referred to as 'cases', 'units of analysis', 'observations' or 'subjects'. In a moment, we will be using the term 'case' in a different and more specific sense, and in Chapter 8 the term 'unit' will be used to refer to sampling units.

Government surveys tend to have large numbers of respondents, for example, the *General Household Survey*, which is undertaken annually by the Office of National Statistics, has a sample size of over 17 000 individuals in nearly 10 000 households. Surveys carried out by market research agencies typically have between 1000 and 2000 respondents. Student projects are more likely to be confined to around 150–300. How many respondents you need for your analysis is an issue that is taken up in Chapter 12. The number of respondents entered into a data matrix is usually denoted by the lower case letter n or the capital N. So you might see '$n = 365$' or '$N = 829$' at the foot of a table or in the text of a research report. In principle, the capital 'N' is used to denote the total survey population and the lower case 'n' to denote a sample. In practice, life is never that simple.

If we now introduce the term 'case' we can use this to mean *any* member of the survey population (whether or not they have responded; respondents may be seen as cases who have provided usable return questionnaires). Sometimes researchers attempt to obtain questionnaires or interviews from a total population of cases in which they are interested, for example, all members of a fitness club. Such attempts at a census, of course, are seldom 100 per cent successful so the 'census' will be incomplete. Some researchers will nevertheless regard the achieved number of cases as a 'sample' and will, for example, write $n = 412$ when in fact there are, say, 560 members. Strictly-speaking, our population is $N = 560$, but $n = 412$ is not really a 'sample' in the sense of being a set of cases selected at random to represent a population of cases. It is, rather, an incomplete census. Any calculations performed will, of course, be made on $n = 412$, but this does not necessarily signify that this is a random sample, or indeed that it is any particular kind of sample, or even that the researcher regards it as a 'sample' at all.

For a variety of reasons, researchers may not attempt to contact the total population of cases, but will take a representative sample that is to be used for the purpose of analysis and for making statements about the population from which the sample was drawn (the topic of sampling is taken up again in Chapter 8). Sometimes the researcher has a complete, accurate and up-to-date list (a 'sampling frame') of members of a population, such as a list of members of the fitness club. Often, however, the list is not complete or up-to-date, so the set of cases from which the sample is to be drawn does not equal the population of interest. So, now we have two 'populations' – the theoretical population of interest (some researchers will call this the 'universe') and the population from which the sample was actually drawn. This is what any statistician will mean by 'population'.

Sometimes the researcher's definition of the population is conceptual rather than operational, for example, 'all single mothers in the UK'. In this situation, the total number of cases may be unknown and there is probably no list, although there may be estimates. In a more extreme situation, the researcher selects cases from a particular list (or lists), but regards these lists as somehow 'representative' or 'indicative' of other similar lists. So our $n = 412$ members of a fitness club may be regarded as somehow 'representative' of members of fitness clubs elsewhere – maybe elsewhere in the city, elsewhere in the region or elsewhere in the country.

Researchers often draw a given number of cases from a list either using a randomised technique or a systematic method of selection (like taking every 10th name). The cases selected constitute the 'target' sample – the sample attempted. However, there is usually a fair amount of non-response (through refusals, non-contacts and so on) so the 'achieved' sample will usually be a subset of the target sample. To add a further complication, not all returned questionnaires or completed interview schedules are usable. Some may be discarded because, for example, the information given is inconsistent. So, the number of usable returns may not equal the achieved sample. Whereas we had two kinds of 'population', we now have three kinds of 'sample' – target, achieved and usable. Unfortunately, researchers often use the word 'sample' to refer to any of these somewhat different sets of cases.

The researcher now has a set of cases that represents the number of usable returns. These are the respondents whose responses we enter into the data matrix. However, not all of the respondents will have answered all the questions (for example because the question does not apply to them, because they refuse to answer that question, or because the respondent does not know the answer or forgets to answer). So, the number of respondents for whom values have been recorded will vary from question to question. Where no value has been recorded for a particular variable it is usually described as a 'missing value'.

Finally, although the researcher will now have a set of cases for each variable for which values have been recorded, he or she will not necessarily use all these values for the final calculation. Thus 'don't know' answers or neutral answers might be excluded from the analysis and become 'user-defined' missing values. If, furthermore, we use two variables for a table or a calculation, the set of cases will be based on the number of cases for which we have (and use) *both* pieces of information. Many of these sets of cases will therefore be some subset of the number of usable returns. How to handle missing values is considered in Chapter 12.

In short, the situation regarding the number of cases that are the focus of a particular piece of research is quite complex. There are few agreed uses of the term 'sample' or 'population'. What we have in practice in many pieces of research is a variety of 'sets' of cases, for example:

■ the total number of cases in which the researcher is interested,
■ the set or list of cases from which a sample is drawn,
■ the set of cases drawn from the list,
■ the achieved sample or total number of questionnaires returned,
■ the number of usable returns (the respondents),
■ the number of cases for which scale values are recorded for a particular variable,
■ the number of cases for which a particular calculation is made or a particular table is constructed.

Warning

Beware the situation when a researcher reports his or her 'sample' as the number of questionnaires sent out, but a particular calculation is based on a small fraction of that number when non-response, unusable questionnaires and missing values are taken into account.

Where the specification of the survey population is conceptual (so there is no list) or where the list that defines the population is large, it will be necessary for the researcher to make a selection of respondents. How this is done is considered in Chapter 8.

The variables

The next task in the design of a data matrix is to decide which variables are to constitute its columns. Variables are the characteristics or dimensions that respondents are responding about. Each variable takes up a column in the data matrix and may relate either to characteristics of the respondent himself or herself, or to characteristics of other people, social groupings, organisations or situations about which the respondent is imparting information or giving a viewpoint. Thus respondents may be asked not only about themselves – their age, their educational background, their use of the media and so on – but also about their families, their households, their networks of friends, their work organisation, the clubs and societies to which they belong, or what happens (or happened) on specified occasions.

Variables vary at a minimum between two values, for example, between male and female or 'yes' and 'no' in answer to a question. At the other extreme, variables may take on a very large – potentially an infinite – number of values. For example, if we record the amount of time it takes to pass through a supermarket checkout in minutes, seconds and even fractions of a second, then each shopper will have a different value recorded. There are many different kinds of variable, but as far as market and social survey research is concerned, there are two key dimensions:

- the type of characteristic being measured,
- the role or roles the variable plays in the research.

Type of characteristic

Characteristics that variables measure may be put into three broad groups:

- demographic,
- behavioural,
- cognitive.

Demographic variables measure 'factual' properties that tend to be fixed, slow to change or are beyond the ability of the individual to change at will, for example, a person's sex or educational background. Some may change slowly, for example age, social grade or income. Some may be subject to sudden changes interspersed with periods of stability, for example, marital status, family size or area of residence. While 'demographics' are normally thought of as pertaining to individuals or groups of individuals, organisations, too, can be measured in terms of a range of demographic features like the type of industry, size, age, profitability, growth and so on.

Suggestion

What are known as 'geodemographics' are based on the demographic composition or structure of a small local area or neighbourhood. All households and all individuals in a neighbourhood are given the 'average' characteristics for that area. These characteristics may be used as a basis for drawing samples, market segmentation, targeting, the planning of store locations, or, more recently, for database marketing. CACI Limited, an international firm of management consultants, was the first agency to develop a classification of residential neighbourhoods in a system it called ACORN (A Classification of Residential Neighbourhoods). This is based on the principle that knowing where people live enables them to be defined as living in a certain type of area, and hence are likely to have certain social characteristics, lifestyles, or buying habits that are of interest to marketers. CACI developed 38 neighbourhood types, for example, 'cheap modern private housing' or 'recent council estates'.

Behavioural variables may relate to what people actually did in the recent past, to what they usually or currently do, or to what they might do in the future. Typical measures in marketing, for example, relate to the purchase and use of products and brands like purchase/non-purchase of a product or brand over a specific time-period, brand variant purchased, quantity/size of pack, price paid, source of purchase, other brands bought, nature of purchase, and use/consumption of the product. These measures may, in turn, be used to generate calculations of brand loyalty, brand switching behaviour and frequency of purchase. If the research is a product test or product concept test, consumers may be asked about future behaviour, for example, likelihood of trial of a new product and likely frequency of purchase.

Cognitive variables relate to mental processes that go on within the individual and include attitudes, opinions, beliefs and images. Attitudes are relatively enduring likes or dislikes, preferences or other positive or negative evaluations of objects, persons, organisations, events or situations. While attitudes do not always correspond directly with behaviour, they are, by definition, 'predispositions' to act in particular ways, and hence strongly influence behaviour. This means that when attitudes of a large number of people are measured or estimated, then predictions about future behaviour can usually be made with some degree of accuracy.

Opinions are somewhat different from attitudes. They do not necessarily have a directional quality and may express feelings or views about what other people should or should not do in the world. Beliefs refer to what people think they know about social situations, products or communications, but which cannot usually be underscored by factual evidence, while knowledge refers to awareness or memory of such factual knowledge. Images are somewhat vaguer than beliefs, being representations in the mind of the character or attributes of a person, object or organisation. The measurement of cognitive variables is thus very complex and is considered in more detail later in this chapter.

Warning

The term 'attitude' is sometimes used in a wider sense than that described here to include all kinds of cognitive processes.

Role in the research

In terms of the various roles variables may play in research, we can distinguish variables being used as:

■ descriptors,
■ independent variables,
■ dependent variables.

Variables used as *descriptors* in a piece of research are not being studied for their relationships to other variables. Demographic variables in particular are often used (a) to provide a framework for defining and describing a range of characteristics of the respondents in a survey, (b) to serve as a basis for sample design, or (c) to act as weights or controls to ensure that the results represent the population correctly. Behavioural and cognitive variables, however, may also be used for such purposes.

Alternatively, variables may be used for the purpose of exploring their relationships to other variables. In some research the purpose of the study may be to explore the degree of statistical association or correlation between specified variables. Some researchers would probably regard this as 'descriptive', that is, describing the observed patterns. Going beyond description would involve examining whether some variables have some influence or impact on other variables, or even whether one variable 'causes' another. Variables treated as causes or influences are known as *independent* variables. Such variables may be seen as, (a) necessary preconditions for some outcome to happen, (b) sufficient by themselves to bring such an outcome about, or (c) just one influence amongst many, that is, they are neither necessary nor sufficient conditions. Variables treated as the effects or outcome are the *dependent* variables. These are the variables the researcher is trying to explain, understand or predict.

Behavioural, cognitive and some demographic variables may be used in any of the three roles in research. Some demographic variables, however, are difficult to conceive as being used as 'dependent' variables, for example, trying to 'explain' a person's sex or age! Some variables may be used in more than one role in a piece of research. Thus some demographics may be used for both structural and for analytic purposes, for example using age both to describe the sample of respondents and also using it to see how far it explains variation in one or more of the dependent variables. Some variables may be used as both dependent and independent variables in the same piece of research. Thus customer satisfaction may be seen both as a result of a customer's prior expectations about the product or service (it is a dependent variable) and at the same time as causing or influencing repeat purchase behaviour (it is also an independent variable).

Which particular variables are going to be used in a given piece of research is a decision that the researcher will make based on the survey objectives that have been already defined (review pp. 7–9 if you have forgotten what these objectives are). Remember that there will usually be a number of demographic variables in addition to those variables specifically mentioned in statements of research objectives, research questions or research hypotheses. A survey will typically have between about 50 and 200 variables, so there could be a large number of columns in the data matrix.

The process of measurement

In common with all scientists, market and social researchers must face the problem of how to go about measuring the variables that are at the centre of their investigations, whether they are demographic, behavioural or cognitive, or whether they are to act as descriptors, independent or dependent variables. However, unlike natural scientists, social scientists need in addition to contend with the fact that the subjects of interest – the respondents – are human beings, and that many of the variables which are the focus of their research have to do with the ways in which they perceive and define their own behaviour and with the ways in which they think. Furthermore, individuals do not always make willing subjects and may (and often do) refuse to answer questions put by the researcher. There is always some non-response in any survey and its implications for measurement are, as we shall see, far from clear or obvious.

Measurement is concerned with spelling out the characteristics or properties of respondents that are to be used as variables for a given concept. It is the process by which we develop our 'yardsticks', but before we can decide how to measure something we need to be very clear about what it is we want to measure. We tend to think about our experiences of the world around us in terms of abstract ideas, or concepts. Concepts are formed from numerous particular observations or events. Thus our concept of a 'bicycle' refers to generalisations we make about the characteristics that all bicycles have in common. We use this concept to decide when an object *is* a 'bicycle' and not something else. If we took our favourite mountain bike and put some motorised assistance on it, is it still a 'bicycle' or have we changed it to a 'moped'?

We use concepts not only to classify things, but to organise our experience of the world and maybe think about processes like socialisation or privatisation, about relationships between people (like hostility or friendship), or about groupings of disparate characteristics that we call 'social class' or 'brand loyalty'.

Before we measure we need to define the concept involved. This is often very difficult when there is no physical referent, and may still be quite complex even when there is. Some concepts like age have no physical or observable referent, but are nevertheless fairly easy to define because people probably understand the concept in more or less the same way. For example, if we said that age is 'the number of calendar years since birth rounded off to the last birthday', then most people would probably agree. If, however, we use a term like 'brand loyalty' we may need to spell out what we mean by it. We would need a conceptual definition that defines our idea in terms of other concepts, the meaning of which is assumed to be more familiar to the reader. So, we might define brand loyalty as 'the preferential attitudinal and behavioural response towards one or more brands in a product category expressed over a period of time by a consumer (or buyer)' (Engel and Blackwell, 1982). Such definitions are a bit like dictionary definitions which aim to capture the essence or key idea of a concept and distinguish it from other similar but distinct concepts. Box 2.1 outlines some of the problems in measuring something as basic – and apparently straightforward – as newspaper readership. Have a look at this if you have not already done so.

Even when we are clear about a concept, however, there will nearly always be several ways in which it can be measured. Take what appears to be the relatively simple concept of the size of a firm. We could measure size in terms of sales volume, sales value, number of employees (and how do we handle part-time employees?); or perhaps we should look at the value of the firm's assets, which could be gross, net, and maybe include intangibles like brand equity. We could even measure age in several ways: we could ask people their age in years, or in years and months, or in age groupings like 25–29. We could ask them their date of birth and make our own calculation, or ask them to show us their birth certificates!

The problem of how we get from concepts to variables is illustrated in Figure 2.7. The research concepts are illustrated as C_1, C_2 and C_3. Suppose a researcher is studying the relationship between customer loyalty, customer satisfaction and social class. C_1 is customer satisfaction, which is conceptually defined as post-purchase feelings of pleasure or disappointment (C_4). C_2 is social class, which is defined conceptually as persons sharing a common position in the economic

Figure 2.7   *The problem of measurement*

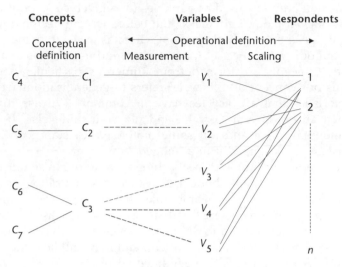

order (C_5), and C_3 is customer loyalty, which is defined, as above, in terms of two constitutive concepts, C_6 and C_7, namely preferential attitudinal response and behavioural response. Suppose now the researcher decides to measure satisfaction *directly* by asking a sample of customers (respondents 1, 2 . . . *n*) how satisfied they are with the product by mapping individuals into three categories of very satisfied, fairly satisfied and dissatisfied (V_1). The mapping of respondents 1 and 2 onto V_1 is shown. These respondents, along with all the other respondents, will need to be mapped onto all the other variables as well. This is a process called 'scaling' and it is discussed in some detail in the next section. Social class is to be measured *indirectly* by asking about the customers' occupational status (V_2). For customer loyalty the researcher uses three variables, V_3, V_4 and V_5. V_3 is image of the company, V_4 is image of the product and V_5 is the number of repeat purchases of a brand. These are to be added together to *derive* an overall measure of loyalty.

Notice that the lines connecting concepts C_2 and C_3 to variables V_2 and V_3–V_5 are dotted. These variables represent only one of many ways in which the concepts could be measured since the concept and the variable are not universally agreed to be the same entity. We cannot 'prove' that the variables we have chosen to measure the concepts are the correct ones. All we can do is gather evidence to prove that the variables are useful or meet specified criteria. These criteria are discussed later on pp. 208–10. In the case of C_1 we have *defined* customer satisfaction as stated satisfaction using the scale we have provided for V_1, hence the solid line.

The process of measurement may, in fact, be of four main kinds:

▨ direct,
▨ indirect,
▨ derived,
▨ multidimensional.

Direct measurement

Direct measurement is possible when one of two circumstances holds. First, a 'true' value, which is unambiguous (or relatively unambiguous), may be held to exist independently of the researcher's attempts to measure it and which is approximated by the value of the variable recorded. This may arise either because the characteristic may be observed, as in colour of packaging, or because some record exists which verifies the recorded value, such as a Birth Certificate. Second, where individual cognition or interpretations of behaviour are involved, the researcher may want a direct record of what these are and may ask respondents directly. In a survey the researcher might ask: 'How satisfied are you with the quality of the food in this café; very satisfied, somewhat satisfied or dissatisfied?' The implication here is that we have defined satisfaction in terms of self-reported levels of satisfaction. We are assuming a literal one-to-one (or 'isomorphic') correspondence between the concept and the recorded scale value. The concept is *defined* by the way we choose to measure it. We take what individuals say at face value and accept their answer as a 'true' record of their feelings. If a respondent says he is 'very satisfied', then this is the 'correct' scale value.

This is fine if, as researchers, what we wish to measure is perceived satisfaction, or perceived loyalty or self-defined social class. But different individuals will define satisfaction in different ways and what one person means by 'very satisfied' may not be the same as another person giving apparently the 'same' answer. Furthermore, for various reasons, the respondent may give a 'wrong' answer, for example because he or she has incorrect recall, has misinformation, is exaggerating or fabricating. The respondent's answers are also likely to be affected by mood, situational factors, willingness or reluctance to impart feelings or information, the wording of the question, the way it was addressed, or the understanding of the question.

In these circumstances, researchers may seek a more 'objective' measure – one that tries to take measures that are comparable across respondents. There are two possibilities: first, the researcher may take some kind of indirect indicator of the concept he or she is trying to measure or, second, the researcher may derive a measure from the combination of two or more items.

Indirect measurement

Indirect measurement entails taking an indicator of the concept rather than the concept itself. Thus the number of defective products returned or the number of complaints received are commonly taken as indicators of customer satisfaction. When the bus company *Stagecoach* won the franchise to run *South West Trains* (SWT) in 1996, its chairman, Brian Souter, paid a visit to his new business. He was amazed to discover that *SWT* received 40 000 letters of complaint a year from passengers. *Stagecoach*, apparently received no such letters. Souter summarised his approach somewhat pithily: 'We judge customer satisfaction by the number of bricks we get through the window'. Occupation is commonly taken as an indicator of social class (as with variable V_2 in Figure 2.7) and repeat purchase is taken as an indicator of brand loyalty.

Indirect measurement assumes that there is a degree of correspondence between the concept and the indicator deployed, but recognises that the indicator is not the concept itself, but only a reflection of it. Such measurement depends on the presumed relationships between observations and the concept of interest. It has been described as 'measurement by fiat' (Torgerson, 1958) because the choice of indicator is usually arbitrary.

With concepts as complex as customer satisfaction, social class, or brand loyalty, asking just one question of respondents or taking just one measure may, however, be insufficient. Such concepts will have several if not many aspects or facets. It may be necessary in respect of many cognitive variables to ask several questions, each relating to a slightly different aspect of the item (or items) being evaluated. If this is the case, then we might need to think about using derived measurement.

Derived measurement

Measurement is derived when we conceive of a property as consisting of two or more dimensions that are used to create a new measure. The process of combination may involve adding up scores and then taking an average, it might entail subtracting scores to derive differences, or it may mean using more complex statistical techniques like conjoint analysis, regression analysis or structural equation modelling. One of the most commonly used methods of derived measurement in the social sciences is the summated rating scale. These are created by allocating numerical scores to responses for each item being measured. These scores are then totalled for each case. Suppose 150 respondents in a survey are asked to rate their level of satisfaction with five aspects of a service from very satisfied to very dissatisfied and scores are allocated as illustrated in Figure 2.8. Total scores can now be added up. The maximum a customer can give is 5 on each aspect, totalling 25. The minimum total is 5. These totals can then be divided by 5 to give an average score for each case.

A particular version of a summated rating scale to measure attitudes was developed by Likert in 1932. This is based on getting respondents to indicate their degree of agreement or disagreement with a series of statements about the object or focus of the attitude. Usually, these are on 5-point ratings from 'strongly agree', through 'agree', 'neither agree nor disagree', 'disagree' to 'strongly disagree'. Likert's main concern was with unidimensionality, that is, making sure that all the items would measure the same thing. Accordingly, he recommended a series of steps.

Figure 2.8   *A summated rating scale – customer satisfaction with service provided*

'How satisfied were you with the performance of our staff on each aspect of service when you last telephoned us?'

	Very satisfied	Fairly satisfied	Neither	Fairly dissatisfied	Very dissatisfied
Speed of getting through	5	4	3	2	1
Getting the right person	5	4	3	2	1
Politeness	5	4	3	2	1
Staff knowledge of products	5	4	3	2	1
Efficiency	5	4	3	2	1

Figure 2.9   *A Likert measurement*

Below is a series of statements that people have made about the call centre. Please indicate to what extent you agree or disagree with each statement by putting a circle around the appropriate number

	Strongly agree	Agree	Neither	Disagree	Strongly disagree
I get through very quickly	5	4	3	2	1
I always get the right person	5	4	3	2	1
The staff are not very polite	1	2	3	4	5
Staff know their products well	5	4	3	2	1
The staff are not very efficient	1	2	3	4	5

1. A large list of attitude statements, both positive and negative, concerning the object of the attitude is generated, usually based on the results of qualitative research.
2. The response categories are assigned scores, usually 1–5, but some researchers prefer −2, −1, 0, +1, +2. These may need to be reversed for negative statements.
3. The list is tested on a screening sample of 100–200 respondents representative of the larger group to be studied and a total score is derived for each respondent.
4. Statements that do not discriminate (that is, everybody gives the same or similar answers) or that do not correlate with the overall total score, are discarded. This is a procedure called item analysis and it avoids cluttering up the final scale with items that are either irrelevant or inconsistent with the other items. Correlation is considered later in Chapter 7.
5. The remaining statements, such as the ones in Figure 2.9, are then administered to the main sample of respondents, usually as part of a wider questionnaire survey. Usually the statements will be randomly ordered to mix positive and negative ones. The items in Figure 2.9 were generated by 'converting' the items in Figure 2.8 into a set of Likert items.
6. Totals are derived for each respondent.

There are a number of fairly fundamental problems with Likert – and indeed all – summated rating scales.

■ The totals for each respondent may be derived from very different combinations of response. Thus a score of 15 may be derived either by neither agreeing nor disagreeing with all the items or by strongly agreeing with some and strongly disagreeing with others. Consequently, it is often a good idea also to analyse the patterns of each response on an item-by-item basis. The analysis of data from summated rating scales is considered in some detail in Chapter 12.
■ The derived total scores are not in any sense absolute, so that a respondent scoring 20 is not 'twice' as favourable as another scoring 10. All we can really say is that a score of 20 is 'higher' than a score of 10 or 15 or whatever.
■ The screening sample and subsequent item analysis are often omitted by researchers who simply generate the statements, probably derived from or based on previous tests, and go straight to the main sample. This is in many ways a pity, since leaving out scale refinement and purification will result in more ambiguous, less valid and less reliable instruments.

▣ The process of summating the ratings is potentially imposing a number system that forces scale characteristics (see scaling below) onto concepts that may not inherently possess these characteristics.

▣ Such scales assume that individuals lie along a dimension from positive to negative when he or she responds to a 5- or 7-point rating scale.

In addition to these problems, the current standard format of Likert scales has been recently criticised by Albaum (1997), who argues that the standard five-point scale confuses two dimensions: the direction (positive or negative) and the strength of the attitude held. Thus a person may like or dislike particular changes in society, but may hold this attitude with varying degrees of intensity or conviction. The responses agree/disagree show direction, but when 'strongly' is added to these it implies intensity. Albaum suggests a two-stage process in which respondents are asked first whether they agree, disagree, neither agree nor disagree or have no opinion, and second whether they hold their opinion very strongly or not very strongly. The traditional one-stage format is likely to under-report extreme positions since they represent the 'ends' of a scale. The two-stage format, argues Albaum, is a better predictor of preferences and results in higher quality data. A major drawback to this procedure, of course, is that it will considerably lengthen any questionnaire.

How data derived from summated rating scales are analysed will be considered in Chapter 12.

Multidimensional measurement

Derived measurement creates a single total or mathematically-generated score – a unidimensional measure. Multidimensional models, by contrast, allow for the possibility not only that there is more than one dimension underlying a set of observations, but also that these cannot be summed or transposed into a derived score. Sometimes these dimensions need first to be identified and some statistical techniques like factor analysis are geared to this end (factor analysis is explained on pp. 129–31). Once they have been identified, there are two main possibilities. One recognises that each dimension is independent of the other dimensions and cannot be added together or transposed into a single score. Rather, a profile of each dimension is described separately in order to present a more complete picture. The other approach sees the respondents as being represented by a single point, but in three-dimensional or multidimensional space.

It would be possible to use Likert-type items for profiling by calculating an average across cases separately for each item, so that, for Figure 2.9, there would be an average score for 'I get through very quickly' and another for 'I always get the right person', and so on. There would be no attempt to add up scores for the five items. A more common way of obtaining a profile is to use a semantic differential. These measures were developed by Osgood et al. (1957) and were designed originally to investigate the underlying structure of words, but have subsequently been adapted to measure images of stores, companies or brands and attitudes. They present dimensions as a series of opposites, which may be either bipolar, like 'sweet . . . sour', or monopolar, like 'sweet . . . not sweet'. Respondents may be asked to indicate, usually on a 7-point rating where between

Figure 2.10   *A semantic differential*

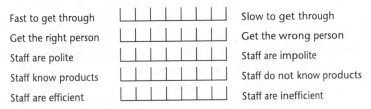

Please put an X at a point between the two extremes which
indicates your view about the service you receive from the call centre.

Fast to get through		Slow to get through
Get the right person		Get the wrong person
Staff are polite		Staff are impolite
Staff know products		Staff do not know products
Staff are efficient		Staff are inefficient

the two extremes their views lie, as illustrated in Figure 2.10. In most semantic
differentials there are three groups of adjective pairs:

■ an evaluation dimension such as 'good . . . bad' or 'sweet . . . bitter'.
■ a potency dimension such as 'strong . . . weak', or 'deep . . . shallow',
■ an activity dimension such as 'fast . . . slow', or 'noisy . . . quiet'.

Unlike Likert items, which may be classified into positive and negative
statements, semantic differentials may not be classifiable in this way, for
example 'bitter . . . sweet' – which is the 'positive' one? For this reason there may
be no attempt to add the items together, but to present them as a 'snake' diagram
as in Figure 2.11. The seven positions on the rating will be scored 1–7 (or −3 to
+3) and an average taken separately for each item across the respondents. It is
then possible to compare profiles of two or more brands, stores or companies.

If the items *are* to be added up, they must be clearly classifiable into positive
and negative and subject to an item analysis procedure on a screening sample as
for Likert procedures. In practice this is often not done, which, again, is a pity
because the potential for error is considerable.

An alternative to profiling is to locate each respondent as a single point in
multidimensional space. What is known as multidimensional scaling (often
referred to as MDS for short or as perceptual mapping) refers, in fact, to a series
of techniques that help the researcher to identify key dimensions underlying
respondents' evaluations. They attempt to deduce the underlying dimensions
from a series of similarity or preference judgements of objects, products, services,
organisations and so on made by respondents. The results are then presented as a
two-dimensional map, which takes account of the multidimensional distances

Figure 2.11   *A snake diagram*

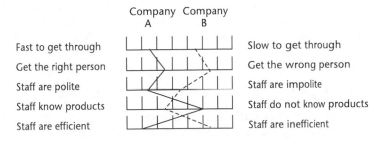

	Company A Company B	
Fast to get through		Slow to get through
Get the right person		Get the wrong person
Staff are polite		Staff are impolite
Staff know products		Staff do not know products
Staff are efficient		Staff are inefficient

between cases. The technique is highly specialised and is explained briefly on pp. 132–3, but for those interested in pursuing MDS, consult Hair *et al.* (1998).

Scaling

Scaling is a process by which researchers select a value to enter into the data matrix for a particular variable for a particular respondent. For example, we might enter the value 56 for the variable age for a respondent. The selection is made from a *scale* of values that represents a continuum or dimension on which responses can be located. The scale must meet certain logical requirements, which will be outlined later in this section. The selection is made on a basis that reflects the response given by a respondent, and must both be relevant to the survey research objectives and accurate as an account of the demographic characteristics, behavioural properties or cognitive processes of the respondent.

Warning

It is unfortunate that the word 'value' has many different connotations in everyday use – worth, goodness, usefulness, esteem, price, price in relation to quality or quantity, moral principles or standards. In most sciences 'value' stands for the exact amount of a variable quantity in a particular case. In the social sciences it would include, besides an exact amount, a clearly defined category or classification of an object, person, organisation or group. The word 'value' is used in this book to mean what we actually record in the process of record-keeping. We might, indeed, record an exact amount, like 56 743 employees; alternatively, we might record as a value a category like 'yes', 'male', 'very dissatisfied' or 'strongly agree'. It is possible, of course, to assign a number to these categories, so we allocate 1 = yes, 2 = no and 3 = don't know. Most survey analysis packages such as SPSS require that all values are given a number before they can be entered. The verbal descriptions of the allocated numbers are usually referred to as 'value labels', making it clear that we are using the numbers only as labels, not as an exact amount of a variable quantity.

There are, in fact, many different types of scale into which values of the variables may be recorded. A fundamental distinction is between scales that are sets of values that are recorded into categories like 'very satisfied', 'strongly disagree', 'large', 'male' or 'strawberry flavour' and scales that arise from a process of calibration or counting. The first type we will call *categorical* scales and the second type *interval* scales. With the latter type of scale there may be some kind of metric like money in Pounds Sterling or US Dollars, or age in years with which we can calibrate the size of intervals between values. Alternatively, we can count up the number of individuals, objects or events as a measure of size, like taking the number of employees as a measure of organisational size, and treating that as our metric. There are, in fact, several different kinds of categorical scale and two main kinds of interval scale. It is to these that we now turn.

Categorical scales

Categorical scales are sets of scale values that at a minimum meet three criteria:

- they are exhaustive of all the possibilities,
- they are mutually exclusive, that is, non-overlapping,
- they refer to a single dimension.

The first criterion means that all the observations that we make must fit somewhere on the scale. To make a set of values exhaustive, it is sometimes necessary to have an 'other' category for observations that do not fit into any of the scale values specified, for example, the answers to the question, 'For which of the following purposes do you mostly use cooking fat?' may be categorised into:

Deep frying	☐	1
Shallow frying	☐	2
Roasting	☐	3
Pastry making	☐	4
Other uses	☐	5
(please specify)		

By adding the 'other uses' category, the set of values is now exhaustive of all the possibilities and there is no answer that cannot be put into a category.

The second criterion means that all observations should fit into one and only one category. If the set of categories is overlapping, then the value of measurements taken is severely limited. Consider the following set of categories for Region of Head Office:

- England,
- Wales,
- Scotland,
- Northern Ireland,
- London and the South East.

An office in or around London will get counted twice, once in England and once in London, making analyses of head office location statistics dubious, to say the least. Such a scale would thus be exhaustive, but not mutually exclusive. In short, exhaustiveness and mutual exclusivity have to be achieved – they do not arise automatically.

All scales, whether categorical or interval, must be *unidimensional*, that is, there must be a single dimension along which the scale values vary. If we classify yoghurt into strawberry, raspberry, blackcurrant, fruits of the forest and so on, the underlying dimension is fairly clear. However, many marketing people, for example, make a distinction between different types of consumer goods into:

- convenience goods,
- shopping goods,
- speciality goods.

Quite apart from the fact that these categories may be overlapping for many products, there are two very different dimensions implicit here. One refers to the degree of search behaviour involved in selecting a brand (convenience goods versus shopping goods), while the third category, speciality goods, has more to do with brand loyalty. The fact that more than one dimension is being referred to is not always obvious.

There is no 'test' or measure of dimensionality for single variables. We have to rely on our intuitive understanding of the concepts involved to be clear about what the underlying dimension is. All the extant literature on dimensionality concerns itself with derived measurement where we are combining two or more variables. Here the issue is whether or not there is a single underlying continuum which all the variables being added together, or otherwise mathematically connected, reflect. If this is so, then the cases can be represented by points along a single dimension through a process of addition, subtraction or other mathematical procedure that generates a single final score, value or index.

Warning

A dimension is different from a variable in that it is a construct – it is a result of the derivation process, whereas a variable is the recorded or measured characteristic. Being a construct means that the dimension is not directly observable, so proof of unidimensionality is not always easy to obtain. The concept of dimensionality in this context is, in fact, quite complex, largely because the substantive and technical meaning of the term is specific to the particular scaling model being used. Thus in the Likert measures previously described, it is assumed that unidimensionality is achieved through item analysis. Thus items that correlate with the total score are assumed to be measuring the same dimension. This may not be the case, however, where there are several subsets of inter-correlated items and each item appears to correlate with the total score, but in fact is related to only a subset of items in the scale. In other models, unidimensionality is determined from the way in which scale items correlate with each other.

Once exhaustiveness, mutual exclusivity and unidimensionalty have been established, a number of different sub-types of categorical scale can arise. At the most basic level we can assign a unique number, letter or other symbol to each respondent like registration number, payroll number, Social Security number or hotel room number. Each number is unique: it identifies one particular respondent and there are as many scale values as there are respondents. The set of numbers used will, however, be both exhaustive and mutually exclusive. The scale values, although they often appear as numbers (they may also be a mixture of numbers and letters like car registrations), are being used solely for identification – as labels. So we can call these *labelling* scales. Statistically, we can do very little with labelling scales. We cannot add up the values; in fact we cannot summarise them in any way by drawing graphs or creating summary tables. We might be able to group them in some way, like taking student registration numbers and grouping them by year of entry. This transformation of the data would, however, create a different kind of scale.

Some people would argue that labelling scales are not really 'scales' at all since they do not classify cases in terms of equivalence or non-equivalence. The simplest form of scale that does this is the *binary* scale where there are just two categories, one for cases that possess a characteristic and one for cases that do not. There are many examples of these scales in social and market research – in poverty/not in poverty; employed/unemployed; married/not married; purchased a particular brand in the last seven days/did not do so; answered yes/no to a question; male/female. To make these proper binary scales we would assign the number one to those cases that possess the characteristic and zero to those that do not. Binary scales (which are sometimes called 'dichotomies', but that sounds like a painful Victorian operation!) have interesting statistical properties not possessed by scales which have three or more categories. We can, for example, use them as proportions by taking the proportion possessing a characteristic as opposed to the proportion not possessing it. We can also use the binomial distribution, which is based on the probability of 'success' and 'failure' in a specified number of trials.

Where there are three or more categories into which cases are classified, but there is no implied order in the way categories are listed, then we have a *nominal* scale. However, some researchers would consider binary scales as just a special form of nominal scale. Others treat binary scales as having special characteristics that make considerations of the 'level' of measurement inappropriate, since, for example, we cannot put two values 'out of order', nor can we compare the 'distances' between two values with other distances. The main feature of nominal scales (and the illustration of the uses of cooking fat is a good example) is that the ordering of the listing makes no difference to any statistical operations we might perform on the data.

Some sets of scale values define the relationships between the scale values not only in terms of equivalence, but also in terms of order. This means we can define the relationships between scale values in terms of greater than and less than, although there is no metric that will indicate by how much. Thus if we classify product usage into 'Heavy', 'Medium', 'Light' and 'Non-user', then there is an implied order, but no measure of the actual usage involved. These are *ordinal* scales. Social class groupings used by social scientists and by market researchers are commonly used examples of such ordinal scales going from 'high' to 'low' social class or social status.

In ordinal scales there is usually a limited number of ordinal categories into which we map a large number of respondents. So we might map 200 respondents onto five degrees of customer satisfaction. However, in other situations it may be possible to rank order each respondent. In *ranking* scales each respondent being measured is given his or her own ranking. Thus 30 customers may be ranked 1–30 on the basis of their attitude scores to a supplier. We would normally rank order only a fairly limited number of people or objects. To rank order 300 people 1–300 would be rather cumbersome. Alternatively, respondents in a survey may be asked to rank order a number of items, for example, customers may be asked to rank seven brands 1–7 in terms of value-for-money. Ranking scales have particular numerical characteristics, however, which mean that special statistics can be applied to them, for example there is a special statistic for measuring rank order correlation between two ranking scales. This is explained in Chapter 7.

Warning

Many statisticians and writers of textbooks on statistics refer to categorical data as 'qualitative' data. This is a bit confusing because such data still involve numbers, for example the numbers of males and females who respond in particular ways to a survey question. Such data are very different from the qualitative data that for example emerge from open-ended questions. Even more confusingly, some statisticians will refer to each category as a 'sample', so a set of respondents divided into males and females will be called a 'two-sample' situation. Actually, I suspect that this is a ploy to obscure the fact that statisticians sometimes have to soil their hands with data that are less than the full, glitzy interval stuff.

Categorical scales may, in short, be labelling, binary, nominal, ordinal or ranking scales. The differences between them are important because the statistics we can apply to them differ, in some cases quite dramatically. What they have in common, however, is that there is no metric that can be used to gauge distances between scale values.

Interval scales

Categorical scales are sets of values that, while they meet certain criteria, do not possess any metric or unit of measurement with which it is possible to say anything about the distances between the scale values. Interval scales, by contrast, arise when there *is* such a unit of measurement or metric and the scale values represent the result of a process of either calibration using some measuring instrument, or counting the number of people or items involved as a measure of size. The metric can be units of time like minutes, days, weeks, years; it can be units of currency; it may be units of weight, size, distance and so on. Alternatively, the metric may be units that arise from counting numbers of people, objects or events taken as a measure or size or magnitude. Think about how we might measure the size of a car park. We could either measure the area in square metres, or we could count up the number of parking spaces it provides. The first procedure might give any value in square metres and fractions of a square metre up to however many decimal places required. The second method will produce only whole numbers or integers. In statistical parlance, the first is usually called a 'continuous' variable and the second a 'discrete' variable.

In summary, *all* scales must at a minimum be sets of exhaustive and mutually exclusive values that represent a single dimension. Sets of values that do *not* represent a metric and where there is, furthermore, no sense of order may be labelling scales, binary scales or nominal scales. Those scales that have no metric, but where there *is* an implied order may be ordered categories or ranking scales. Interval scales may be discrete or continuous. Figure 2.12 summarises the various scale types. This set of scales may themselves be seen as an ordinal scale that goes from low to higher levels of measurement. Box 2.2 illustrates tables that present data at each of these levels. Notice in particular that there are situations where

Figure 2.12 *Summary of scale types*

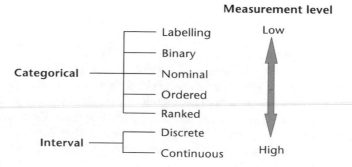

the distinctions between the various different types of scale are by no means clear-cut. Chapter 12 shows how, when we are analysing a data matrix, we may wish to transform the data in such a way that may upgrade (or downgrade) these scales before we undertake any statistical analyses.

Warning

Statisticians – or at least writers of statistics books – seem to get very confused about the distinction between discrete and continuous variables. Some argue that categorical variables, like sex of respondent, are inherently discrete, and so include such variables in the 'discrete' category. Others distinguish categorical variables from numeric ones, and say that only numeric variables may be discrete or continuous. Most books take the latter view and consider only what I have called interval variables in their treatment of statistics. Some, however, define discrete variables as numerical responses that arise from the counting process, while continuous variables arise from the measuring process. Others say that discrete variables are variables that can take only a limited number of values, while continuous variables can take an unlimited number. Some admit that the distinction is sometimes a little difficult to draw. For example, although it is not possible to have a fraction of the smallest unit of currency, it may nevertheless be treated as continuous since there are many possible values. Some admit that, because of the limitations of any measuring instrument and the consequent necessity of rounding at some point, empirical data always arise in discrete form, but that in many cases it is at least possible to *imagine* a continuous distribution.

Yet others will see the process of rounding off, or grouping into sets of values, like taking ages 20–29, 30–39 and so on to create a limited number of values, as creating discrete data. Many statisticians talk about discrete and continuous probability distributions. Among the former are included the binomial distribution and the Poisson distribution. Continuous probability distributions include the normal distribution, the t-distribution and the F-distribution. Oddly, while the binomial distribution relates to binary variables, they are still often regarded as appropriate for 'discrete' data, even though, apparently, only 'numeric' variables (as opposed to categorical ones) can be discrete or continuous.

There are two sources of confusion here. The first is whether we are really saying that the important point is whether the scale values are necessarily integers (whole numbers) or whether the number of scale values being used is very small. In practice, *both* these ideas really need to be combined so that the distinction becomes important only when the scale values *in principle* can only be whole numbers (like number of employees) and, furthermore, are few in number (for example, number of children in a household). If we create whole numbers for continuous variables by rounding off, that does not make them discrete. If the number of discrete scale values is small, then calculating an average size (for example, 2.47 children) may not be appropriate or meaningful. If the number of discrete values is large, then the distinction is not important.

The second source of confusion is the failure to distinguish between scale values and frequencies. The distinction between discrete and continuous applies only to features of the set of scale values – that they are limited in number and can in principle only be integers. To define discrete in terms of the process of counting confuses situations where, on the one hand, we count the number of instances as a numerical measure of size, and, on the other, where we count the number of times a categorical scale value occurs, for example numbers of males and females in a group. In the latter case, the scale value recorded will be either 'male' or 'female' and the number refers to a frequency; in the former case the scale value recorded will be the number of employees in an organisation.

Box 2.2   Some examples of the different types of scale

Data, at any of the levels of measurement, will normally be laid out as a table, so they will be illustrated here as tables, even though we have to look in more detail at tables and table construction in Chapter 4 for categorical variables and Chapter 5 for interval variables. Labelling scales will appear as lists of numbers against each case, as in Table 2.2. A labelling scale might appear in a data matrix that lays out the raw data so that each case is numbered 1, 2, 3, . . . n, or each case may have its own identity number such as a payroll number. Table 2.3 shows what a simple table of binary data would look like, while Table 2.4 illustrates nominal data.

Table 2.2   *Students by identification number*

Student	ID number
Ahern	985672
Brown	975539
Crimp	985792

Table 2.3   *Respondents by sex*

	Frequency	Percentage (%)
Male	138	44.5
Female	172	55.5
Total	310	

Table 2.4   *Respondents by ethnic group*

Ethnic group	Frequency	Percentage (%)
European	356	42
Afro-Caribbean	284	33
Indian or Pakistani	173	20
Other	39	5
Total	852	

Notice that with all of these tables we could put the categories in any order and it would not change the sense of the table. We need to arrange the categories in some way, even if it is arbitrary or random. Thus Table 2.2 lists the students in alphabetical order and this makes sense, while Table 2.4 puts the categories in order of the frequencies involved with the biggest at the top. However, changing the order say, to alphabetical, will not affect the interpretation, only its appearance. We shall see later that this means that any statistics we calculate on the data are unaffected by the order in which they are laid out.

cont.

Box 2.2 continued

Table 2.5 shows ordinal data – the categories are arranged in order of degrees of agreement with a statement. This is a natural ordering inherent in the meaning of the categories. Statistics appropriate for ordinal scales will be affected by the ordering of the categories. Table 2.6 shows six students who have been ranked according to their performance in two examinations in Maths and English. You can see that the rankings are very similar, and we could calculate a special statistic – Spearman's rho – to show how strongly the rankings agree.

Table 2.5 *Respondents' agreement with the statement:*
'This is a first class service'

Strongly agree	23
Agree	56
Neither	45
Disagree	78
Strongly disagree	12

Table 2.6 *Ranking of 6 students by performance in Maths and English*

Student	Maths, rank order	English, rank order
A	1	1
B	2	3
C	3	2
D	4	5
E	5	4
F	6	6

Table 2.7 illustrates discrete interval data whereby size of household is measured by the number of individuals in it. Finally, Table 2.8 shows continuous interval data in which the ages of respondents have been grouped into class intervals of ten years.

Table 2.7 *Household size*

Household size	Frequency
One person	45
Two people	68
Three people	74
Four or more	51

Table 2.8 *Age distribution of respondents*

Age of respondents	Frequency
20–29	46
30–39	58
40–49	69
50–59	44
60–69	31
70+	15

Remember that what characterises all interval data and distinguishes them from categorical is that we can add up the quantities involved. Thus we can add up amounts of money to get a total, or we can add up the number of employees in different factories to obtain a total of corporation size. Categories cannot be added in this way. This means that how we handle categorical data statistically is very different from how we handle interval data. Chapters 4–7 and 9–11 in this book treat operations we can perform on these different types of data in separate chapters. Chapter 4, for example, considers tables and charts for categorical variables while Chapter 5 reviews tables and charts for interval variables.

Warning ⟩ **Data, variables and scales**

Researchers sometimes distinguish different types of data on the basis of the kind of characteristic being recorded, so they might, for example, refer to 'demographic' data, 'behavioural' data or 'attitudinal' data. They might refer to different kinds of data depending on the kind of scale used, so there may be references to 'categorical' data or 'interval' data. Finally, they might distinguish data based on the role they play on research, so there might be 'descriptive' data, and 'analytic' data. Bear in mind that the words 'data', 'variable' and 'scale' are often used interchangeably, so some researchers might refer to categorical data, categorical variables or categorical scales.

Remember that survey data arise only when there are many respondents and we have recorded a value for each one. Variables arise from the process of measurement and may play different roles in the research. So we *can* refer to 'data', 'variables' or 'scales' depending on whether we wish to emphasise the numbers of respondents, the processes of measurement, or the requirements met by sets of values. Notice that we 'record' a scale value, we 'measure' a variable, but 'construct' data.

THE QUALITY OF DATA

Constructing survey data means designing a data matrix before it can be filled with data. We can now see that this is a very human activity that requires that a series of decisions be taken – decisions for which there is usually no scientific template for making the 'correct' decision. These decisions will, furthermore, be influenced by researchers' own wishes, prejudices and agendas, and by the circumstances in which they find themselves with careers to foster, deadlines to meet, or research grants to be obtained. Furthermore, they work within a structure of sometimes competing interests – there are the commitments and ambitions of the researcher's colleagues, the goals of organisational administrators, the objectives of clients and funding bodies, and the concerns of those to whom the data relate. Data construction thus takes place in a social, moral, political, economic and historical context.

We must remember, furthermore, that survey data are constructed using the medium of the respondent to obtain information. In most surveys the respondents are inexpert informants – they are members of the public selected often by chance or by using some randomised method of selection. They therefore cannot be presumed to possess any expert knowledge on the topic of the survey, but can relate only their own everyday knowledge or experiences of the world, or report in a non-expert way on circumstances or behaviours of those in their immediate environment. Respondents in surveys are selected for their representativeness, not their expertise, knowledge or ability to communicate with the researcher. Respondents may, furthermore, be addressed or approached in several different ways, for example in face-to-face situations by an interviewer, or they may be contacted by telephone, by post or by e-mail.

The quality of survey data derived from inexpert respondents – as measured by their relevance to the research objectives and by their accuracy in reflecting the world of the respondent – is very much more difficult to establish than for directly observed data. This is because many more factors can intervene to affect how good the data are. We have seen what some of these factors are in this chapter, and in Chapter 3 we will be looking at those factors that arise in the process of filling the data matrix.

Sometimes mistakes are made in the data construction process. Different researchers are likely to produce very different results, apparently from observing the 'same' things or events. Even government statistics are often based on questionnaire surveys, and, as we shall see in Chapter 3, there are many errors that can arise in this process. This does not imply that data are meaningless artefacts, but the implication is that few data are perfect and that data produced by research activity will vary considerably in terms of quality from one piece of research to another. We, both as data producers and as data users, need to judge this quality; but bear in mind that we probably cannot give any particular set of data a 'score out of ten' for quality. We would at least wish to give the data different 'ratings' on different dimensions, for example on accuracy, completeness, timeliness or relevance to the research objectives. Furthermore, the 'quality' of research data may be judged in different ways according to the perspective of the researcher or of the user of the data. According to one perspective, 'good' data have been collected using the correct scientific procedures; according to another, 'good' data help to solve problems, whatever procedures were used to obtain them; and according to a third perspective, 'good' data allow for complete sympathetic emotional understanding of social actors, buyers, sellers, volunteers, donors or whoever is the focus of the research.

Where measurement is derived from the combination of several scale items, then the 'quality' of such measurements is usually judged against two key criteria: reliability and validity. These terms are considered in some detail in Chapter 12, pp. 208–10.

BACKGROUND DISCUSSION: THE CURRENT 'THEORY' OF MEASUREMENT

What is taken to be the current 'theory' of measurement emerged in the 1950s, reputedly from the work of the physicist Norman Campbell. It has since been developed by social psychologists, but largely in the context of psychological measurement and the measurement of attitudes in particular. A consequence of this has been that most authors on social research and marketing research consider the topic of measurement within a chapter on attitude measurement as if attitudes were the only things that needed to be measured. In reality, *all* quantitative data arise from the measurement process, including not just attitudes (and other kinds of cognitive variables), but also demographics and behavioural variables.

According to the theory, measurement is the assignment of numbers to represent the properties of objects, people or events according to rules. These rules are cumulative and define four levels of measurement. The first rule is that the assignment of numbers represents categories that are distinct or mutually exclusive and which furthermore exhaust all the possibilities. So, if we ask people in a survey whether or not they are currently paying tax at the 40 per cent rate, we might allocate the numbers 1 = yes, 2 = no, 3 = not sure and 4 = won't say, then we have probably met the criteria of the first rule. This is usually called the 'nominal' level of measurement. If we add another rule that, besides being mutually exclusive and exhaustive, there is an implied order in the categories to which the numbers refer, then we have an 'ordinal' level of measurement. Thus if we ask people in our survey how satisfied they are with the service they have just received and allocate 1 = very satisfied, 2 = satisfied, 3 = neither satisfied nor dissatisfied, 4 = dissatisfied and 5 = very dissatisfied, then there is an implied order in terms of degrees of satisfaction or dissatisfaction.

A third rule adds to the other two rules that we can compare the distances or intervals between the categories. This gives us 'interval' measurement. Thus the difference between a temperature of 18°C and 20°C is the same as the difference between 24°C and 26°C, that is, two units of degrees Centigrade. A final rule adds that there is a non-arbitrary zero, so if we are measuring quantities of money in Pounds Sterling, then having no money is a meaningful (and possibly painful!) situation. By contrast, 0°C is an arbitrary point on a scale and we cannot have 'no temperature'. Having a non-arbitrary zero means that we can say, for example, the £20 is 'twice' as much as £10. In other words, we can calculate ratios and this level of measurement is accordingly usually called the 'ratio' level.

In short, according to the theory, the numbers we assign to the properties of objects, people or events progressively add identity, order, distance and origin to create four levels of measurement – nominal, ordinal, interval and ratio. The levels are cumulative so that ordinal scales possess the properties of nominal scales plus order. Interval scales possess the properties of ordinal scales plus distance, while ratio scales possess all the properties, including a non-arbitrary zero. This means that treating an ordinal scale at the nominal level is a legitimate operation, although it means throwing away information. Similarly, treating interval scales as ordinal is also legitimate, but information on distances is not being utilised. The 'levels' of measurement are, furthermore, themselves an ordinal scale going from low to high – from nominal to ratio. At the nominal level the numbers are used only to identify categories. They may be assigned arbitrarily and it does not matter if we assign 1 = male and 2 = female or 1 = female and 2 = male or even 26 = male and 39 = female. What we certainly cannot do, for example, is, if we take 1 = male and 2 = female and we have 60 males and 40 females, calculate the 'average sex' as 1.4! As we will see later, any self-respecting computer will happily perform this calculation for you: the trick is to realise that the result is total nonsense.

At the ordinal level, again we can assign the numbers arbitrarily, but they must preserve the order. So, we can assign the numbers 1–5 to represent the degrees of satisfaction, or 5–1, or 1, 3, 5, 7, 9, but to put 1, 5, 3, 9, 7 would be 'out of order'. As soon as we add distance the numbers we assign are no longer arbitrary, but must represent accurately the number of units of measurement that we are using. What we *cannot* do at this level is say, for example, that 18°C is 'twice' as hot as 9°C. To talk about ratios we need ratio scales.

This is the theory of measurement as it currently exists. It all seems nice and logical, even seductive, but, unfortunately, it is of limited practical value. Furthermore, it manages to confuse a really useful distinction that could (and should) be drawn between the separate processes of measurement and scaling. It also has to be said that many texts on statistics, whether on social statistics or business statistics, fail to mention even this theory. The focus is usually on ratio data and so-called 'parametric' statistics, even though the vast majority of data collected by social scientists is only at what current theory would describe as the nominal or ordinal levels. Some statistics books give the standard theory an airing in an introductory chapter and then proceed never to mention it again. Some make a passing reference to 'non-parametric' statistics and may give an example of one or two such statistics, but never a comprehensive treatment. Nominal and ordinal scales are often considered to result in 'qualitative' data and are thereby dismissed as inferior citizens, not worthy of further or detailed treatment.

So, what, then, is wrong with the current theory? Here are a few pointers:

- it focuses only on the process of scaling, not measurement,
- in terms of statistical analysis there are few differences between interval and ratio scales,
- there are, in any case, few examples of genuine interval scales – once a unit of measurement – a metric – exists, it is nearly always possible to conceive of 'zero' units. The measurement of temperature is usually the only example of an interval scale that is ever suggested, although it is possible to add calendar time, index numbers and some measures of attitudes that utilise rating scales,
- statisticians will tend to treat rating scales and various forms of psychological and attitude measurement as producing ordinal data,
- psychologists, sociologists and market researchers tend to assume that such scales produce interval or ratio data,
- there are other forms of scale that do not fit easily into the current classification,
- most discussion of measurement ignores a key precondition of all types of scale, namely, unidimensionality.

This list is by no means exhaustive, but it should suffice to show the limitations of the theory as it is usually presented. It should also mean that if you come across nominal, ordinal, interval and ratio scales in the literature you will know to what it is referring and you should have some idea of how the approach suggested in this book differs from it.

SUMMARY

Data arise from the human activity of systematic record-keeping. They are not 'the facts' or 'things given'; rather they are constructed by individuals for their own purposes within a structure of diverse interests. Data construction may be seen as involving the separate, but related, activities of designing and then filling a data matrix. Data come in different qualities, are judged according to different criteria and are of different types. A basic distinction is between qualitative and quantitative data. The former are non-numerical, while the latter arise as numbers. All quantitative data have a tripartite structure consisting of respondents, variables and values, and for the purpose of analysis of survey data should be laid out as a data matrix. The design of a data matrix entails:

■ specifying the type, number and selection of respondents,
■ deciding which variables are to be measured,
■ working out how each variable is to be measured,
■ being clear about the scales onto which responses are to be mapped.

Measurement is concerned with specifying the characteristics of respondents that will be used a variables. This may be achieved directly, indirectly, derived or treated multidimensionally. Scales are sets of values that meet specific logical requirements and may be categorical or interval. Categorical scales may in turn be labelling, binary, nominal, ordinal or ranked, while interval scales may be discrete or continuous.

Exercises

1. Think of the concept degree of religiousness. How could this be measured in a way that is (a) direct, (b) indirect, (c) derived, and (d) multidimensional?
2. Table 2.9 shows some summary results from the study of table tennis in Northern Ireland, which is the focus of the dataset included with this book. The background to the study is explained on pp. 68–9, but you do not need to read them to answer the questions below.

   ■ How many respondents are there?
   ■ What are the variables to which the data refer?
   ■ Which ones are demographic, which ones are behavioural and which are cognitive?
   ■ What kind of scale is being used for each variable?

Table 2.9 Some results from a survey

	Count	Percentage (%)
In which league do you compete?		
Bangor and District	46	38.3
Belfast	37	30.8
Greystone	30	25.0
Antrim	7	5.8
Total	120	100.0
In which division do you compete?		
first	38	31.7
second	41	34.2
third	36	30.0
fourth	5	4.2
Total	120	100.0
What sex are you?		
male	103	85.8
female	17	14.2
Total	120	100.0
How many times do you play per week?		
once	43	35.8
twice	52	43.3
three times	18	15.0
four or more times	7	5.8
Total	120	100.0
Social benefits		
unimportant	11	9.2
fairly unimportant	18	15.0
neither unimportant or important	41	34.2
fairly important	37	30.8
very important	13	10.8
Total	120	100.0

Points for discussion

1. Disraeli is reputed as having once said in the House of Commons (although he was quoting Mark Twain at the time) that there are 'lies, damn lies, and statistics'. Consider the extent to which the arguments put forward in this chapter give weight to this viewpoint.
2. If all survey data are in one way or another 'manufactured', are there any data that we *could* accept as 'the facts', as 'things given'?
3. Is the distinction between discrete and continuous metric scales any more (or less) useful than the distinction between interval and ratio scales?
4. Is direct measurement any more (or less) 'scientific' than indirect or derived measurement?
5. The unidimensionality of scales is commonly assumed rather than demonstrated. Why do you think this may be so?

Further reading

Bowers, D. (1996) *Statistics from Scratch: An Introduction for Health Care Professionals*, Chichester, John Wiley and Sons.
    See Chapter 2 on types of variables, which explains the different types of scales very clearly.
Churchill, G. (1979) 'A Paradigm for Developing Better Measures of Marketing Constructs', *Journal of Marketing Research*, Vol. XVI, pp. 64–73.
    For more serious/advanced reading.
Spector, P. (1992) *Summated Rating Scale Construction: An Introduction,* London, Sage.
    Covers all the basic ground on summated rating scales.
Traylor, M. (1983) 'Ordinal and Interval Scaling', *Journal of the Market Research Society*, Vol. 25, No. 4.

References

Albaum, A. (1997) 'The Likert scale revisited: an alternative version', *Journal of the Market Research Society*, Vol. 39, No. 2, pp. 331–48.
Brown, M. (1994) 'Estimating newspaper and magazine readership', in R. Kent (ed.), *Measuring Media Audiences*, London, Routledge.
Engel, J. and Blackwell, R. (1982) *Consumer Behaviour*, 4th edn, Chicago, Dryden Press.
Hair, J., Anderson, R., Tatham, R. and Black, W. (1998) *Multivariate Data Analysis*, 5th edn, London, Prentice Hall International.
Likert, R. (1932) 'A technique for the measurement of attitudes', *Archives of Psychology*, No. 40.
Miles, M. and Huberman, A. (1994) *Qualitative Data Analysis*, 2nd edn, London, Sage.
Osgood, C., Suci, G. and Tannenbaum, P. (1957) *The Measurement of Meaning*, Chicago, Univeristy of Illinois Press.
Torgerson, W. (1958) *Theory and Methods of Scaling*, London, Wiley.

chapter 3

Filling the Data Matrix

INTRODUCTION

The last chapter explained how to design a data matrix. In this chapter we look at what is entailed in filling the matrix with good quality data. Essentially this means that the survey must be designed and carried out in ways that avoid as far as possible some of the main problems that can arise. The data can then be entered into the matrix using SPSS or some other computing package.

SURVEY DESIGN AND EXECUTION

Anything that can go wrong with a survey is a potential source of error. While it would be a futile venture to attempt to discuss every possible pitfall, the discussion below selects some of the more common factors that can result in data being of a quality that is lower than can reasonably be expected.

Aspects of survey design that often cause trouble include:

■ the specification of the population of cases to be studied,
■ the frame used for the selection of respondents,
■ the design of the questionnaire.

Aspects of survey execution that sometimes give rise to problems include:

■ non-response,
■ inaccurate, inappropriate or incorrect responses,
■ interviewer error,
■ editing,
■ coding,
■ data entry.

Population specification

What is often referred to as the 'target population' is the set of cases that the researcher would, ideally, like to study. This should be defined carefully and should include:

■ a specification of the type of case which is the focus of the research,
■ the geographical extent or location of the study,
■ the time frame involved.

An example might be a study of 'all private motorists in England and Wales who have driven their own, a rented or a borrowed car in the last four weeks'. Any element in this specification that is left out will result in an incomplete definition of the population to be studied, yet it is surprising how many researchers do not specify their population very carefully and in some published research there is no specification at all. Ideally, too, there should be some statement or estimate of the numbers of cases involved.

Researchers sometimes specify an inappropriate set of cases from which to collect data. Thus the relative ease of contacting housewives has resulted in perhaps too much reliance on responses from this quarter. Many household decisions, for example, are made by husbands, working females or children, and treating the housewife as the key decision-maker, or even key informant on the decisions of others, may give rise survey error. A lot of published academic research involves taking students as cases for further study, presumably because they are at hand and are more easily persuaded to complete questionnaires or take part in group discussions, experiments or depth interviews. This is acceptable if the focus of the research is one that relates specifically to students, but all too often students are taken as a 'sample' of the general public. If the limitations inherent in doing so are explained by the researcher and the possible effects on the results are seriously considered this may be acceptable. What is certainly less acceptable is where the population specification fails to justify the exclusion of certain types of cases where these might reasonably be included, for example restricting a study to adults defined as 18 or over when the views of younger teenagers may well be very important. Sometimes a specification of the population is entirely absent from the report of research findings and the researcher just refers to his or her 'sample' without saying what it is a sample of.

Frame error

Even if the survey population is adequately specified, the total set of cases will, for most research, still need to be identified. This may entail using one or more lists. Suppose we wanted to study males who are currently in paid employment in Scotland who suffer from osteoporosis. How could we identify such a population? Since no lists currently exist, or are not accessible to the researcher, a total list – a 'frame' – will need to be constructed. Candidates for frames might include lists of businesses in Scotland, lists of General Practitioners, lists of hospitals, the telephone directories or the Electoral Registers depending on whether the researcher tries to identify cases at work, through Medical Centres, through hospitals, by telephoning individuals at home. Some of these procedures may be combined. The frame or frames chosen will, clearly, affect the quality of the survey results. Some of the frames will include large numbers of people who are not of interest to the researcher and will need to be screened out; some lists may miss out members of the survey population.

The frame plays a fundamental role when cases in the population are to be sampled (see Chapter 8). Probability sampling involves selecting a subset of cases from a finite set – a sampling frame – in a way that allows for the calculation of the probability that any one case will be selected. The sampling frame, as we saw in the last chapter, may not be identical to the target population, but will, nevertheless, constitute the set of cases about which inferences are made from the sample. Some writers have called this the 'inferential' population. To make life even more complicated, the researcher may make inferences about various sub-groups in the population, so there may be several inferential populations.

Ideally, the nature of the target population should determine the type of frame. In practice it may be the other way round. Thus a researcher wishing to study *people* who have been discharged from hospital over a period of time in a specified area, will find that hospital lists only consist of discharges, and people may have been discharged more than once or discharged in a different area or in a different hospital. So, the frame forces the researcher to study discharges rather than unique individuals who have been discharged within the time frame.

Constructing a frame may be one of the most difficult tasks the survey designer faces. The cost in terms of time and money in constructing the frame must be weighed against the gains in the efficiency and accuracy of the survey results. Deficiencies in the frame can (a) introduce error where the frame is to be used for a census, and (b) may cause bias in survey estimates when the frame is to be used for sampling. Frame errors may be grouped into six main categories:

- missing population cases,
- inclusion of non-population cases,
- duplication,
- failure to account for clustering,
- incorrect auxiliary information,
- incorrect accessing information.

Failure to include some members of the population of cases is probably the most serious type of frame error since it can be extensive, difficult to detect and difficult to measure. It is often referred to as 'under-coverage', 'non-coverage' or 'incomplete coverage'. Frames may, alternatively, contain cases that are not part of the target population, sometimes called 'over-coverage'. This is usually not too serious since non-population cases (and non-existent cases like empty houses or deceased persons) can normally be recognised. In some surveys under-coverage and over-coverage will tend to cancel each other out. Thus, in a population census, a person erroneously omitted from one enumeration distract may be erroneously included in another. The end result is 'net coverage error'.

Duplication of cases in a frame, such as will occur in the *Yellow Pages*, will, clearly, produce frame error for censuses and will undermine probability of inclusion calculations for samples. Clustering – the selection of cases within small geographical areas – may cause errors where frame elements include clusters of target population cases. This often happens where the researcher samples households, but households may contain more than one population target case. For censuses this may not be a problem, but as a sampling frame may well result in bias.

Incorrect auxiliary information is only a problem if such information is to be used for special sampling techniques, but incorrect accessing information will have the same effect as under-coverage since the result may be a non-contact. Thus a university wishing to survey its alumni may well have a full and correct list of names, but addresses may well be out of date or unknown.

It is often necessary to use imperfect frames for a survey. This may be a conscious decision in view of the time or expense of building a better frame. One way of dealing with the problem is to redefine the target population – the target population is simply considered to be the population that can be accessed by the frame. In terms of simplicity and cost it has a lot to recommend it – and it is not always a poor technique. Sometimes the result still enables the survey to obtain its objectives. A possible alternative is to add a rule that will identify missing population cases. Thus telephone directories will, by definition, miss out all ex-directory numbers. However, by adding a digit – usually one – to each number selected, the correct proportion of directory and ex-directory numbers will be included. Finally, it may be possible to integrate more than one frame to create a master frame that is more correct than any of the constituent frames. Failing these techniques, the researcher will just have to live with the frame limitations, warning the reader of some of the inadequacies.

Questionnaire design

There are many things that can go wrong in the design of questions and the overall design of questionnaires. These might include, for example:

◼ questions that are understood or interpreted in ways that the researcher did not intend,
◼ questions that people fail to understand or find too difficult,
◼ questions to which everybody gives the same answer, that is, do not discriminate,
◼ questions which give response categories that do not allow some respondents to answer in ways that are relevant to them,
◼ questions that do not provide sets of categories that are exhaustive, mutually exclusive, and which refer to a single dimension,
◼ questionnaires that have routings that leave the respondent 'stranded' in the middle of the questionnaire or lead them into inappropriate sections of the questionnaire.

Any of these problems will result in errors of various kinds and their extent is unlikely to be known. It has been shown many times over that the responses people give to questions is notoriously sensitive to question wording. However, answers are also affected by (a) the response alternatives they are given in fixed-choice questions, (b) whether or not there is a middle category in a rating scale or a 'don't know' filter, or (c) by the ordering of the questions, the ordering of the responses, or their position on the page. All the researcher can do is to minimise the likelihood of errors arising from poor questionnaire design through design improvements.

There are many excellent sources on questionnaire design, for example, Hague (1993), Evans (1995) and Oppenheim (1993). For the moment, bear in mind the following ideal steps in the process of designing questionnaires.

1. Review the research objectives. These should spell out what the research is designed to explore, measure or explain. If these objectives are unclear then think about them again before proceeding with designing the questionnaire – there is little point in doing so if you are not clear what it is meant to achieve. Review the discussion in Chapter 1 on survey research objectives. If the research is exploratory, the questions are more likely to be open-ended. If the research is descriptive, investigative or hypothesis-testing, then the key variables will need to be carefully measured and issues of scaling become important. The issues of measurement must be clarified before you proceed to designing questionnaires. It may well be, furthermore, that using questionnaires is only part of the overall research programme – keeping the role and purpose of these other aspects in mind will also be important.

2. Generate a list of topics to be covered by the questionnaire and think about the order in which they could or should be approached

3. Decide whether the questionnaire is to be self-completed or interviewer-completed. This will influence a number of aspects of questionnaire design. Think about the questionnaire from the point of view of the likely respondents – what is their level of knowledge and interest likely to be? Think about the likely interviewers if the questionnaire is interviewer completed. Will they be experienced and well trained? These considerations may influence your view on the kind of wording and instructions that may be needed. If you were thinking of interviewing children as respondents, think again! The process of interviewing children is highly specialised and includes many more pitfalls.

4. Think about how the data will be processed. If you are using a survey analysis package like SPSS you will need to be clear which variables you intend or wish to be interval and which ones categorical. If the technique of analysis that you intend to use presupposes interval data (for example, factor analysis) then you will need to design your questionnaire in ways that will generate such data. That means, for example, asking people for their actual ages and not in broad groups. It means that, if you are using summated rating techniques, you need to design your categories so that they can be assumed to have almost equal intervals between the categories. If you wish to use a package like Pinpoint, which allows you to design and print the questionnaire, then you need to be aware of the design possibilities and limitations of the package (see Appendix 2 for an introduction to the package).

5. Now you are ready to attempt drafting the questionnaire itself. Do not expect this to be easy. You may need several drafts, which you can do either on paper or directly into a package like Pinpoint. The advantage of the latter is that you can change things and edit as you go along, and you can always print off the latest draft at any point.

6. When your draft is complete, it is time for a bit of testing. First, try it out on some of your friends or colleagues and perhaps also on a 'pilot' group of respondents similar to those who will be used in the main study. The questionnaire is likely to go through further drafts before reaching its final form.

The piloting of questionnaires is frequently short-changed, but it is, however, critical for successful research. Once the questionnaire has been taken forward into the main data collection phase it is too late to make any changes. There are three main kinds of pilot study:

■ qualitative research amongst the target population to check language and the range of likely opinions,
■ pre-testing the questionnaire to see how it works,
■ a small scale pilot survey to obtain approximate results.

Many errors of design are often uncovered at the pilot stage, particularly if it has not been preceded by qualitative research, or based on questionnaires that have already been tried. Small-scale pilot surveys are often regarded as a luxury except for large projects.

Non-response

A source of error in virtually all survey research is non-response. It is seldom that all individuals who are selected as potential respondents are successfully contacted, and it is seldom that all those contacted agree to co-operate. In coping with non-response error it is difficult to appreciate all the many things that can go wrong with an attempt to contact a designated individual. Figure 3.1 illustrates a variety of outcomes of an attempted telephone contact.

Non-contacts are unlikely to be representative of the total population of cases. Married women with young children, for example, are more likely to be at home during the day on weekdays than are men, married women without children or single women. The probability of finding somebody at home is also greater for low income families and for rural families. Call-backs during the evening or at weekends may minimise this source of bias, but it will never be eliminated.

The contact rate takes the number of eligible cases contacted as a proportion of the total number of eligible cases approached. Interviewers may be compared or monitored in terms of their contact rates. Those with low rates may be required to

Figure 3.1   *Telephone survey contact outcomes*

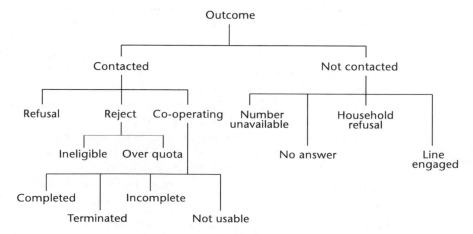

undergo further training if, on investigation, it appears not to be the result of working in a difficult area. Attempts have been made to adjust for non-contact bias by weighting answers against the probability of respondents being at home. The weightings are derived by asking respondents on how many days they were at home during the five preceding days. The answers of those who were less likely to be at home are given more weight than those who are at home most days on the basis that these are the ones likely to be missed out.

Potential respondents who have been contacted may still refuse co-operation for a whole variety of reasons including inconvenience, the subject matter, fear of a sales pitch, or negative reaction to the interviewer. The refusal rate generally takes the number of refusals as a proportion of the number of eligible cases contacted. Once again, refusals are unlikely to be representative. Refusals are more likely amongst women, non-whites, the less educated, the less well off and the elderly (De Maio, 1980). The detection of refusal bias usually relies on checking differences between those who agreed to the initial contact and those who agreed only after later follow-ups on the assumption that these are likely to be more representative of refusals.

Most researchers report a response rate for their study and this will normally combine the ideas of a contact rate and a refusal rate. However, in terms of its actual calculation a bewildering array of alternatives is possible. At a minimum it is:

$$\text{response rate} = \frac{\text{number of completed questionnaires}}{\text{number of cases approached}}$$

Some researchers will argue, however, that it is misleading to include those approached but found to be ineligible for the study as a 'non-response' so,

$$\text{response rate} = \frac{\text{number of completed questionnaires}}{\text{number of cases successfully contacted and deemed to be eligible} + \text{non-contacts}}$$

Yet others will argue that the same applies to non-contacts, terminations and rejects. The result will be dramatically different calculations of the response rate. Whichever of these is reported, however, what is important as far as error in measurement is concerned is the extent to which those not responding – for whatever reason – are in any way systematically different from those who successfully completed. Whether or not this is likely to be the case will depend substantially on whether or not there were call-backs and at what times of the day and days of the week individuals are approached.

The UK, as in most countries, has experienced a decline in response rates over the years. Meier (1991) reports that the 30-year trend between 1960 and 1990, as experienced by the National Readership Survey (NRS), shows a drop in response rates from 77 per cent to 62.6 per cent. Most of this is accounted for by an increase in refusals, which now accounts for 50 per cent of the non-responses. This is despite an increase in the number of call-backs made by interviewers from an average of 2.4 in 1983 to 3.4 by 1989. The NRS is generally regarded as a 'model' of sampling and survey analysis and its response rate is somewhat higher than many interview surveys. Thus even the Government's National Food Survey manages only just over 50 per cent. For mail surveys, the response rate is often under 30 per cent.

Apart from total non-response there will, in addition usually be item non-response where individuals agree to participate in the survey, but refuse to answer certain items. A refusal to answer is not always easy to distinguish from a 'don't know', but both need to be distinguished from items that are not responded to because they have been routed out as inappropriate for that respondent. All, however, are instances of 'missing values', which is a topic taken up in Chapter 12.

Researchers faced with non-response have a number of options:

- simply report the response rate as part of the findings,
- try to reduce the number of non-respondents,
- allow substitution,
- assess the impact of non-response,
- compensate for the problem.

Many researchers choose to report survey results based only on data derived from those responding and simply report the response rate as part of the results. This shows that the researcher is unaware of the implications of non-response, believes them to be negligible, or has chosen to ignore them. Non-response may not itself be a problem unless the researcher ends up with too few cases to analyse. What is important is whether or not those responding are in any significant ways different from those who do not respond. It has been argued above, however, that non-contacts and refusals are likely to be unrepresentative. In postal surveys typical response rate are 20–30 per cent and it is unlikely that there will be little or no non-response error.

The number of non-respondents can usually be reduced through improvements in the data collection strategy. This might entail increasing the number of call-backs, using more skilled interviewers, or offering some incentive to potential respondents. The effort to increase the rate of return becomes more difficult, however, as the rate of return improves and cost will rise considerably. Allowing substitution can sometimes be a sensible strategy in a sample survey provided the substitutes are selected in the same way as the original sample. This will not reduce bias from non-response, but it is a useful means of maintaining the intended (or needed) sample size. For censuses, substitution is, of course, not an option.

Assessing the impact of non-response calls for an analysis of response rates, contact rates and so on, plus an investigation of potential differences between respondents and non-respondents, and some model of how these relate to total survey error. There are various ways of checking for non-response bias. Researchers sometimes take late returns in a postal survey as an indication of the type of people who are non-responders. These are then checked against earlier returns. In an interview survey, supervisors may be sent to refusers in an attempt to obtain some basic information. Interviewers can also be sent to non-responders in a postal survey. Another technique is to compare the demographic characteristics of the sample (age, sex, social class and so on) with those of the population. If this is known, the comparison is relatively straightforward, although deciding on how 'similar' they should be to be acceptable is not clear-cut. If the demographic of the population from which the sample was drawn is unknown, then Census or other data thought to characterise the population may be used.

If differences are discovered then, again, this can simply be reported along with suitable caveats applied to the results. Alternatively, the researcher may try to compensate for the problem by using a weighted adjustment of responses. A weight is a multiplying factor applied to some or all of the responses given in a survey in order to eliminate or reduce the impact of bias caused by types of case that are over (or under) represented in the sample. Thus if there are too few women aged 20–24 in a sample survey compared with the proportions in this age group known to exist – for example, only 50 out of a required 60 are in the achieved sample – the number who purchased brand X in a measurement period of, say, four weeks, will be multiplied by a weighting which is calculated by taking:

$$\frac{\text{target sample number}}{\text{actual sample number}} = \frac{60}{50} = 1.2$$

This means that if, for example, this group are heavy purchasers of brand X, then estimates of sales of brand X will not be underestimated because that group is under-represented in the sample from which the estimate is to be made.

Response errors

Response error deals with differences between respondents' reported answers and actual (or true) values of a survey item. Actual values can be obtained only by external validation such as checking shelves in the household for items that have been reported as having been purchased, or through access to confirmatory sources like sales records, savings account balances, telephone bills and so on. Lacking any actual or true value, response errors arising through dishonesty, forgetfulness, faulty memories, unwillingness or misunderstanding of the questions being asked are notoriously difficult to measure. Research on response error, furthermore, is limited due to the difficulty of obtaining external validation.

Response error is affected by a large number of factors that will include:

- demographic characteristics of the respondent,
- perceptions, attitudes, expectations or motives of respondent,
- temporary situational circumstances,
- interviewer characteristics,
- interviewer–respondent interaction.

Both interviewer and respondent bring certain background characteristics and psychological predispositions to their interaction. The face-to-face interview and the telephone interview is an interactive process with each participant perceiving and reacting to the specific behaviours of the other. Evidence suggests that for face-to-face interviews, better co-operation and more information is obtained when backgrounds are similar and, furthermore, that interviewers opinions, perceptions, expectations and attitudes all affect the responses they receive.

At the end of the day, individuals do as they please and attempts to isolate variables that change behaviour in a consistent manner are fraught with difficulties. The so-called 'Hawthorne effects', where it was found that any changes made to experimental conditions increased productivity largely on account of the extra attention given to participants, are evidence of such problems.

Interviewer errors

In interview surveys, whether face-to-face or by telephone, interviewers may themselves misunderstand questions or the instructions for filling them in, they may be dishonest, inaccurate, make mistakes or ask questions in a non-standard fashion. Interviewer training, along with field supervision and control can, to a large extent, remove the likelihood of such errors, but they will never be entirely eliminated, and there is always the potential for systematic differences between the results obtained by different interviewers.

Editing

Questionnaires (either respondent-completed or interviewer-completed) are returned to the researcher for every respondent successfully contacted. Editing is the process of scrutinising completed data collection forms and taking whatever corrective action is required to ensure that the data are of high quality. It is a kind of quality control check on the raw data to ensure that they are complete, accurate and consistent.

A preliminary or field edit is a quick examination of completed data collection forms. Its purpose is twofold: to ensure that proper procedures are being followed in selecting respondents, interviewing them and recording their responses, and to remedy fieldwork deficiencies before they turn into a major problem. Speed is crucial and it needs to be done while the fieldwork is still in progress. Typical problems that are discovered in field edits include:

■ inappropriate respondents,
■ incomplete questionnaires,
■ illegible or unclear responses.

When any of these arise, the errors will be traced back to the interviewers concerned who will be advised of the problems and, if necessary, undergo further training.

A second stage of editing, a final or office edit, is undertaken after all the field-edited questionnaires are received. It involves verifying response consistency and accuracy, making necessary corrections, and deciding whether some or all parts of a questionnaire should be discarded. Some of these checks include:

■ **logical checks** – for example, the 17 year old claiming to have a PhD or the male claiming to have had an epidural at the birth of his last child,
■ **range checks** – for example, a code of '8' is entered when there are only six response categories for that question,
■ **response set checks** – for example, somebody has 'strongly agreed' with all the items on a Likert scale.

Where a question fails a logical check, then the pattern of responses in the rest of the questionnaire may be scrutinised to see what is the most likely explanation for the apparent inconsistency. Range check failures may be referred back to the original respondent. Response set checks may indicate that the respondent is simply being frivolous and the questionnaire may be discarded.

Coding

The tasks involved in transforming edited questionnaires into machine-readable form are generally referred to as coding. Most survey analysis packages will accept responses or other data that are in various forms. A key distinction is normally between numeric and alphanumeric or 'string' variables (which are strings of letters). This corresponds to the distinction we made in Chapter 1 between quantitative and qualitative variables. All quantitative variables should, ideally, be entered into the data matrix in numeric form – there is little point in typing in 'male' or 'female' if you can type in '1' or '2'. Thus binary variables should be coded into 1 or 2 and the categories for nominal and ordinal variables numbered 1, 2, 3, 4 and so on. Answers to open-ended questions will either need to be classified and coded, or left as strings, in which case the original comments will simply be listed. Interval data already have numerical scale values that can be entered directly, for example, a person's age as '59'.

Some, if not all, of the categorical responses will usually be pre-coded, that is, they are numbered on the questionnaire. If not, they need to be coded afterwards by the researcher. Qualitative responses to open-ended questions may be classified into categories, and the categories then numbered. The procedures for doing this are considered in Chapter 13.

For some survey analysis packages it is necessary to keep a separate record of what response categories each code refers to for each question. Such a record is normally referred to as a 'code book'. More modern survey analysis packages, however, tend to keep labels, or labels in words can be added to both the questions and responses, so code books are not needed because the labels are printed out with the results.

If a cell is left blank, a system missing value (indicated in SPSS by a period) is supplied. Alternatively, the researcher may enter a zero to indicate missing values or may wish to distinguish different reasons for the missing value, for example:

90 = not applicable,
91 = refused to answer,
92 = don't know,
93 = forgot to answer.

Data entry

When editing and coding is complete, the data are ready to be keyed into an analysis package. Mistakes can, of course, occur in this process. In SPSS, any entry that is outside the stated range of codes will quickly show up in a table. Thus if, for the variable sex of respondent, we allocate 1='male' and 2='female', then entering a '3' or a '4' will show up as a label in the table, as in Table 3.1. Three '3's and one '4' have been erroneously entered. Provided the questionnaires have been numbered it would be a simple matter the check the number of the respondent from the data matrix where the wrong codes have been entered and find what the code should have been from the questionnaire.

Clearly, however, if any '1's or '2's had been entered as mistakes, then this would not be apparent. To overcome this, data may be subjected to double-entry

Table 3.1   *Errors in data entry*

Sex of respondent	Frequency	Percentage (%)
Male	10	41.7
Female	10	41.7
3	3	12.5
4	1	4.2
Total	24	100.0

data validation. In effect this means that the data are entered twice, usually by two different people, and any discrepancies in the two entries are flagged up by the computer and can be checked against the original questionnaire. Some market research agencies do this, but only on a sample basis so that, for example, only 10 per cent of the questionnaires may be subject to double-entry data validation.

It is normal nowadays to enter data directly from the questionnaires. For some packages like SPSS or Minitab this means entering the appropriate values row-by-row, that is, questionnaire by questionnaire, directly into the data matrix. Some packages like Pinpoint allow the researcher to enter the data by clicking the appropriate box with a mouse on an electronic version of the questionnaire. A worksheet is then created which functions like a data matrix and can be saved in a format that can be transferred to other packages. The particular procedures for entering data into SPSS are explained later in this chapter.

The number of cases entered into the data matrix will usually be the number of usable returns. Missing values will either be left blank or a special code will be entered. For non-missing values, what is entered for each variable is a number. If the scale is continuous interval, each scale value may be a unique number, each having a frequency of one and perhaps measured to several decimal places. We could, however, round off, round down or round up each scale value, for example to the nearest whole number, in which case a scale value may happen more than once. Thus in a group of 130 people, there may be 6 persons recorded as aged 23 (age in years rounded down to age last birthday). The number of times a scale value happens is the *frequency* – in this example the frequency of people aged 23 is 6. If the scale is discrete interval the scale values will be whole numbers anyway and we could record the number of times each value occurs. The result, however, may still be a very large number of scales values. For observed price of brand X, for example, there may be many different prices observed on the shelves in shops. One way of reducing the number of scale values, but keeping an overall view of the distribution, is to group values together. The number of shops selling brand X at various prices may be grouped into under 40p, 41–45p, and over 50p. We can then produce a frequency for each grouping.

For categorical scales there will usually be a limited number of categories used as scale values, so it makes sense to report the frequency with which each occurs. The results will often be laid out as a table, the scale values forming the rows, and the frequencies (and perhaps relative frequencies) the columns. Frequency tables are considered in detail in Chapter 4.

If respondents are allowed only one response category for a question (a single-answer question), then, by definition, the total number of recorded answers plus the total number of missing values should for each variable always equal the number of usable returns. If it does not, then values have either been omitted or duplicated. For multiple response questions where respondents can tick as many boxes as apply to them, then clearly, the total number of recorded answers may considerably exceed sample size. How such questions are analysed is considered in Chapter 12.

USING COMPUTER PACKAGES

Fortunately, long gone are the days when you needed a large mainframe computer to perform any kind of analysis on survey data. That usually entailed learning how to use a mainframe 'editor' whose arcane rituals were devised by computer 'nerds', and the term 'user-friendly' had not even been coined. Nowadays, practically any program you are likely to need will be available on your PC, using the familiar 'Windows' format. There are three main kinds of package that are likely to be of interest to you:

■ spreadsheets,
■ statistics packages,
■ survey analysis packages.

Spreadsheets *look* like a data matrix with rows and columns. There, the similarities begin to fade out fast. The rows do not necessarily represent respondents and the columns do not necessarily relate to variables. The key facility of a spreadsheet is that it can link individual cells or groups of cells by formulae so that changes in one cell entry will cause other cell entries to change. The cells themselves can contain text (labels), values or formulae. They were designed essentially for use in accounting, not for the analysis of survey data. Most spreadsheets do have a 'database' function that allows calculations to be performed on rows or columns of values, but be warned that the values will be treated as interval, so if you have entered values as labels (for example, 1='Female', 2='Male') then the values 1 and 2 will be treated as the numbers 1 and 2, and you might end up with an 'average' sex of 1.634! There is usually a 'count' function that will tell you how many '1's and how many '2's there are in a column, but it will not produce a nice labelled table with counts, percentages and cumulative percentages, as SPSS does, for example, nor will any spreadsheet allow you to recode any variables or group them as multiple response questions. Microsoft's Excel does have a Pivot Table function that produces a table that summarises information about different variables, including a count of entered values, and it will crosstabulate two variables, but three-way or *n*-way tables are not possible and there are no accompanying statistics that measure the degree of association or that will calculate Chi-square for you. It is also the case that the data have to be laid out in a particular fashion, otherwise the table rows and columns will not be labelled properly. In short, spreadsheets are not really recommended for analysing survey results.

Statistics packages like Minitab and Statgraphics can handle categorical data and thereby are more suited to survey analysis. Minitab in particular is very user-friendly and it will produce crosstablations and calculate Chi-square for you. It has a very wide range of statistical and graphical functions, but it cannot handle multiple-response questions. If you have a number of these in your questionnaire, this can be a severe limitation. For an introduction to using Minitab for survey analysis see Bryman and Cramer (1996).

Survey analysis packages fall into two main groups. There are those packages like SPSS and SAS that take data entry (or the import of data) as the first step; and those like Marquis and Pinpoint which allow you to type in, format and print out the questionnaire. These have the advantage that the data matrix is formatted for you because it knows what the value labels are (from the response categories you have typed in) and how many values there are associated with each variable. You can also specify a variable name and identify whether the question is single response or multiple response. There are many options for printing out the questionnaire and in Pinpoint, items can be moved around like a desktop publisher. Data entry is made simple by clicking on the screen with a mouse to indicate the response category for each question. The statistics and graphics produced by Pinpoint, however, are rather limited, although it will create crosstabulations with no problem (crosstabulations are explained in Chapter 4). The more recent versions of Pinpoint allow you to save the worksheet it creates as an SPSS file, so you can use all the SPSS procedures. If you have access to both Pinpoint and SPSS, then this is an ideal combination – enter data on Pinpoint – provided you have generated the questionnaire on it – and then transfer to SPSS. (An introduction to using Pinpoint for survey analysis is to be found in Appendix 2.)

ENTERING DATA ON SPSS

The first step is getting into SPSS. Log on to your system and open the SPSS application. This may entail double-clicking on the SPSS icon or going into the Start/Programs from your desktop window. The first SPSS window you will see is the Data Editor window (Figure 3.2). The window is a data matrix whose rows represent cases (no row should contain data on more than one case) and whose columns will contain the values of the variables for each case. No cell can contain more than one value.

Imagine now that we have done a very short customer satisfaction survey in which 20 respondents have filled in a brief questionnaire that records sex, age in years, and their response to a 5-point rating of satisfaction on each of 5 dimensions as illustrated in Figure 3.3.

Figure 3.2   *The 'Data Editor' window*

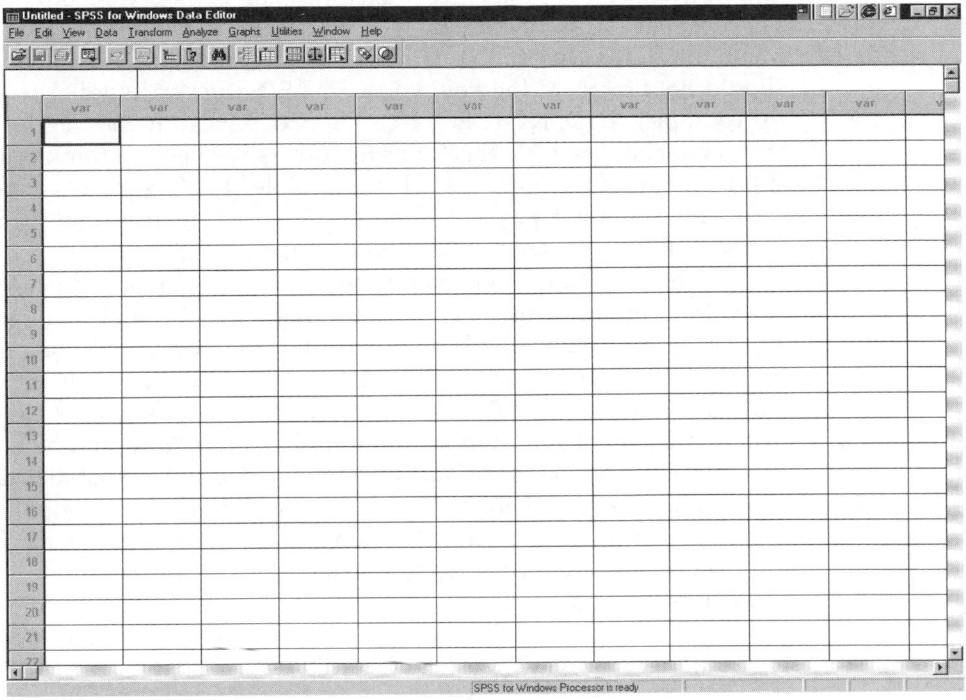

Figure 3.3   *The completed data matrix*

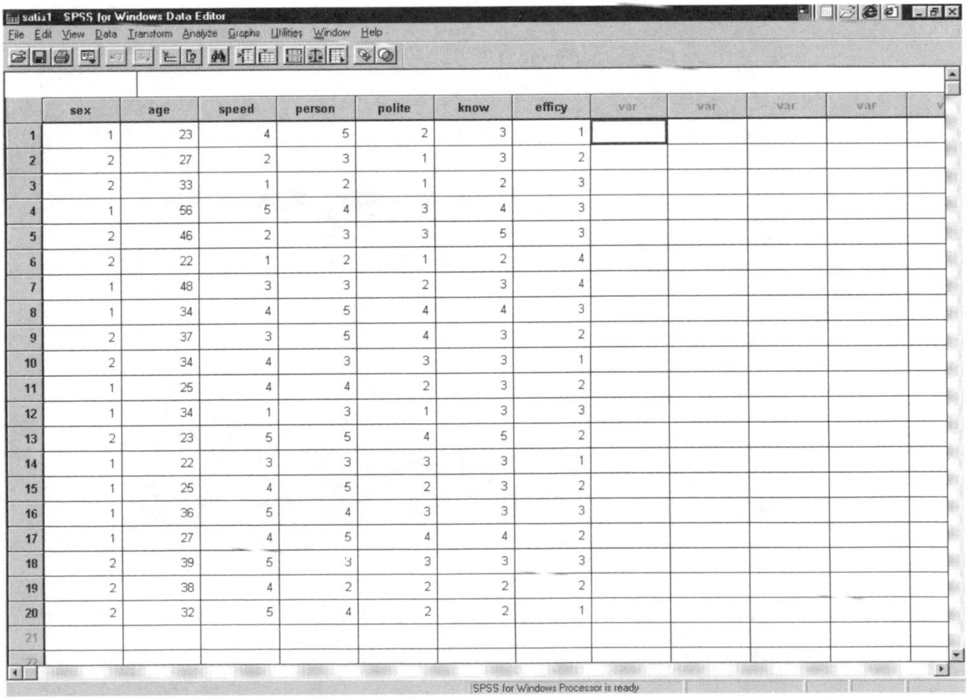

	sex	age	speed	person	polite	know	efficy
1	1	23	4	5	2	3	1
2	2	27	2	3	1	3	2
3	2	33	1	2	1	2	3
4	1	56	5	4	3	4	3
5	2	46	2	3	3	5	3
6	2	22	1	2	1	2	4
7	1	48	3	3	2	3	4
8	1	34	4	5	4	4	3
9	2	37	3	5	4	3	2
10	2	34	4	3	3	3	1
11	1	25	4	4	2	3	2
12	1	34	1	3	1	3	3
13	2	23	5	5	4	5	2
14	1	22	3	3	3	3	1
15	1	25	4	5	2	3	2
16	1	36	5	4	3	3	3
17	1	27	4	5	4	4	2
18	2	39	5	3	3	3	3
19	2	38	4	2	2	2	2
20	2	32	5	4	2	2	1

Before entering any data it is advisable first to name the variables (if you do not, you will be supplied with exciting names like 'var00001' and 'var00002') These names must not exceed eight characters, they must begin with a letter and must not end with a full stop. There must be no spaces and the names chosen should not be one of the key words that SPSS uses as special computing terms, for example, AND, NOT, EQ, BY, ALL. So, we can name the first variable 'sex' and the second variable 'age'. For the others we need to think of names that are short and which remind us which variable it refers to. For 'speed of getting through' we might just call this 'speed', 'getting the right person', call that 'person'; the others we can call 'polite', 'know' and 'efficy'.

To enter the first variable name ('sex'), double click on the grey area at the top of the first column. This will obtain the Define Variable dialog box (see Figure 3.4). The Define Variable dialog box can also be obtained by selecting Define Variable from the Data drop-down menu. The Variable Name text box contains a default variable name, 'VAR00001'. Delete this by typing in 'sex' and the default will be overwritten. A longer, more meaningful label can, however, be attached to each variable. Click on the Labels button in the Change Settings subdialog box. This will produce the Define Labels dialog box. Type in 'Sex of respondent' in the Variable Label box. The rules governing the naming of variables do not apply to labels, for example, there may be spaces, the letters are case sensitive, and up to 120 characters may be used.

Since the variable 'sex' is categorical, it is necessary to give each value a label, for example, 1 = 'Male', 2 = 'Female'. In the Value box, type in '1' (the lowest code

Figure 3.4   The 'Define Variable' dialog box

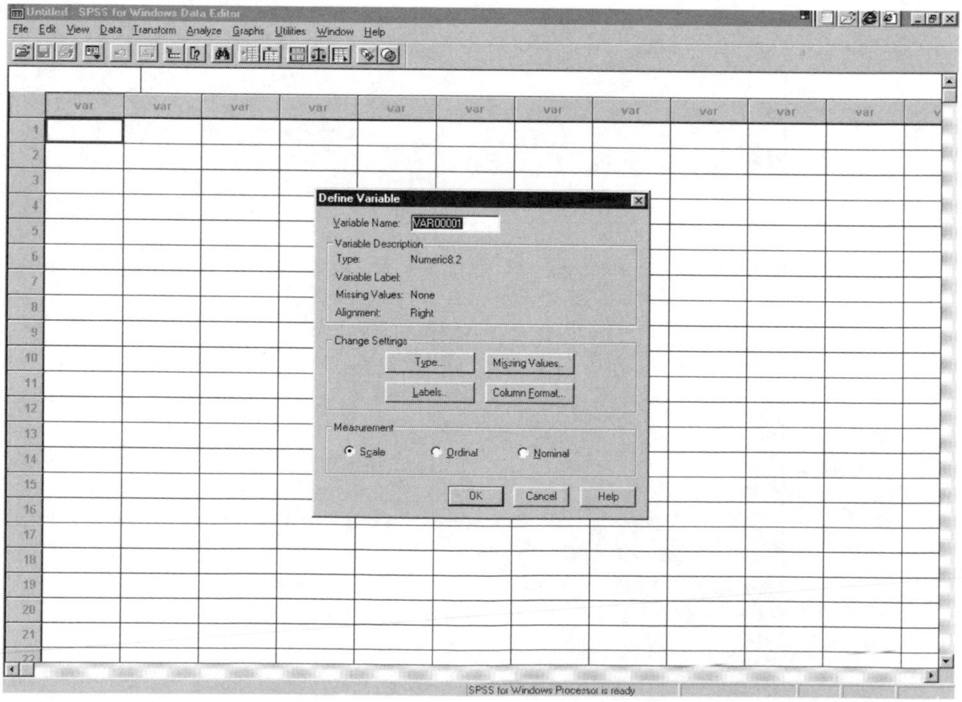

number) and in Value Label type in 'Male'. (Note that to move between boxes click on the mouse in the appropriate box or use the Tab key to move to the box below). Click on the Add button and '1="Male"' will appear in the lowest box. Now add 2=Female using the same procedure and then click on Continue. Now name the other six variables, adding variable labels and value labels. Note, however, that age is an interval variable and does not require value labels. Notice, too, that there is a Measurement box in the Define Variable dialog box, enabling you to choose between Scale, Ordinal and Nominal. Scale is the equivalent of an interval scale. In SPSS versions 8.0 and earlier, these were indeed called 'Interval'. Ordinal and Nominal are both categorical scales, but SPSS does not make a distinction, as we did earlier, between ranking and ordinal scales, or between nominal and binary scales. The default setting is Scale. Changing the setting to Ordinal or Nominal makes very little difference to SPSS operations except for some chart drawing commands. It is, however, worthwhile making the changes, even if only to force you to think about what kind of scale is attained by each variable.

Suggestion

If you have a number of variables each with the same set of values and value labels, try using **Data/ Templates** instead of re-entering the same labels for each variable. First, highlight the variables concerned by dragging the pointer across the grey areas at the top of the columns. Then select **Templates** from the **Data** drop-down menu. Click on **Value Labels** in the **Apply** box and on **Define**. Click on **Value Labels** and enter these as above. Click on **Continue** then on **OK**.

Warning

If you have Version 10.0 on SPSS there is a totally different way of defining and labelling your variables and you no longer need a template procedure for repeating sets of labels. See Appendix 3 on Version 10.0.

You are now ready to enter some data. This will normally be done row by row, that is, case by case or questionnaire by questionnaire. Figure 3.3 shows the completed data matrix which actually contains 'spoof' data, but imagine that you are taking each questionnaire in turn and putting the appropriate codes for each case. Put the cell highlight on the cell into which you wish to enter a value (begin top left) and simply type the number (always enter the codes, not the value labels). Move the highlight using the direction keys. Notice that the process of entering is completed simply by moving the highlight to another cell. You could press the Enter key instead. If your system is set up with a default with decimal places, you can change the number of decimal places for any variable by clicking on the Type button in the Define Variable window. Click on the Decimal Places box and change to '0', click on Continue then OK. Alternatively, you can alter the default to zero, but you must do this *before* you enter any data or define any variables. From the menu bar at the top of the application window select Edit and then Options. Click on the Data tab and change Decimal Places to '0'. Click on OK.

Notice that just above the grid is a white bar – this is the Status bar. This shows your entry as you type it and indicates the cell position on the left. The usual Windows editing functions are available, for example, you can cut, copy and paste in the usual way. To change a value in a cell once it has been entered, simply highlight the cell, type in the new value and press Enter.

Note that SPSS assumes that all data matrices are rectangular. If you press Enter before you get to the end of the second or subsequent rows a period is entered in each of the remaining cells in that row. There can be no empty cells. If no value has been entered, the system supplies the system missing value.

SAVING YOUR WORK

Remember that SPSS does not have an automatic timed backup facility. You need to save your work regularly as you go along. Use the File/Save sequence as usual for Windows applications. The first time you go to save you will be given the Save As dialog box. Make sure this indicates the drive you want. Drive a: for your floppy disk, Drive c: for you hard disk or Drive h: if you are on a networked system. File/Exit will get you out of SPSS and back to the Program Manager or windows desktop.

Warning

Unlike most other applications, SPSS does not allow you to have several files open at once. You will need to save everything you wish to save before moving to another file or opening a new one.

INTRODUCTION TO THE TABLE TENNIS STUDY

Now that you have entered some data for yourself on SPSS, it is time to access some more extensive data that have already been entered for you. These data are from a study of table tennis in Northern Ireland. The table tennis dataset is available on the Palgrave website, the address of which is given on the back cover of this book. The site gives you instructions on how to download the data into your SPSS program. Table tennis in Northern Ireland has been in decline for a couple of decades. The number of people playing the game is getting smaller while the adult male is dominating the sport. The standard of club and league table tennis playing is well behind most other countries. Table tennis desperately needs more younger players, but attempts to recruit new players have so far been largely unsuccessful. The purpose of the research was to produce data that would help promoters to target the sport to a wider audience. More specifically, the research objectives were to:

- identify who plays table tennis and why,
- determine when and where the sport is first played,
- establish the perceptions of non-players and their level of awareness of the sport,
- examine the extent to which table tennis is played in primary schools.

The data in *tabten.sav* relate to the first two of these objectives. Other stages of the research looked at non-players and at primary schools. The questionnaire to players, which is reproduced in Appendix 1, was generated following preliminary qualitative interviews with a cross-section of those who have a direct role in the game as a competitive sport. The population being studied is all members of table-tennis clubs in Northern Ireland in 1996. A representative random sample of 150 such members was drawn from membership lists after stratifying by the major leagues in Northern Ireland and then by the four divisions within each league to represent all standards of player. Self-completed questionnaires were mailed and 120 usable returns were received. Such a size of sample is the absolute bare minimum that will allow for quantitative analysis. The topic of sample size is taken up in more detail in Chapter 12, although some of the implications of sample size – in particular the limitations imposed by having a sample as small as 120 – will emerge during the chapters that follow.

The questionnaire consists of 19 questions, but some of these produced more than one variable, giving 30 variables in total. Once you have accessed the data, you should obtain a screen the same as Figure 2.2. Now have a look at some of the data.

- If you position the pointer over the grey area that contains the variable name but without clicking, SPSS will show you to what question the variable relates.
- Now double-click on the grey area that contains 'league' and on Labels in the Change Settings box. You will now see how the four main leagues in Northern Ireland have been coded.
- Now check out some of the other variables.
- Notice that 'agebegan' is an interval variable, so there are no value labels.
- Notice that 'agenow' is grouped into intervals of 10 years.

SUMMARY

Getting good quality data with which to fill the data matrix means:

- paying attention to the design of the survey, including a precise specification of the survey population, a good frame for selecting cases, and the design of a good questionnaire,
- having a clear policy for the execution of the survey that minimises the potential for error from non-response, respondent answers, interviewers, editing, coding and data entry.

For analysing survey data, spreadsheets and statistics packages have their limitations and dedicated survey analysis packages are almost certainly better. The chapter concluded by showing you how to enter data into SPSS, how to save your work, and introduced the table tennis study that will illustrate most of the techniques and procedures used in the remainder of this book.

Exercises

1. Pick out three articles that present the results of survey research in the area you are studying and check out the definition given by the author(s) of the population of cases being studied. How do these definitions stack up against the elements suggested on p. 52? Have one or more frames been used as lists for selecting cases and has the author made any comments on the quality of such lists?
2. Using the same articles, look at the response rate. Does the author explain how it was calculated?
3. Can you make some overall assessment of the quality of the data?

Points for discussion

1. Researchers often report a response rate which is the number of refusals (or refusals plus non-contacts) as a proportion or a percentage. But should this be of the target, the achieved or the usable set of cases? Should response rates be calculated on a question-by-question basis?
2. Why might the researcher wish to classify and keep a record of the reasons for missing values?
3. It might be concluded from this chapter that no survey is free from error. If so, what faith can be placed on the findings of survey research?

Further reading

Good introductions to SPSS are:

Babbie, E. and Halley, F. (1998) *Adventures in Social Research: Data Analysis Using SPSS for Windows 95*, Thousand Oaks, California, Pine Forge Press.
  Like this text, the focus is on the logic of survey analysis using SPSS (7.5 or 8.0) as a vehicle for putting that logic into practice. However, it is based around the key concepts being illustrated – religiosity, political orientation and attitude towards abortion – and shows how SPSS procedures can be used to explore them. The coverage of SPSS operations, however, and the coverage of statistical procedures is not systematic other than by a loose grouping into univariate, bivariate and multivariate procedures. It contains lots of examples and screen shots of SPSS,

Bryman, A. and Cramer, D. (1999) *Quantitative Data Analysis with SPSS Release 8 for Windows*, London, Routledge.
  This contains a substantial two-chapter introduction to using SPSS followed by explanations of statistical operations and how they may be accessed from SPSS. The book, however, is not focused specifically on survey data, so there is rather more on the kinds of statistics that might be used in experimental set-ups. Thus there is rather more on exploring the statistical significance of discovered differences between variables and rather less than in this text on handling categorical data descriptively.

Foster, J. (2000) *Data Analysis Using SPSS for Windows Versions 8.0–10.0: A Beginner's Guide*, 2nd edn, London, Sage.
  Very much a 'how to use SPSS' book. A very useful supplement to this text if you want to know a bit more about actually using SPSS.

Kinnear, P. and Gray, C. (1999) *SPSS for Windows Made Simple*, 3rd edn, Hove, Psychology Press.
  Designed for those with no prior knowledge even of using computers before. The first couple of chapters tell you about personal computers and the Windows operating environment. All SPSS operations are very simply explained with lots of screen shots and examples. There is limited explanation of the statistics themselves and the structure of the book reflects a concern mainly for experimental designs and significance testing. The third edition uses SPSS 8.0, but a new edition recently published covers Release 10.0.

In addition, have a look at the Website produced by the Social Science Research and Instructional Council, *SPSS for Windows, Version 9.0: A Brief Tutorial*, available from <http://www.csubak.edu/SSRIC/Modules/SPSS/SPSFirst.htx>.

Have a look at the suggested references below on what is sometimes called 'non-sampling' error:

Churchill, G. (1999) *Marketing Research: Methodological Foundations*, 7th edn, Fort Worth, Texas, The Dryden Press, pp. 452–564 and Chapter 12.
  Chapter 12 is a 'must read' on non-sampling error. There are also lots of references to other sources in Churchill's chapter.
Armstrong, J. and Overton, T. (1977) 'Estimating Non-response Bias in Mail Surveys', *Journal of Marketing Research*, Vol. XIV, August, pp. 396–402.
  This article, although a bit dated, gives a clear account of ways of estimating both the direction and magnitude on non-response bias.

On questionnaire design, consult one of the following:

Evans, N. (1995) *Using Questionnaires and Surveys to Boost Your Business*, London, Pitman Publishing.
Hague, P. (1993) *Questionnaire Design*, London, Kogan Page.
Oppenheim, A (1993) *Questionnaire Design, Interviewing and Attitude Measurement*, 2nd edn, London, Pinter.
  Each of these books has lots of examples and offers some very sound advice on designing question and designing questionnaires. Oppenheim was originally published in 1966, but has re-emerged as a second edition.

References

Bryman, A. and Cramer, D. (1996) *Quantitative Data Analysis with Minitab: A Guide for Social Scientists*, London, Sage.
De Maio, T. (1980) 'Refusals, Who, Where, and Why', *Public Opinion Quarterly*, Summer, pp. 223–33.
Meier, E. (1991) 'Response rate trends in Britain', *Marketing and Research Today*, Vol. 19, June, pp. 120–3.

part II

Analysing Survey Data

Choosing the Right Data Analysis Techniques

Introduction to Part II

In data construction the focus is on the entry of a single value at a time for a single respondent on a single variable. The focus of data analysis, by contrast, is upon data in the aggregate, and the individual respondent along with his or her associated values 'disappear' in the sense that they can no longer be identified from the results. While data construction and data analysis are separate processes, they are nevertheless interdependent. Both the design of the data matrix and its analysis must reflect the objectives of the research as outlined by the researcher or as agreed between researcher and client. The particular analysis procedures deployed must reflect a clear understanding of how the data were constructed, and in particular the measurement and scaling procedures used. The fact that data construction and data analysis are separate processes, however, means that good quality data can be used for a number of purposes using a variety of different data analysis techniques. What is called 'secondary analysis' and the emergence of large data archives depend on this ability to separate data construction and data analysis.

Data analysis is the process whereby researchers take the raw data that have been entered into the data matrix and create information that can be used to tackle the objectives for which the research was undertaken. The raw data are of little informative value themselves until they have been structured, summarised and a range of conclusions drawn from them. Such conclusions, furthermore, need to be relevant to the objectives of the research.

Data will have been entered row by row, and analysis now proceeds by performing a range of operations on the columns. Before any researcher can decide what analysis techniques to deploy, three key questions need to be answered:

- What does the researcher want to do with the data?
- On what type of scale are the data recorded?
- How many variables are to be entered into the analysis?

Answering these questions may be seen as three key steps that have to do with establishing the objectives of the analysis, the scale type and the number of variables.

ANALYSIS OBJECTIVES

The researcher may wish to do one or more of three main things with the data in the data matrix:

- display the data,
- summarise the data,
- draw conclusions from the data.

Data display takes the raw data and presents them in tables, charts or graphs so that it is possible for readers to 'eyeball' the total distribution on a single variable or to observe the pattern of relationships between two or more variables. Chapters 4 and 5 look at tables and charts for categorical and for interval variables respectively.

Summarising data uses statistical methods like calculating an average on a single variable, or measures of association or correlation on two or more variables to reduce the data to a few key summary measures. Chapters 6 and 7 explain summary measures, again respectively, for categorical and for interval variables.

Data display and data summaries are components of what is commonly referred to as 'descriptive' statistics. Drawing conclusions may involve one or more of three main activities:

- statistical inference,
- evaluating hypotheses against the data,
- explaining discovered relationships between variables.

Sometimes the data in the data matrix relate to a set of respondents who are part of a sample that was chosen using probability (random) methods. The issues of when survey researchers take samples, sample design and the errors that may arise from the sampling process are taken up in Chapter 8. The researcher who has taken a sample may wish to make estimates based on the sample of total, proportional or average values for the population of cases from which the sample was drawn. Alternatively, the researcher may wish to test statements or hypotheses made about the population of cases against the probability that survey research findings were, in fact, a result of random sampling fluctuations. Chapters 9 and 10 explain how researchers make inferences, again respectively, for categorical and for interval variables.

These procedures are known variously as 'inferential' statistics, 'statistical inference', 'significance testing' or 'testing statistical significance'. Making estimates is, unsurprisingly, generally referred to as 'estimation'. However, the second procedure is almost universally called 'hypothesis-testing', which in many ways is unfortunate, because testing the statistical significance of a statement is only one of several ways in which hypotheses may be evaluated.

In evaluating hypotheses, the researcher is more concerned about the extent to which the data in the data matrix 'fit' or support his or her initial ideas, hunches or formally stated hypotheses. Hypotheses come in many different forms, they may be stated formally before the data analysis begins, or they may emerge during, or even after, the analysis. All these different circumstances affect the ways in which they may be appropriately evaluated. The first part of Chapter 11 takes up the theme of evaluating hypotheses in rather more detail.

Once hypotheses have been evaluated, it might still be necessary to explain why the research findings appear to be as they are. What counts as an 'explanation', however, can vary enormously from causal analysis to providing understanding or discovering a dialectic. The second part of Chapter 11 looks at these issues.

SCALE TYPE

Chapter 2 introduced you to different types of scale. It made a basic distinction between categorical and interval scales with the former sub-divided into labelling, binary, nominal, ordinal and ranked, and the latter sub-divided into discrete and continuous. The type of scale crucially affects the kind of statistical operations that may be performed on the data, so after clarifying what he or she wants to do with the data, the researcher must be very clear about the nature of the scale for *each* variable being mapped into the matrix. Chapters 4, 6 and 9 deal specifically with categorical variables and what can be done with them by way of tables, charts, summaries and statistical inference. The various sub-types of categorical scale also assume an important role. Chapters 5, 7 and 10 look at interval variables and what can be done with these by way of tables, charts, summaries and statistical inference.

THE NUMBER OF VARIABLES

When approaching a data matrix the first thing a researcher needs to do is to look at the distribution of each variable, one at a time. This is usually called 'univariate' analysis. So, the researcher might use data display, data summary or statistical inference separately on each variable. Which particular techniques are used depends on the scale involved. For categorical variables it would be usual to get SPSS to create univariate (or 'one-way') tables, bar charts or pie charts. Chapter 4 explains how this is done. For interval variables it is also possible to create one-way tables for discrete variables, but for continuous variables it would normally be necessary to group the values into class intervals before this can be done. The procedures are explained in Chapter 5 along with other ways of displaying interval variables. Which summary measures and what procedures for statistical inference can be used on variables one at a time similarly depend on the scale involved. Chapter 6 deals with summary measures for categorical variables and Chapter 7 with summary measures for interval variables. (Univariate statistical inference is explained in Chapters 9 and 10.)

Univariate analysis, however, tells the researcher nothing about the relationships between the variables. 'Bivariate' analysis takes variables two at a time to see whether there is any pattern in the way the values of the two values jointly occur. If the two variables are categorical it is possible to display the relationship between them in a crosstabulation. Crosstabulations are explained in Chapter 4, while Chapter 6 considers how it is possible to calculate summary measures for two crosstabulated variables. If both are interval then the relationship may be graphed in a scattergram. (These are explained in Chapter 5.) Relationships between two interval variables may be summarised by using correlation and regression. Similarly, it is possible to undertake statistical inference for bivariate relationships (Chapters 9 and 10).

Bivariate analysis is limited to looking at the relationships between variables two at a time; multivariate analysis techniques allow the analysis of three or more variables simultaneously. It has a number of advantages over univariate and bivariate procedures, namely:

- it permits conclusions to be drawn about the nature of causal connections between variables (establishing causality is discussed in Chapter 11),
- it facilitates the grouping together of variables that are inter-related, or cases that are similar in terms of their characteristics,

■ it provides the ability to predict dependent variables from two or more independent variables and hence improve on predictions made on the basis of only one variable.

Where all the variables to be used in multivariate analysis are categorical, then it is possible to 'layer' or 'control' the relationship between two variables by a third, fourth, fifth variable and so on in the process of crosstabulation. How this is done is explained in Chapter 4. Where all the variables are interval then much more sophisticated techniques like multiple regression, factor analysis, and cluster analysis are possible. This book considers these techniques briefly and shows you how to obtain them using SPSS. However, for a more detailed consideration, other sources are recommended.

Where variables to be used in multivariate analysis are a mixture of categorical and interval then other techniques like analysis of variance may be used. (This is explained in Chapter 10.)

CHOOSING DATA ANALYSIS TECHNIQUES

Data analysis is not a 'one-off' enterprise that a researcher undertakes on one single occasion. Rather, it is an iterative process in which the researcher moves backwards and forwards between the objectives of the research and a number of 'sessions' of analysing data from the matrix. For each session, the researcher needs to answer the three question posed at the beginning of this section:

■ What do I want to do with the data – display, summarise or draw conclusions?
■ Onto what type of scale are the variables recorded – categorical or interval?
■ How many variables do I want to enter into a single analysis – one, two or more than two?

Thus a researcher in one session may wish to display the relationship between two categorical variables and in another may wish to summarise a single interval variable. The various factors that will affect the researcher's choice of technique are summarised in Figure ii.1, which can be seen as a kind of 'map' of the rest of this book. Notice that, for the sake of completeness, there is a fourth element in Figure ii.1, namely respondents. If these constitute a random sample then it is possible to deploy statistical inference. If the sample is non-random or is a census or an attempt at a census, then such techniques are not appropriate.

Further reading

Fink, A. (1995) *How to analyse survey data*, London, Sage.
   A very simple and straightforward introduction to the types statistics that are useful for analysing data from surveys. A good book to begin with if you are approaching statistics for the first time. However, there is little on analysing categorical data and no mention of crosstabulation. Selecting statistical methods for surveys appears to entail picking your test of statistical significance. There is a brief introduction to SPSS output, but it refers to SPSS/PC+, which is little used these days.

Figure ii.1   *Factors determining choice of technique*

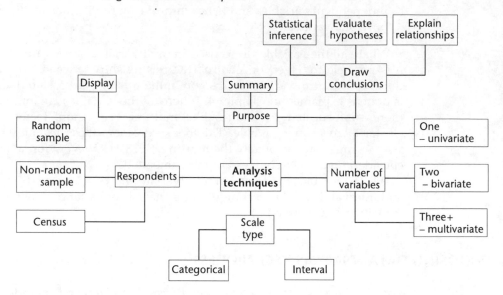

chapter 4

Tables and Charts for Categorical Variables

Learning objectives

In this chapter you will learn how to begin your analysis of the data matrix you have created for your survey research. In particular this chapter will help you to:

■ appreciate the general layout of tables,

■ understand the construction of univariate, bivariate and multivariate tables for categorical variables,

■ be aware of the different types of chart that can be used for such variables,

■ produce edited tables, bar charts and pie charts using SPSS.

INTRODUCTION

This chapter is the first of eight chapters that look in detail at the use of tables and charts, summary measures and drawing conclusions for categorical and for interval variables. We begin by looking at the different kinds of tables and charts that can be used for categorical variables, and then show you how to produce them all using SPSS. All the illustrations use the *tabten.sav* file that was introduced in Chapter 3.

UNIVARIATE FREQUENCY TABLES

You should recall from Chapter 2 that categorical variables are mapped onto sets of values that represent categories that are exhaustive, mutually exclusive and refer to a single dimension, but which possess no metric with which to measure distances between scale values. They may, furthermore, be sub-divided into binary, nominal, ordinal or ranked scales. A first stage in analysing any data scaled in this way is to display them in the form of tables or charts. In the first instance, this display will be univariate – treating variables one at a time. (Univariate analysis was explained in the introduction to Part II.)

A table is any layout of two or more values in rows, columns, or rows and columns combined. For categorical data, we can display the frequencies or relative frequencies (percentages) of the various categories. Tables for univariate analysis are often called 'one-way' or single-variable frequency tables. Clearly, for binary variables there will be only two categories giving, for example, the number of people saying 'yes' and the number saying 'no' to a question in a

Table 4.1   *A frequency table for a binary variable*

Do you read articles on table tennis in local papers?

	Frequency	Percent
Yes	109	90.8
No	11	9.2
Total	120	100.0

survey, as illustrated in Table 4.1, which is taken from the table tennis survey introduced in the previous chapter. The table was produced using SPSS. Note that the layout is rather different from Table 3.1 on page 62, which is in the standard publisher's format. Most tables from now on will look as they are produced by SPSS so that you can get used to its layout.

For nominal data there will be three or more categories. Precisely because the scale is nominal it does not matter in what order the categories are placed. However, if the number of categories is large it may make sense to list or group them in a particular way, for example, alphabetically or by frequency. For ordinal data the scale values should be in the intended order of magnitude, usually with the highest, largest, fastest and so on at the top. Table 4.2, for example, shows the level of importance respondents give to the social benefits arising from playing table tennis.

Table 4.2 illustrates a number of points about table layout:

■ the response categories, the frequencies and the percentages are usually in columns,
■ the columns are labelled at the top so that we know to what variable the categories refer and whether the figures represent frequencies, percentages or proportions,
■ totals are given at the bottom of the columns,
■ there is a table number and a title, which is usually at the top of the table,
■ there may be a source of the data at the bottom of the table if these data were derived from other than the results of the research being reported.

Table 4.2   *A frequency table of ordinal data*

Social benefits

	Frequency	Percent
Unimportant	11	9.2
Fairly unimportant	18	15.0
Neither unimportant or important	41	34.2
Fairly important	37	30.8
Very important	13	10.8
Total	120	100.0

Table 4.3   *A multi-variable frequency table:*
respondents by sex, social class and age

	Frequency	Per cent
Sex		
Male	104	52
Female	96	48
Social Class		
AB	30	15
C1	50	25
C2	70	35
DE	50	25
Age		
20–29	10	5
30–39	30	15
40–49	64	32
50–59	56	28
60+	40	20

Some tables may contain two or more adjacent univariate distributions, as in Table 4.3. Such multi-variable tables do not relate or interlace the variables. Thus we do not know from Table 4.3 which males are in which social classes or in which age groups.

Looking at one-way tables enables the researcher to do two main things. First, the researcher can see whether any variables are failing to discriminate between respondents. If all (or most) respondents give the same answer, then, while it may be an 'interesting' finding, such a variable will be of limited value for further analysis. The findings in Table 4.1, for example, are no great surprise and may really just confirm what the researcher would have anticipated anyway – that table tennis players will normally read (or say they read) articles on table tennis in local papers. However, since only 11 respondents said they do not read articles on table tennis in local papers, then these 11 cannot sensibly be compared with the other 109 respondents against another variable.

Second, and this is clearly related to the first point, if any categories are empty or very low in frequency, then the researcher will need to consider whether the variable can be sensibly collapsed into a smaller number of categories. Thus in Table 4.2 we may want to add together the unimportant and fairly unimportant categories, and add together the fairly important and important categories to generate Table 4.4. How to do this on SPSS is explained at the end of this chapter.

Table 4.4   *Table 4.2 regrouped*

	Frequency	Percent
Unimportant	29	24.2
Neither	41	34.2
Important	50	41.7
Total	120	100.0

BIVARIATE CROSSTABULATION

To display the relationship between two categorical variables a bivariate crosstabulation is required. These are sometimes referred to as 'contingency' or 'two-way' tables. A crosstabulation is a particular kind of table in which the frequencies or proportions of cases that combine a value on one categorical variable with a value on another are laid out in combinations of rows and columns. In other words a crosstabulation presents the frequencies of two variables the values of which are interlaced. Thus in Table 4.5 there are 42 individuals who combine the characteristics of being both male and answered 'yes' to the question about other members of the household playing table tennis. The combination of a row and a columns creates a 'cell'. There are four cells created by two variables, each having two categories, creating what is called a 'two-by-two' table. The totals at the end of each row (52 and 68 in this table) are called 'row marginals', and the totals at the bottom (103 and 17) are 'column marginals'.

Table 4.5   *A crosstabulation of other household players by sex of respondent*

Count

		What sex are you?		Total
		Male	Female	
Does anybody else in your household play table tennis?	Yes	42	10	52
	No	61	7	68
Total		103	17	120

Crosstabulations may be of any size in terms of rows and columns. Thus Table 4.6 is a 'seven by eight', having 56 cells. As tables get larger they become increasingly difficult to interpret and they require many more cases to avoid having very small numbers in most of the cells. As you can see in Table 4.6 there are many empty cells. It is almost impossible to see whether or not there is any connection between the two variables. With 56 cells and 120 cases there is an average of only two cases per cell! The only solutions are either to increase the number of cases or to reduce the size of the table. To do this, 'age' would need to be regrouped into two or three categories and 'where first played' into, for example, school, club, or elsewhere.

Where the totals at the ends of the rows or the foot of the columns (the 'marginals') are unequal (as they are in Table 4.5), direct comparison of cell frequencies is difficult to make. If, however, we standardise the frequencies to a common denominator, the patterns of association become more apparent. The best solution is to calculate percentages, either down the columns or along the rows. Which of these is appropriate depends on how the researcher wishes to interpret the data.

Table 4.6 *A crosstabulation of 'where table tennis was first played' by 'age'*

Count

		What age are you?							Total
		under 15	15-24	25-34	35-44	45-54	55-64	over 65	
Where did you first play the sport?	Primary school	2	5	6					13
	Secondary school	1	3	3	3	2			12
	Youth club	1	8	9	1	5	1		25
	Youth organisation		4	2	4	2	2		14
	Table-tennis club	2	4	8	1	6	3	2	26
	Coaching scheme	1							1
	Leisure centre		1	3					4
	Other		6	5	5	5	2	2	25
Total		7	31	36	14	20	8	4	120

Suppose we hypothesise that males are more likely than females to have somebody else at home who plays table tennis. Since there are many more males it is difficult to compare the frequencies in the table. What we need to do is compare the percentage of the males who answer 'yes' with the percentage of females who answer 'yes'. This means calculating percentages down the columns as in Table 4.7. This shows that, contrary to expectation, a higher percentage of females (58.8 per cent compared with 40.8 per cent for males) have somebody else in the household who plays table tennis (but remember that this is based on very few females).

Notice here that we have percentaged downwards in the direction of the 'independent' variable, sex. It is independent in the sense that it is not the variable we are trying to investigate or explain, which is table-tennis playing. It is not that we are necessarily saying that the sex of the player determines or has some effect on whether or not there are other players in the household. It could just as easily be the case that the existence of other players in the household is more likely to encourage females. The normal assumption that 'independent' means cause and 'dependent' means effect does not necessarily hold. It is a convention (not universally followed, but useful nevertheless) that the independent variable forms the columns of the table, and the dependent variable the rows. So, as a general rule, put the independent variable at the top and percentage downwards. Notice also that the comparison was made across the direction of percentaging.

Table 4.7 *Table 4.5 expressed as column percents*

% within What sex are you?

		What sex are you?		Total
		Male	Female	
Does anybody else in your household play table tennis?	Yes	40.8%	58.8%	43.3%
	No	59.2%	41.2%	56.7%
Total		100.0%	100.0%	100.0%

THREE-WAY AND *n*-WAY TABLES

Bivariate analysis is limited to looking at the relationships between variables two at a time; multivariate analysis techniques allow the analysis of three or more variables simultaneously. Where all the variables are categorical, it is possible to conduct a series of three-way analyses. Four-way, five-way up to any number or '*n*-way' analyses *are* possible, but they become exceedingly complex and require very large sample sizes as the number of sample splits grows. An example of a three-way cross tabulation is illustrated in Table 4.8. This shows the relationship between the age at which respondents began playing table tennis and whether or not anybody else in the household plays, 'layered' by whether or not they said they were encouraged to take up the sport.

Table 4.8 *Age began playing table tennis and other household players layered by whether or not they were encouraged to take up the sport*

Count

Were you encouraged by anyone to take up the sport?			Does anybody else in your household play table tennis?		Total
			Yes	No	
Yes	Began table tennis	Under 12	25	18	43
		12 and over	19	22	41
	Total		44	40	84
No	Began table tennis	Under 12	4	7	11
		12 and over	4	21	25
	Total		8	28	36

As you can see, amongst those who were not so encouraged, there is a stronger relationship between beginning age and the existence of other players in the household. In other words, where players were not encouraged by anybody, the existence of other players in the household had a greater effect – as you would expect. This is an example of what would usually be called a 'three-way' analysis. It is quite possible to layer by more variables, but the sample is getting split into smaller and smaller sub-groups, so it really requires a much larger size of sample. This layering can be done very easily on SPSS and you will see how later in this chapter.

The control or layering variable will often be a demographic so that we might, for example, check the association between two variables, first for males and then for females. Ideally, all the key bivariate relationships that are the focus of the research should be checked in this way against all variables that potentially might affect that relationship. The implications of the results of doing so will need to wait until we have looked at causal analysis in rather more detail in Chapter 11.

BAR CHARTS AND PIE CHARTS

'Chart' and 'graph' are terms that are often used interchangeably to refer to any form of graphical display. Charts for categorical variables are limited largely to bar charts and pie charts. In bar charts each category is depicted by a bar, the length of which represents the frequency or percentage of observations falling into each category. All bars should have the same width, and a scale of frequencies or percentages should be provided. What each bar represents should be clearly labelled or given a legend. A simple bar chart produced by SPSS is illustrated in Figure 4.1, which shows the distribution of age groups of table tennis players.

The bars will sometimes be constructed horizontally rather than vertically for categorical data and the actual figures for each bar may be written at the end of the bar, as illustrated in Figure 4.2. However, SPSS 9.0 does not have the facility to present bar charts in this way. Figure 4.2 was created by entering the frequencies and the scale values from Table 4.2 into an Excel spreadsheet and using its graphics facility. It is possible to represent a second categorical variable in one chart using a component, or 'stacked', bar chart, as in Figure 4.3, but there should not be more than three or four categories in the second variable. Component bar charts are sometimes a little difficult to interpret particularly when the variable being used as a component has very variable proportions within each bar. An alternative way of presenting two variables in a bar chart is in a 'clustered' bar chart, as illustrated in Figure 4.4.

As well as providing summaries for groups of cases, as above, a bar chart can be used as summaries for separate variables, as in Figure 4.5. This shows the average (mean) of each respondent's perceived importance of the five aspects of playing table tennis. Finally, it is possible to provide a chart of the values of individual cases, as in Figure 4.6. This shows the responses for all 120 cases for the variable social benefits.

Figure 4.1   *Bar chart: the age distribution of players*

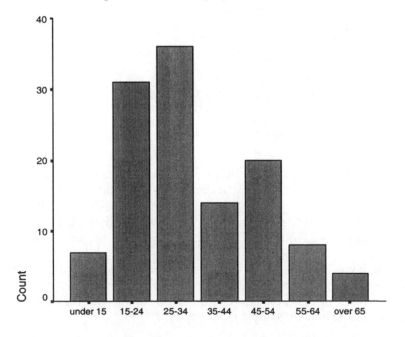

Figure 4.2   *A horizontal bar chart: importance of perceived social benefits*

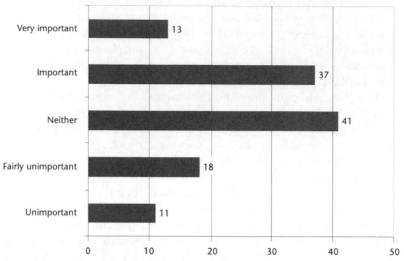

Figure 4.3   *A stacked bar chart: importance of perceived social benefits by sex of player*

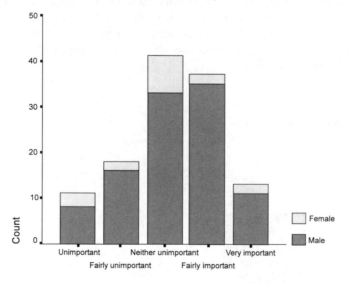

In a pie chart the relative frequencies are represented in proportion to the size of each category by a slice of the circle, as is illustrated in Figure 4.7, which shows the proportions who are in the various table tennis leagues. It is also possible to illustrate summaries of separate variables, as in Figure 4.8. A pie chart of individual cases would not be a sensible option here as there would be too many slices.

The bar chart is normally preferred to the pie chart because the human eye can more accurately judge length comparisons against a fixed scale than angular measures. However, pie charts are more aesthetic and they clearly show that the total for all slices adds up to 100 per cent.

Figure 4.4   *A clustered bar chart: importance of perceived social benefits by sex of player*

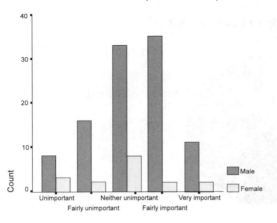

Figure 4.5   *Importance of aspects of playing table tennis*

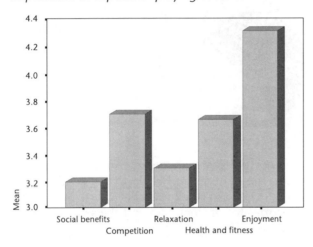

Figure 4.6   *The social benefits of playing table tennis by individual case*

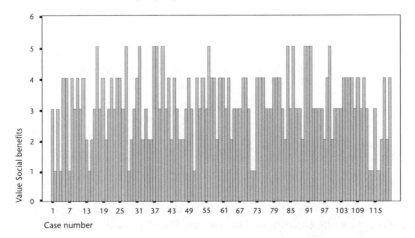

Figure 4.7   *A pie chart*

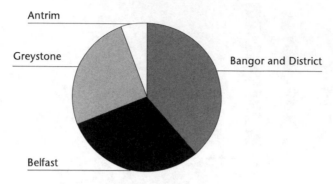

Figure 4.8   *Summaries of separate variables as a pie chart*

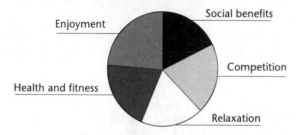

Neither bar charts nor pie charts, however, are particularly useful for binary data. For nominal data they can certainly help to display the data where there are between about four and 12 or so categories. Bar charts in particular can preserve the order of the categories for ordinal data, but the sense of ordering may be lost in pie-charts.

USING SPSS 'FREQUENCIES', 'GRAPHS', 'CROSSTABS' AND 'RECODE' PROCEDURES

Frequencies

To obtain one-way descriptive summaries for categorical variables, you will need the SPSS Frequencies procedure. This is in the Analyze/Descriptive Statistics drop-down menu from the menu bar at the top.

Warning

In versions 8.0 and earlier for SPSS these menus were called **Statistics/Summarize**

So, access the *tabten.sav* file as explained in the previous chapter, click on Analyze, then move the pointer to Descriptive Statistics and then to Frequencies and click.

Figure 4.9   The SPSS 'Frequencies' dialog box

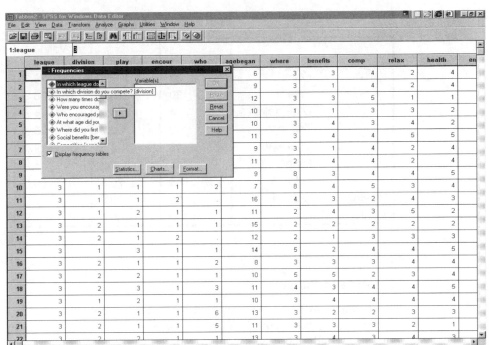

The Frequencies dialog box will appear (see Figure 4.9). All variables are listed in the left box. To obtain a frequency count for any variable simply transfer it to the Variables box by highlighting it, then clicking on the direction button in the middle. If you hold down the left mouse button while dragging the mouse you can highlight adjacent variables in one move. Click on OK and you instantly obtain a frequency count for each variable. Table 4.9 illustrates the default table, which gives you Frequency, Percent, Valid Percent and Cumulative Percent. Notice that there are 35 Missing and 85 Valid cases in this table. That means that 35 people did not answer this question. So the 33 cases who said they were encouraged by a friend represents 27.5 per cent of the total sample of 120, but 38.8 per cent of the 85 valid cases – this is the Valid Percent. The Cumulative Percent accumulates the Valid Percents so that, for example, a total of 74.1 per cent were encouraged either by a friend or by a parent. Since the scale here is nominal, the order is not important and reflects the order in which the value labels were entered.

Where there are no missing cases the Percent and Valid Percent are the same. You can edit the table to remove these columns if you wish. Just double-click on the table. Click on Valid Percent and hit Delete. Then highlight the figures in the column and hit Delete and the column will disappear and the table will close up. You can do the same with the Cumulative Percent column. To get out of edit mode just left-click outside the table area. With the table highlighted (there will be a frame around it and a red arrow to the left) you can select Edit and Copy and then Paste it into any other application like Word or Powerpoint.

Table 4.9   *An SPSS 'Frequencies' output*

Who encouraged you?

		Frequency	Percent	Valid Percent	Cumulative Percent
Valid	Friend	33	27.5	38.8	38.8
	Parent	30	25.0	35.3	74.1
	Other relative	4	3.3	4.7	78.8
	Teacher	2	1.7	2.4	81.2
	Club leader	15	12.5	17.6	98.8
	Other	1	.8	1.2	100.0
	Total	85	70.8	100.0	
Missing	System	35	29.2		
Total		120	100.0		

Graphs and charts

If you click on Charts in the Frequencies dialog box you obtain the Frequencies: Charts dialog box. Simply click on Bar Chart or Pie Chart as appropriate and indicate whether you want the axis label to display frequencies or percentages, click on Continue and then OK. This will give you a basic bar chart or pie chart in addition to the frequencies table. To obtain the stacked or clustered bar charts you will need to select the Graphs/Bar drop-down menu to give you the Bar Charts dialog box. In this box you can in addition also choose between Summaries for groups of cases (which is the usual, default option, giving you bar charts like Figure 4.1), Summaries of separate variables (giving charts like Figure 4.5), or Values of individual cases (like Figure 4.6).

Once you have obtained your chart you can edit it by double-clicking in the chart area. The will give you the SPSS Chart Editor. Try clicking on the Bar Style button and change the bars to a 3-D effect. You can change the colours and a number of other chart features from the editor. Close the Editor when you have finished. If you single-click on the chart area you highlight it. If you now select Edit/Copy you can copy the chart into other applications.

Crosstabs

The next stage in any data analysis is to look at the relationships between variables. For example, is there any relationship between whether anybody else in the household plays and how often they play per week? For this you need the Crosstabs procedure. This generates contingency tables for non-metric variables. Select Analyze/Descriptive Statistics/Crosstabs to obtain the Crosstabs dialog box. (See Figure 4.10.) Enter your dependent variable ('play') in the Row(s): box so it will appear at the side, and the independent variable ('else') in the Column(s): box. The result is in Table 4.10. If you put several variables in each box, then you will obtain a crosstabulation of each combination. To obtain column percentages, click on the Cells button in the Crosstabs dialog box to obtain Crosstabs: Cell

Figure 4.10   *The 'Crosstabs' dialog box*

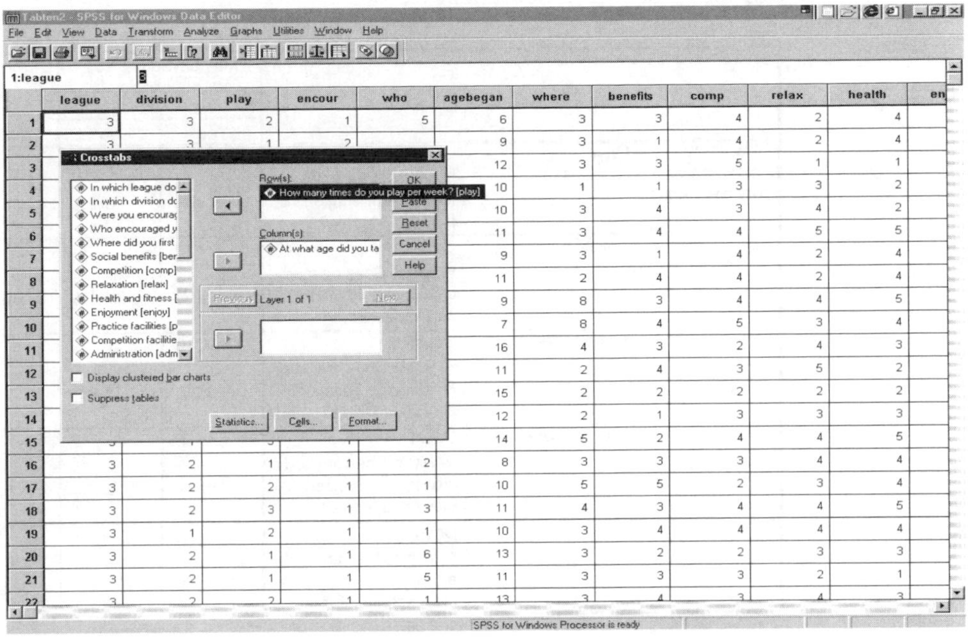

Display. Click on Column in the Percentages check box, then on Continue, then on OK. The result is shown in Table 4.11. Notice that the frequencies (called Count) and the percentages to one decimal place are shown in each cell. The frequencies can be edited out if you want to display just the percentages.

To obtain 3-way and *n*-way tables put the 'control' variable, for example, sex of respondent, in the Layer box and click on OK. You will, in effect, obtain two crosstabulations, one underneath the other, one for males and one for females. You can layer by more than one variable, but the frequencies in the cells get very low and the whole thing becomes more difficult to interpret. Try it and see what happens!

Table 4.10   *'Play frequency' by whether anybody else in the household plays*

Count

| | | Does anybody else in your household play table tennis? | | Total |
		Yes	No	
How many times do you play per week?	Once	15	28	43
	Twice	22	30	52
	Three times	10	8	18
	Four or more times	5	2	7
Total		52	68	120

Table 4.11   Column percentages: 'how many times played per week' by whether anybody else in the household plays

| | | | Does anybody else in your household play table tennis? | | |
			Yes	No	Total
How many times do you play per week?	Once	Count	15	28	43
		% within Does anybody else in your household play table tennis?	28.8%	41.2%	35.8%
	Twice	Count	22	30	52
		% within Does anybody else in your household play table tennis?	42.3%	44.1%	43.3%
	Three times	Count	10	8	18
		% within Does anybody else in your household play table tennis?	19.2%	11.8%	15.0%
	Four or more times	Count	5	2	7
		% within Does anybody else in your household play table tennis?	9.6%	2.9%	5.8%
Total		Count	52	68	120
		% within Does anybody else in your household play table tennis?	100.0%	100.0%	100.0%

Recode

If you need to transform a variable by regrouping categories, then it is the SPSS Recode procedure that you need. Select Transform/Recode/Into Different Variables. To create Table 4.4 from Table 4.2 it was necessary to add together 'unimportant' and 'fairly unimportant' into a new category, and to add together 'fairly important' and 'very important' into another category. To do this, select '*Social benefits*' and put into the Input Variable → Output Variable box. See Figure 4.11. Now click on Old and New Values. We need codes 1 and 2 to become code 1 so in the Old Value dialog area on the left click on the first Range radio button and enter '1' through '2'. In the New Value dialog area on the right enter '1' in the Value box and click on Add. (See Figure 4.12.) This instruction will now be entered into the Old → New box. Code 3 we want to change to 2 so click on the Value radio button under Old Value and enter '3' and '2' under New Value and click on Add. We now want codes 4 and 5 to be code 3. Click on the Range radio button and enter '4' through '5'. Under New Value enter '3' and click on Add. Click on Continue. Give the Output Variable a name in the Name box, for example, 'socben3' and click on Change then OK. The new variable will appear as the last column. (See Figure 4.13.) To add value labels for the new variable, double click on the variable name and on Labels. Under Value Labels enter '1' in Value and 'Unimportant' under Value Label and click on Add. Now enter '2' in Value and 'Neither' under Value Label and click on Add. Finally, enter '3' in Value and 'Important' under Value Label and click on Add. Now click on Continue and OK. You can now check this out using the Analyze/Descriptive Statistics/Frequencies procedure.

Figure 4.11   *The 'Recode into Different Variables' dialog box*

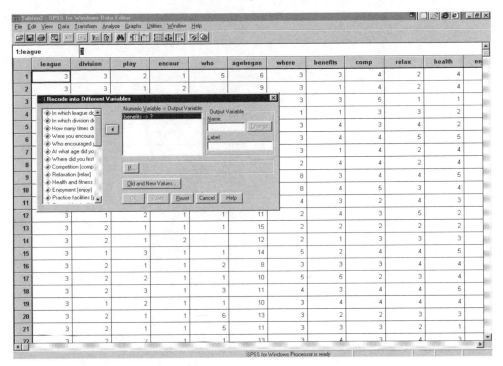

Figure 4.12   *'Old and New Values'*

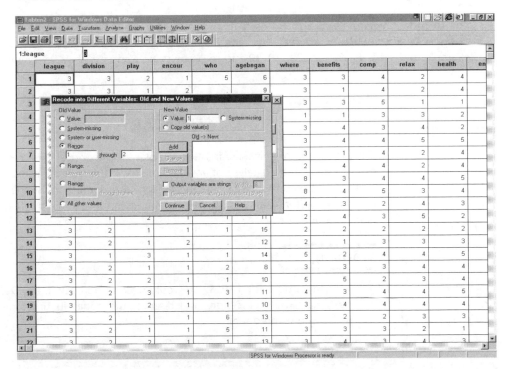

Figure 4.13　　*The new recoded variable*

	else	spend	foot	tennis	squash	badmin	socben3	var	var	var	var	v
1	1	15	1	2	2	2	2.00					
2	2	25	1	2	2	2	1.00					
3	1	63	1	2	2	2	2.00					
4	1	55	2	1	1	1	1.00					
5	2	46	1	2	2	2	3.00					
6	2	30	1	2	2	2	3.00					
7	1	20	2	1	2	2	1.00					
8	2	30	2	1	2	2	3.00					
9	1	28	1	1	2	2	2.00					
10	1	12	1	1	2	1	3.00					
11	2	80	1	2	1	2	2.00					
12	2	60	2	2	2	2	3.00					
13	2	78	2	1	2	2	1.00					
14	2	62	1	2	2	2	1.00					
15	2	70	1	2	1	2	1.00					
16	1	23	1	2	2	2	2.00					
17	1	56	1	2	2	1	3.00					
18	1	67	1	2	2	2	2.00					
19	1	53	1	2	2	2	3.00					
20	1	85	1	2	2	2	1.00					
21	2	71	2	2	2	2	2.00					
22	2	79	1	2	2	2	3.00					

Suggestion

The **Recode** procedure can also be used to group continuous interval variables into grouped categories. You could, for example, put the variable 'agebegan' into groups of 10 years, for example under 10, 10–19, 20–29, 30–39 and so on by using **Range** in the **Old Value** box.

SUMMARY

The production of univariate frequency tables for categorical variables is usually the first stage in the analysis of any data matrix. If the scale is ordinal, then the table should keep the scale values in their logical order, otherwise the order can be changed, for example, to put categories arranged by frequency or in alphabetical order.

Warning

To actually do this on SPSS you would need to go back to the **Define Variable/Labels** procedure and re-enter the codes in the order in which you wanted them.

Summary continued

Univariate procedures are very good at giving the researcher an overview of what the data look like and may be all that is required for a descriptive analysis. To develop the analysis, however, it will be necessary to progress to bivariate and then to multivariate procedures. Crosstabulations need to be limited in size (as measured by the number of cells) for the purpose of analysis, so categories of the variables used may need to be regrouped (using **Recode**) to create fewer categories. As tables get larger, so the number of cases in the dataset needs to grow. As a 'rule of thumb', there need to be 100 cases for every category of the independent variable. So, an independent variable with three categories crosstabulated with any other variable will require 300 cases. This implies that the minimum number of cases where bivariate analysis is to be used should ideally be about 200 for a two by two table. The issue of sample size and the number of cases is taken up again in Chapter 12.

Apart from tables, data display may take the form of bar charts and pie charts for categorical variables. Pie charts are less appropriate for ordinal variables and not particularly helpful for binary ones. Bar charts have the advantage that they can incorporate more than one variable in stacked or clustered charts. SPSS can be used to produce a whole range of tables and charts. These can be edited in SPSS, which is very helpful if they are to be copied across to other applications.

Exercises

1. Recreate Table 4.6 as a two-by-two table using SPSS.
2. Recreate Figure 4.3 and edit out the frequencies. Are there any other improvements you would make to the presentation of the table?
3. Use SPSS to create a bar chart of the importance of the social benefits of playing table tennis clustered by league played in. Use the **Chart Editor** to change/improve the appearance.
4. Use SPSS to create a bar chart comparing the mean satisfaction scores of the various elements of playing table tennis in Northern Ireland (Question 9).
5. Change the output from question 4 above into a pie chart.

Points for discussion

1. Is there a danger that the procedures used to analyse a dataset become largely a function of the procedures that happen to be available on a particular computer package like SPSS?
2. Do pie charts have any advantages over bar charts?

Further reading

Bowers, D. (1996) *Statistics from Scratch: An Introduction for Health Care Professionals*, Chichester, John Wiley and Sons.
See Chapter 3 on Organising Qualitative Data.
Foster, J. (2000) *Data Analysis Using SPSS for Windows Version 8.0–10.0, A Beginner's Guide*, 2nd edn, London, Sage.
Have a look at Chapter 10 on Graphs.

chapter 5

Tables and Charts for Interval Variables

INTRODUCTION

We saw in the last chapter that tables and charts can be used to great effect for categorical variables. You should remember from Chapter 2 that interval scales, although they are distinguished from categorical scales in that they have a unit of measurement for calibrating or counting the distances between observations, nevertheless also possess all the characteristics of categorical scales. This means that it is possible to utilise all the procedures described in the last chapter. However, since there will usually be a large number of scale values (particularly for continuous interval variables), in order to do so it will be necessary first to group observations into class intervals.

Once interval variables are grouped they can then be used to produce univariate, bivariate and multivariate tables, or alternatively bar charts or pie charts. Of course, when interval variables are deployed in this way, the information about distances is being ignored or thrown away. So why would any researcher want to do that? Usually, it is because the researcher wishes to look at the relationship between a categorical and an interval variable. In this situation, the researcher will group the interval variable into class intervals and then crosstabulate with the categorical variable.

Where researchers are dealing with interval variables in isolation (that is, they are undertaking univariate analysis) or where they are relating two or more interval variables, then a rather different range of procedures become appropriate. This chapter looks at how tables for interval variables may be set out and then considers how such variables may be illustrated graphically. Finally, it explains how SPSS can be used to produce the necessary analyses.

FREQUENCY TABLES FOR INTERVAL DATA

In the table tennis survey there are only two interval variables: the age at which respondents began playing table tennis and the amount they spent on table tennis in the last six months. If we did a straight frequency count on these the result would look like Table 5.1, which illustrates a frequency table for 'agebegan'. While most began playing between the ages of 8 and 14, there are many ages with a frequency of only one. There are in fact 21 different ages and if we tried, for example, to crosstabulate this with sex of respondent we would have a 21-by-two table with 42 cells. That would be impossible to interpret and would be fairly useless for any kind of statistical analysis. The solution is to group the ages into what are often called class intervals. These might be classes of equal size, for example, 6–10, 11–15, 16–20, 21–25, but there would still be four people outside this range so we would need a '26 and over' category. That still leaves five groupings, which, for a sample of 120, will still be too many if we want to use it for crosstabulation.

The Cumulative Percent column shows that just under half (45 per cent) began at the age of 11 or earlier and the rest began at the age of 12 or later. So, if we wanted to split them into two roughly equal halves, we could have two categories, '11 and under' and '12 and over'. The result is shown in Table 5.2. This can now be crosstabulated, for example, against sex of respondent, as in Table 5.3.

In short, the researcher may wish to use class intervals or groupings for metric variables if he or she wants to crosstabulate them with categorical variables. If the

Table 5.1   *A frequency table for age began playing table tennis*

agebegan	Frequency	Percent	Cumulative Percent
6	1	.8	.8
7	2	1.7	2.5
8	12	10.0	12.5
9	7	5.8	18.3
10	20	16.7	35.0
11	12	10.0	45.0
12	16	13.3	58.3
13	11	9.2	67.5
14	12	10.0	77.5
15	8	6.7	84.2
16	5	4.2	88.3
17	2	1.7	90.0
18	4	3.3	93.3
19	1	.8	94.2
21	1	.8	95.0
22	1	.8	95.8
24	1	.8	96.7
27	1	.8	97.5
28	1	.8	98.3
32	1	.8	99.2
43	1	.8	100.0
Total	120	100.0	

Table 5.2   *Table 5.1 regrouped into two categories*

Began table tennis	Frequency	Percent
11 and under	54	45.0
12 and over	66	55.0
Total	120	100.0

Table 5.3   *Age groups by sex of respondent*

Count

		What sex are you?		
		Male	Female	Total
Began table tennis	Under 12	44	10	54
	12 and over	59	7	66
Total		103	17	120

sample is quite small then it may be necessary to create only two or three categories. The groupings for Table 5.2 were created using the SPSS Recode procedure, which was introduced in the last chapter.

METRIC TABLES

Sometimes tables are used not to display frequencies of scale values, but to display that actual metric quantities. If you look at a set of company accounts, you will see tables that express turnover, profits, revenue, costs in terms of Pounds Sterling, sales may be expressed in tonnes, kilograms, litres or units sold, while personnel may be expressed in numbers of employees in various categories. The figures in the tables will not be frequencies, but the actual metric values like £5 687 000 turnover or 496 employees.

Data from survey research will normally be displayed in frequency tables, but suppose we take the interval variable, 'amount spent on table tennis in the last 6 months', and calculate a grand total. This comes to £6208.80, averaging at £51.74 per person. We could break this down by sex of respondent and say that the average expenditure of the males was £53.05 and for the females £43.82. There could be further breakdowns by age, what league they compete in and so on. The point is that the figures in the table would relate to Pounds Sterling, not frequencies.

HISTOGRAMS AND LINE GRAPHS

We saw in the last chapter that bar charts and pie charts are appropriate for categorical data. For continuous interval data these do not usually make a great deal of sense. Figure 5.1, for example, shows the continuous interval variable

Figure 5.1   *A bar chart for continuous interval data*

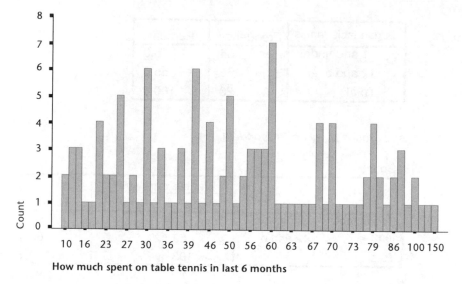

How much spent on table tennis in last 6 months

Figure 5.2   *A histogram for continuous interval data*

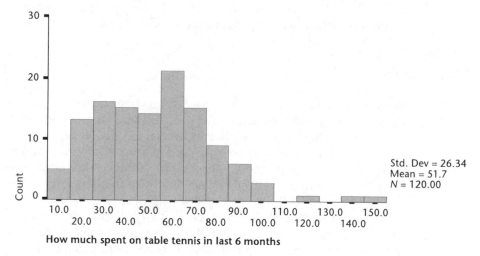

How much spent on table tennis in last 6 months

amount spent on table tennis in the last six months as a bar chart. It shows a separate bar for each quantity mentioned. Notice that a lot of the sums spent are mentioned only once. It is difficult to get a sense of the overall distribution from this chart. The same data are illustrated as a histogram in Figure 5.2. Here, the width of the bars represents class intervals of amounts of spend, giving a good picture of the distribution.

For discrete interval data we can use either a bar chart or a histogram. Figure 5.3, for example, shows the importance of social benefits of playing table tennis as a bar chart. Each bar is treated as a category. If, however, we treat the scores 1–5 allocated to the responses to the importance of social benefits and so on as interval, then there are only whole numbers (1–5). Respondents cannot, for

Figure 5.3   *A bar chart for discrete interval data*

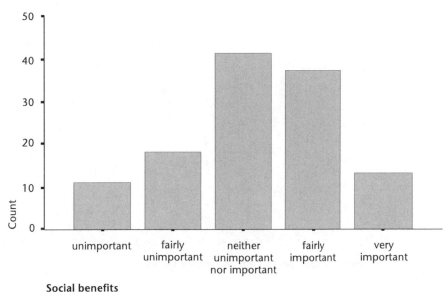

Social benefits

example, score 4.3. Figure 5.4 shows the same data as a histogram. The bars are assumed to be equal distances apart and a mean of 3.2 has been calculated.

A line graph can be used to represent the frequencies or percentages of interval variables, as in Figure 5.5, but this is only an alternative version of Figure 5.1. Line graphs are not particularly helpful for presenting frequencies. They are of more use as time graphs where the X-axis is used for elapsed time or for dates and the Y-axis for the quantities of a variable that are changing over time.

Figure 5.4   *A histogram for discrete interval data*

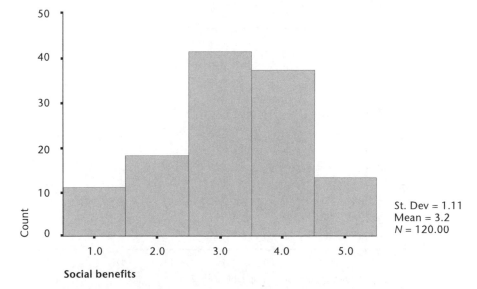

Social benefits

Figure 5.5　　　*A line graph of Figure 5.1*

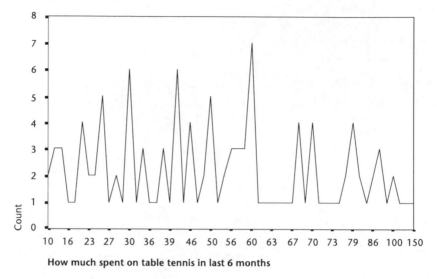

How much spent on table tennis in last 6 months

SCATTERGRAMS

These may be used to illustrate the relationship between two variables where both are interval. The horizontal axis is used to represent the values of one of the interval variables and the vertical axis to represent the other. The combination of two scales values is then plotted for each case, as in Figure 5.6. There are 120 points, one for each respondent. It shows that there is a tendency for those who took up table tennis at a later age tended to have spent more on it in the last six months. It shows, furthermore, that the relationship is approximately linear. We

Figure 5.6　　　*A scattergram of 'spend' by 'agebegan'*

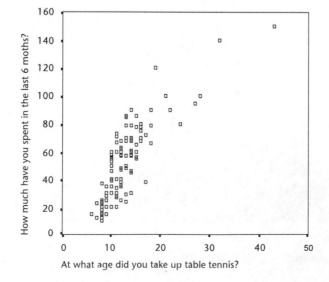

At what age did you take up table tennis?

will see in Chapter 7 how this property can be used to calculate a measure of correlation. It is worth noting that if one of the variables is considered to be independent (like age began playing table tennis) then it is plotted along the horizontal or X-axis. The dependent variable ('spend') is put on the vertical Y-axis.

USING SPSS 'HISTOGRAM', 'LINE' AND 'SCATTER'

These three procedures are contained in the Graphs drop-down menu. Access the *tabten.sav* file, click on Graphs, then Histogram. The Histogram dialog box will allow you to enter only one variable. This should be an interval variable, so try putting in 'agebegan'. You have the option of being able to superimpose a normal curve on the result, so try it. The result should be as in Figure 5.7. Notice that the distribution is not a close approximation to a normal distribution.

The Graphs/Line procedure will give you the Line Charts dialog box. From this you can choose from three types of chart – Simple, Multiple and Drop-line. The Simple chart plots your chosen variable along the X-axis. Enter it into the Category Axis. It will plot the number of cases or the percentage of cases against each scale value. A line graph for 'agebegan' is shown in Figure 5.8. It is possible to plot the results of several interval variables on the same graph by selecting Summaries of Separate Variables. Thus Figure 5.9 was produced by entering the five aspects of table tennis that were rated in terms of importance. As you can see, this is not a particularly helpful graph. A bar chart would have been better. The problem is that the five aspects are not themselves a genuine interval scale.

The multiple line chart enables you to plot the frequencies of one variable against the categories of another, as in Figure 5.10. This shows the frequencies of the various ages at which people took up table tennis separated out by sex of

Figure 5.7   *A histogram of 'agebegan'*

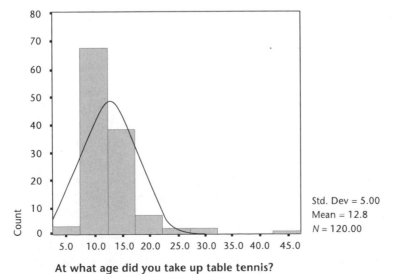

At what age did you take up table tennis?

Std. Dev = 5.00
Mean = 12.8
N = 120.00

Figure 5.8   *A line graph of 'agebegan'*

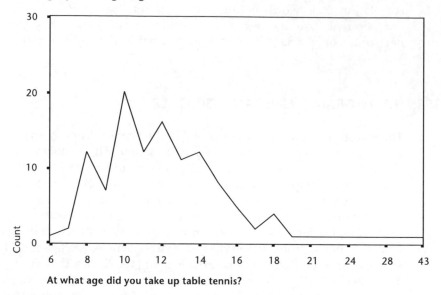

Figure 5.9   *The importance of various aspects of playing table tennis*

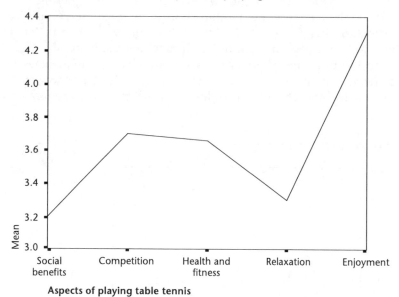

respondent. It is also possible to obtain summaries of separate variables split by the categories of another variables, but, once again, this is not particularly helpful.

The Scatter program allows you to choose between Simple, Matrix, Overlay and 3-D. Thus Figure 5.6 is a simple scatterplot, but it is possible to set markers by another variable, as in Figure 5.11. The scatterplot matrix plots all combinations of two or more variables. The number of rows and columns is equal to the

Figure 5.10   *'Agebegan' plotted by sex of respondent*

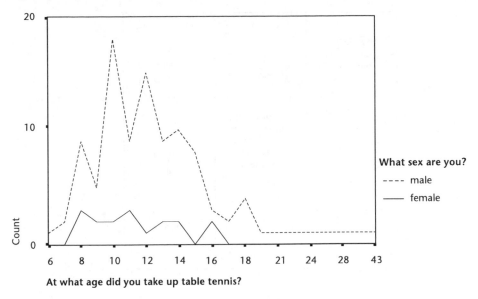

Figure 5.11   *A scatterplot with separate markers for males and females*

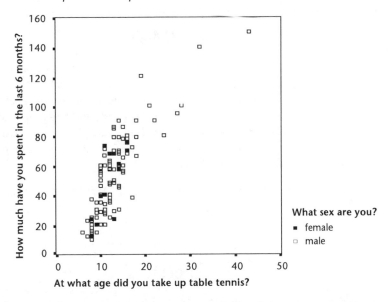

number of matrix variables selected. Thus Figure 5.12 shows three matrix variables. Notice that only 'agebegan' and 'spend' are continuous interval. 'Comp' is discrete interval so does not work in a scatterplot. Overlay plots two or more variable pairs and requires a minimum of four continuous interval variables, which we do not have in the *tabten* dataset. Finally, the 3-D facility plots three continuous metric variables in three dimensions. Again, this cannot be illustrated on our dataset.

Figure 5.12   *A matrix scatterplot with three variables*

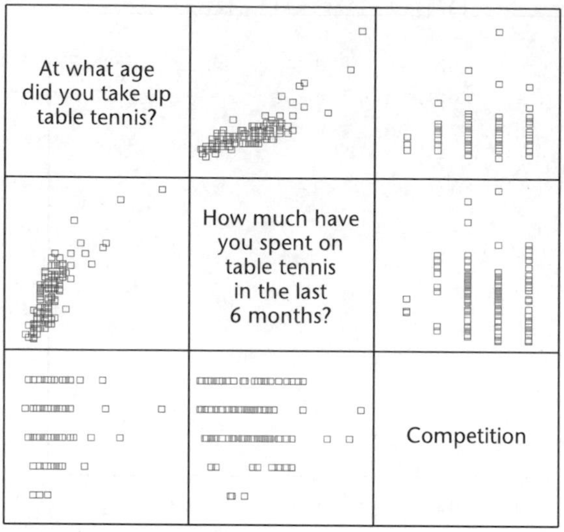

SUMMARY

Where variables are interval it is possible to use them as if they were categorical by grouping scale values into class intervals. Such variables can then be crosstabulated with other categorical variables. However, for univariate analysis it is possible to use histograms rather than bar charts and line graphs instead of pie charts. For bivariate analysis, where both variables are interval then a scattergram can be used to display how the variables are related together. SPSS can be used for all these procedures.

Exercises

1. Regroup the variable 'spend' into three categories and crosstabulate against whether there is anybody else in the household who plays table tennis.
2. Use SPSS to draw a histogram of the variable 'agebegan'. Use the **Chart Editor** to change/improve its appearance.
3. Try plotting a scattergram of the perceived importance of the social benefits of playing table tennis against the importance of health and fitness.

Points for discussion

You can use SPSS to produce any kind of nonsense. The trick is to know what counts as 'nonsense'. Suggest some of the main ways in which the researcher might produce nonsensical tables and charts.

Further reading

Bowers, D. (1996) *Statistics from Scratch: An Introduction for Health Care Professionals*, Chichester, John Wiley and Sons.
See Chapter 4 on Organising Quantitative Data.
Foster, J. (2000) *Data Analysis Using SPSS for Windows Versions 8.0–10.0: A Beginner's Guide*, 2nd edn, London, Sage.
See Chapter 10 in particular.

chapter 6

Summarising Categorical Variables

INTRODUCTION

Chapter 4 looked at tables and charts for categorical variables. This chapter deals with categorical variables by way of reducing the data to a few key summary measures. We begin by looking at what can be done one variable at a time (univariate summaries) and we then turn to how the relationship between two variables can be measured (bivariate summaries). There are many statistics that can be used in this context, but for the purpose of this chapter, however, just one statistic is picked out because it suits most situations.

The statistic selected – Cramer's V – will have to stand as an example of what can be done with bivariate tables. This particular statistic was chosen because of its versatility, but, like all statistics, it is not without its limitations. The treatment of Cramer's V in the following pages is probably far more detailed than you are likely to find in other sources, but it is better at this stage to understand one measure well than to have a superficial acquaintance with a range of measures.

UNIVARIATE DATA SUMMARY

The calculation of univariate summary measures for categorical variables is fairly limited. The SPSS Frequencies procedure offers three measures: Percent, Valid Percent and Cumulative Percent, as illustrated in Table 6.1 for the variable 'division', which is scaled at the ordinal level. Thus 31.7 per cent of respondents compete in the first division, 34.2 per cent in the second, and so on. Valid Percent excludes missing cases, which were explained in Chapter 4 (p. 89). Where there are no missing cases, as in Table 6.1 then Percent and Valid Percent are identical.

Table 6.1   *A univariate table for categorical variables*

In which division do you compete?

		Frequency	Percent	Valid Percent	Cumulative Percent
Valid	First	38	31.7	31.7	31.7
	Second	41	34.2	34.2	65.8
	Third	36	30.0	30.0	95.8
	Fourth	5	4.2	4.2	100.0
	Total	120	100.0	100.0	

Cumulative Percent accumulates the Valid Percent so a total of 65.8 per cent compete in the first or second division and most (95.8 per cent) in one of the first three divisions.

The only other univariate summary statistic that might be appropriate for categorical data is the mode. This is the most commonly occurring value. You can get SPSS to give this to you, but all it will tell you is the category with the highest frequency, which, for example, for Table 6.1, is the second division, which has the highest frequency. For nominal scales the very notion of 'central tendency' does not meaningfully apply. You can hardly have a 'central point' about which values cluster if they cannot be put into any order. For ordinal scales the idea of a central point does make some sense, but if there are very few categories, as for the variable 'division', it does not help very much to say that the second division has the largest number of players when, in this case, numbers are fairly evenly split between the first three divisions. The mode makes more sense with interval data, as we shall see in the next chapter.

BIVARIATE DATA SUMMARY

We saw in Chapter 4 that the relationship between two categorical variables may be displayed in a bivariate crosstabulation. We also saw that calculating percentages enables us to make comparisons between various subgroups, for example comparing males with females. However, what we really need is to be able to measure the strength of the relationship between two variables in a single figure – a measure of association.

Statisticians have developed a mind-blowing array of different measures of association for crosstabulated variables. Each statistic, however, will give a different (sometimes very different) answer. Each statistic will have its own strengths and weaknesses, and there will be circumstances in which its calculation is misleading or inadvisable. The SPSS Crosstabs procedure offers eight different statistics; four for situations where both variables are scaled at the nominal level and four for where both are scaled at the ordinal level. Each of these statistics is explained in detail in Kent (1999). The focus here is on one statistic: Cramer's V. This statistic is suitable for all sizes of table and may be calculated on either nominal or ordinal scales.

Table 6.2　　*How many times per week respondents play crosstabulated by whether anybody else in the household plays*

Count

| | | Does anybody else in your household play table tennis? | | Total |
		Yes	No	
How many times do you play per week?	Once	15	28	43
	Twice	22	30	52
	Three times	10	8	18
	Four or more times	5	2	7
Total		52	68	120

Cramer's V is based on the notion of what statisticians call *departure from independence*. It entails imagining what the data would look like if there were no association at all, and then measuring the extent to which the observed values depart from this. Table 6.2 crosstabulates how many times per week respondents play table tennis with whether or not anybody else in the household plays. Clearly, if there are other people in the household who play, then respondents are likely to play more often. It does indeed seem that where there is somebody else, then respondents are more likely to play two or three times a week. But how strong is this tendency?

52 respondents out of a total of 120 said there was somebody else in the household who plays. That represents a proportion of 0.433 or 43.3 per cent. If there were no association between the two variables, then we would expect the same proportion, 43.3 per cent, of those who played once a week to say 'yes', or $0.433 * 43 = 18.63$. There were in fact 15, which is 3.63 *below* expectation. The difference between the observed frequency and the expected frequency (fo − fe) is, then, −3.63. A quick way of calculating the expectation is to multiply the row and column marginals for that cell and divide by *n*, in this case $52 * 43/120 = 18.63$. For the 'no' respondents, the observed result is 3.63 *above* expectation. All expectations must sum to the same marginal. The total of differences will, then, sum to zero. However, if the differences are squared they all become positive. Furthermore, the importance of the size of this difference will depend on whether the expected figure is large or small, so we divide the squared difference by *fe*:

$$(fo - fe)^2 / fe = (3.63)^2 / 18.63 = 0.71$$

This calculation is made for each cell and the total for all cells is summed. This is the statistic Chi-square. For this table it works out at 4.618. It is an overall measure of the extent to which the observed values in the table depart from expected values. However, as a measure of association it is difficult to interpret. The minimum value Chi-square can take is zero where there are no differences between observed and expected values. The maximum value depends on the number of cases and the number of cells. For a two-by-two table with four cells or for any table where either rows or columns have only two categories (that is, binary) the maximum value that Chi-square can take is always the number of cases.

Measures of association are usually designed in such a way that they vary between zero for no association and plus (or minus) one where there is a perfect association. If we divide Chi-square by the number of cases, then we achieve such a measure. If the maximum value of Chi-square is achieved (for example of 120 where there are 120 cases) then $120/120 = 1$. It reverts to zero if there are no differences between observed and expected values. For Table 6.2 this value would be Chi-square divided by 120 or $4.618/120 = 0.0385$. However, since we have squared all the differences, this value is in squared units, so we need to take the square root to return to the original units, giving a value of 0.196. This is the value of Cramer's V reported by SPSS, as in Table 6.3. Where either rows or columns is a binary scale then this coefficient is identical to a statistic that is called Phi, which is the square root of Chi-square divided by n. Unfortunately, for larger tables where neither rows nor columns is binary, Phi can take on values greater that one. In this situation an adjustment is made for the number of rows or columns. This adjustment is to divide Chi-square not by n but by n multiplied by either rows minus one or columns minus one whichever is the smaller value. Thus in a table with three rows and four columns, Chi-square will be divided by $n * 2$. In a table with six rows and seven columns it will be divided by $n * 5$ and so on. This makes Cramer's V always vary between zero and one. For any table where one variable is binary, then n is multiplied by one and it becomes identical to Phi. So, if you consistently use Cramer's V you do not have to worry about the size of the table.

The achieved value of V is, then, 0.196. This shows that there is a small degree of association between the two variables. It is difficult to give the result a more precise statistical interpretation. However, if, for example, we crosstabulated the number of times respondents reported playing table tennis with another variable, like sex of respondent, we could calculate V and then compare the result. We could then conclude whether the presence of others in the household playing table tennis, or sex of respondent, was more strongly associated with frequency of playing.

Cramer's V is, then, a good statistic. It can be used on any size of table. It can be used for two binary scales, two nominal scales, two ordinal scales or any combination like one binary and one ordinal. It is a fairly robust measure in that it can be applied in a wide range of circumstances and does not produce nonsensical results under certain conditions. For example, unlike some other statistics, it does not revert to zero simply because one or more cells is empty. It also makes no assumptions about the shape of the population distribution of the variables from which it is computed and requires only categorical measurement.

Table 6.3   *Chi-square and Cramer's V for Table 6.2*

Symmetric Measures

	Value
Pearson Chi-Square	4.618
Cramer's V	.196
N of Valid Cases	120

However, Cramer's V is not perfect and it has its limitations. First, although V is always zero when there is a complete lack of association between the two variables, when it is unity there may not be a 'perfect' association. If the table is square (for example, a two-by-two, a three-by-three, a four-by-four and so on) then $V = 1$ does indeed indicate that the variables are perfectly associated. However, if the table is non-square (for example, a three by five) then V can reach unity even when there is clearly not a perfect association.

A second limitation is that since V depends on calculating Chi-square it must be amenable to the use of that statistic. This statistic assumes that the expected values are large. A 'rule of thumb' that is commonly applied is that the statistic should be calculated only if fewer than about 20 per cent of all the cells have expected frequencies of less than 5 and that no cell has an expected frequency of less than one. (As we shall see, SPSS will warn you if this is the case.)

A third limitation is that the magnitude of achieved values of V has no direct interpretation, and, furthermore, it is not directly comparable with any other measure of association, except in the case of the two-by-two table, when it is identical to Pearson's r statistic, which will be explained in the next chapter.

Finally, the statistic is designed for use with nominal scales. When it is being used for ordinal scales it does not violate any statistical assumptions and its use is legitimate, but it may be less informative than measures that are specifically for ordinal data. Thus V does not indicate a direction of association. This is fine for nominal scales where the notion of a 'negative' association does not apply. However, for ordinal scales it could happen that *high* values on one variable are associated with *low* values on the other. This would indicate a negative association, but Cramer's V cannot be negative. Furthermore, the statistic is insensitive to the ordering of categories. Putting the scale values in a different order on either variable will not change the value of V. This again is fine for nominal scales, but for ordinal scales it ignores information that could be derived from the ordering of categories.

Despite these limitations, Cramer's V is an extremely useful coefficient because of its wide applicability. It does not make any distinction between dependent and independent variables. This may be seen as an advantage if the researcher does not wish to make such a distinction, but where he or she does, then other measures of association may be better. (See Kent, 1999 for a fuller explanation.)

RANK CORRELATION

If both scales to be measured for the strength of the association between them are fully ranked with as many rankings as there are cases to be ranked, it is not possible to use Cramer's V. There is, however, one statistic that was developed specifically for this situation by the statistician Spearman at the end of the nineteenth century which he called rho. It is still called Spearman's rho or Spearman's rank-order correlation coefficient. The formula for it was derived from the Pearson product-moment correlation coefficient, so we will look at this statistic in more detail in the next chapter when we consider the uses (and misuses) of Pearson's r. Suffice it to say at this point that the main use of Spearman's rho is for interval data when such data do not meet the requirements of parametric statistics.

USING SPSS 'CROSSTABS:STATISTICS'

The SPSS Crosstabs procedure was described at the end of Chapter 6. If you access the *tabten.sav* file and go to Analyze/Descriptive Statistics/Crosstabs you will obtain the Crosstabs dialog box as before. Now click on the Statistics button and will obtain the Crosstabs:Statistics dialog box as in Figure 6.1. You will see that Cramer's V is in a group of four statistics that are appropriate for nominal data and it is listed alongside the statistic Phi. It was explained earlier that Phi and *V* are the same statistic where either rows or columns is binary. For larger tables, Phi is no longer appropriate, so just stick to *V* and you cannot go wrong! Notice that you can also click on the Chi-square box at top left.

Now crosstabulate whether anybody else in the household plays table tennis by the division in which people compete. (This would be on the hypothesis that those with others in the household who play might be better players and play in a higher division than those who do not have anybody else in the household to play). Put the variable 'else' into the Column(s): box and 'division' into the Row(s): box. Click on Statistics and check the Phi and Cramer's V and the Chi-square boxes. You should obtain the output shown in Tables 6.4 and 6.5. Table 6.4 shows the results of the Phi and Cramer's V calculation. Both are identical at 0.094.

There is virtually no association here. The interpretation of Approx.Sig. we will leave until Chapter 9. Table 6.4 shows that Chi-square (called Pearson Chi-Square in SPSS) is 1.058. However, we are warned that two cells have an expected frequency of less than 5, so we can place no reliance on the result.

Figure 6.1   The 'Crosstabs:Statistics' dialog box

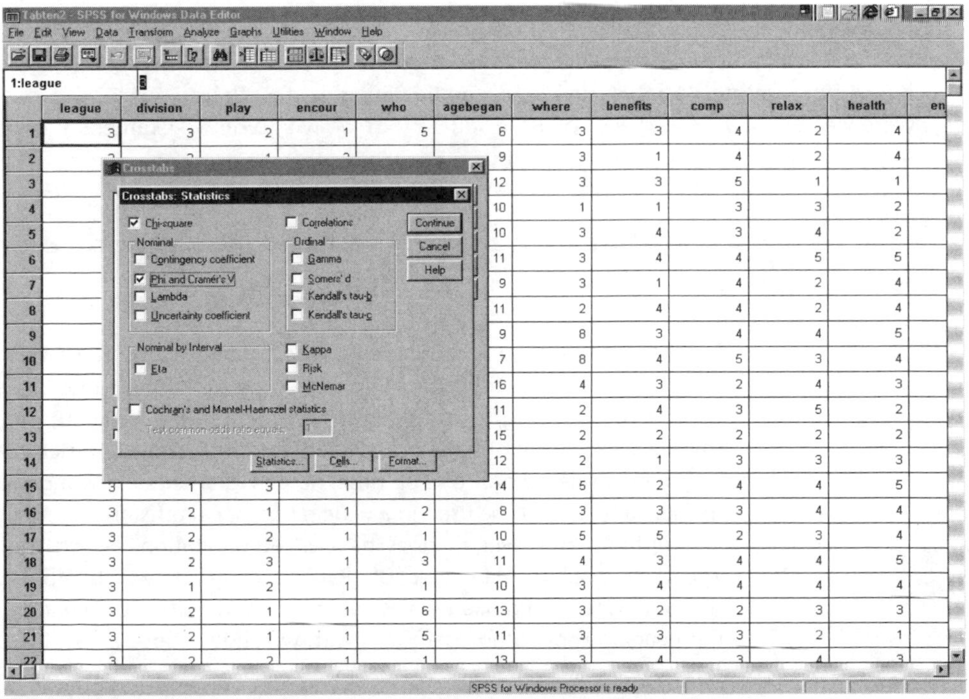

Table 6.4   SPSS output for Phi and Cramer's V

Symmetric Measures

		Value	Approx. Sig.
Nominal by Nominal	Phi	.094	.787
	Cramer's V	.094	.787
N of Valid Cases		120	

Table 6.5   SPSS Chi-square output

Chi-Square Tests

	Value	df	Asymp. Sig. (2-sided)
Pearson Chi-Square	1.058[a]	3	.787
Likelihood Ratio	1.055	3	.788
Linear-by-Linear Association	.862	1	.353
N of Valid Cases	120		

a. 2 cells (25.0%) have expected count less than 5. The minimum expected count is 2.17.

Suggestion

If we exclude the fourth division from the analysis since there are only 5 players in this division, then the result will be to eliminate low expected frequencies. This can easily be done in SPSS by going back to the **Define Variables** dialog box and defining 4 = Fourth as a missing value. Notice that if we divided 1.058 by 120 and took the square root we would derive Cramer's V of 0.094.

SUMMARY

For the purpose of summarising categorical variables one at a time it is possible to use percentages, either for all the cases, or excluding those cases for which that value is missing, or cumulative percentages. For bivariate data summary there is a vast array of statistics. SPSS itself offers eight such measures, but this chapter considered only one of these, namely Cramer's V. It is a good statistic in the sense that it can be used in a wide range of circumstances and it makes few assumptions. However, it does have a few limitations which the researcher would be well to be aware of. Rank correlation, which although strictly-speaking is for two ranked scales, will be treated in the next chapter along with the Pearson correlation coefficient with which it is closely identified.

Exercises

1. Complete the calculation of Chi-square by hand from Table 6.2 to show that it gives the same result as SPSS.
2. Try out more crosstabulations from the *tabten.sav* file, but think about the hypotheses you are implicitly testing. If any of your tables are large, try reducing their size using **Recode** on the variable before crosstabulating.

Points for discussion

1. Bivariate data summary using SPSS is so quick and simple that the temptation must be to crosstabulate everything in sight. Is this a good idea?
2. What result from Cramer's V do you think would count as a 'high' degree of association?

Further reading

Kent, R. (1999) *Marketing Research: Measurement, Method and Application,* London, International Thomson Business Press.

Have a look in particular at pp. 155–74, which takes you through all the statistics on the SPSS **Crosstabs** procedure, explaining their calculation, their strengths and limitations, and the situations in which they may be appropriately used.

chapter 7

Summarising Interval Variables

INTRODUCTION

The statistics considered in this chapter are covered in just about every statistics book you can think of, but they are included here for the sake of completeness. The focus, however, will be on what SPSS provides for summarising interval variables. We begin by looking at univariate measures. We then we turn to bivariate statistics and then introduce a number of multivariate techniques that SPSS offers. Finally, we consider how to use SPSS to generate all these measures.

Warning

This chapter gets complicated quite quickly and if you feel uneasy about symbols and equations you can skip the sections on multivariate analysis and maybe return to them when you have greater familiarity with SPSS

UNIVARIATE DATA SUMMARY

SPSS offers four groups of univariate statistics summarising:

■ central tendency,
■ dispersion,
■ distribution shape,
■ percentile values.

Central tendency

Central tendency focuses on the extent to which the interval values in a set of values are concentrated about a central figure. SPSS offers three measures of central tendency:

- the mean,
- the median,
- the mode.

The mean is commonly what we understand by 'average'. It is calculated by adding all the values together and dividing by the number of values included. Table 7.1 illustrates an SPSS output for the mean, median and the mode. It also gives the sum, which is the total of all the values. For the variable 'agebegan' in our table tennis data the sum of all 120 ages is 1536. There are 120 values recorded, so $1536/120 = 12.8$, which is the mean value. The mean takes account of every value in the distribution. While this is normally seen as an advantage, it may be unduly affected by extreme values. Thus one person began playing table tennis at the age of 43. If we exclude him from the analysis then the mean goes down to 12.55.

Another tricky feature of the mean arises when the scale is discrete rather than continuous. Being discrete, all the scale values will be integers, but the mean may be a fraction, like the average family having 2.4 children. Remember that the mean is appropriate only for interval data, but SPSS is very obliging and will, for example, happily take the variable 'division', which is ordinal, and calculate an average of 2.07. This is nonsense, of course, but you cannot expect SPSS to know this.

The median is the middle value in an ascending or descending series of values. It is that value which splits the observations into two halves. For the variable 'agebegan' the median is 12. You would have to imagine putting respondents in a row in order of the age at which they say they began playing and a line dividing the 60th and the 61st respondent would lie between two people who had given the answer 12. If there had been 121 respondents, then the median would have been the value of the 61st person. One advantage of the median is that it is unaffected by extreme values, so if the person who began playing table tennis at 43 had been 93 instead, this would leave the median value unaffected, but, of course, would have put up the mean age considerably!

Table 7.1   *Measures of central tendency for 'agebegan'*

At what age did you take up table tennis?

N	Valid	120
	Missing	0
Mean		12.80
Median		12.00
Mode		10
Sum		1536

It is commonly argued that to calculate the median you must have at least ordinal data. Strictly-speaking, that is true, but calculating the median on such data is not usually very insightful. If the scale is fully ranked, then the median value is always the middle rank. If we have 300 respondents put into three categories of high, medium and low satisfaction, then – not surprisingly – the median value will probably be 'medium'. Only on metric data can the median be used for its main advantage: excluding outliers, or extreme values.

The mode is the most commonly occurring value. For categorical scales it is that scale value (or category) that has the largest frequency. For metric data, certainly if they are continuous, each scale value may occur only once. If the values are grouped, then there will be a modal class interval, but that may change with different intervals being used. The modal age for 'agebegan' is 10. This is because age ten was reported most often compared with other ages.

Dispersion

Dispersion measures variability or the amount of spread in the data. From Table 7.2 you can see that the youngest age at which respondents began playing table tennis was 6 and the oldest, 43. That is a range of 37, (that is, 43 – 6). The problem with the range, however, is that it does not tell us how far *on average* the individual values are spread out either side of the mean. This is what the standard deviation measures and it tells you the extent to which the set of values tend to be fairly close to the mean of the set or are considerably spread out.

The standard deviation is the average of deviations about the mean. Its calculation involves taking the mean and working out how far each value is above or below the mean. These distances are then squared and added up. Finally this sum is divided by the number of cases and the square root is taken. For the variable 'agebegan', we have seen that the mean age is 12.8. If you look at Table 7.3 you will see that one person began at the age of 6, that is, 6 – 12.8 or 6.8 years below the mean. The square of this is 46.24. There are two respondents who began at the age of 7, so they are both 5.8 below the mean. The square of this is 33.64 and we need to take account of the fact that there are two of them. We do this for all 120 cases and add up the grand total. That comes to 3002.4. Divide by 120 and take the square root and you get a standard deviation of 5, as seen in Table 7.2. It is actually quite a lot of calculation if you are doing it by hand.

Table 7.2   *Measures of dispersion for 'agebegan'*

At what age did you take up table tennis?

N	Valid	120
	Missing	0
Std. Error of Mean		.46
Std. Deviation		5.00
Variance		25.02
Range		37
Minimum		6
Maximum		43

Table 7.3   *A frequency distribution for 'agebegan'*

At what age did you take up table tennis?

		Frequency
Valid	6	1
	7	2
	8	12
	9	7
	10	20
	11	12
	12	16
	13	11
	14	12
	15	8
	16	5
	17	2
	18	4
	19	1
	21	1
	22	1
	24	1
	27	1
	28	1
	32	1
	43	1
	Total	120

Fortunately, SPSS will do it for you in less than a second. The variance is the sum before we have taken the square root. It is this figure that tends to get used in further calculations rather than the standard deviation. The remaining statistic in Table 7.2 is the standard error of the mean. We will be returning to this statistic when we come to deal with statistical inference for interval variables in Chapter 10.

So, the standard deviation of 'agebegan' is 5. So what? To answer this question more fully it will be necessary to wait until we have considered statistical inference. For the moment, we will have to content ourselves with saying that the average of deviations about the mean age of 12.8 years is 5 years. Provided the distribution of values has a central concentration, most of the values will be within two standard deviations of the mean, in this case between 2.8 and 28.8. In fact there is nobody who began playing under three years old and only two who began after the age of 28 (see Table 7.3).

Distribution shape

You can obtain a good idea of the actual distribution of a metric variable by getting SPSS to draw you a histogram, as in Figure 7.1 for the variable 'agebegan'. This distribution would be regarded as skewed to the right or positively skewed. If a distribution is completely symmetrical, then the values of the mean, the median and the mode will be the same. However, if the distribution is skewed,

Figure 7.1   *The distribution of 'agebegan'*

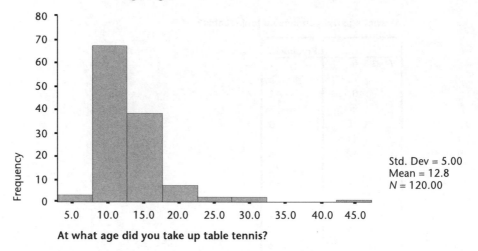

Std. Dev = 5.00
Mean = 12.8
N = 120.00

At what age did you take up table tennis?

they will not. If positively skewed, the mean will be higher than the median and the median will be higher than the mode. The reverse will be true if the distribution is skewed to the left. This gives a basis for a measure of the extent of skewness. This uses simply the difference between the mean and the median and is a measure of the asymmetry of the distribution. It will have a value of zero if the median and the mean are the same. A measure of skewness which is less than one (or minus one) is generally taken as an indicator that the distribution is approximately normal in shape. The value calculated by SPSS for 'agebegan' is 2.869 (Table 7.4), which shows that the distribution cannot be regarded as normal in shape.

The other measure of the distribution shape given by SPSS is *kurtosis*. This is a measure of the extent to which the values cluster more or less about the mean than would a normal distribution. It will have a value of zero for a normal distribution, a positive value for high clustering and a negative value for low clustering. For 'agebegan' it has a high positive value so the clustering is high with a long tail, which you can see from the histogram.

Table 7.4   *SPSS measures of distribution shape*

At what age did you take up table tennis?

N	Valid	120
	Missing	0
Skewness		2.869
Std. Error of Skewness		.221
Kurtosis		12.575
Std. Error of Kurtosis		.438

The normal distribution

Reference has been made in several places above to something called a 'normal' distribution. This is a special kind of distribution that has a number of crucial properties. It has a bell-shaped curve that can be described by a mathematical equation and has a zero measure for skewness and kurtosis. It is symmetrical in shape and its tails never quite touch the base. The last feature means that, in principle, the range is infinite, but in practice nearly all observations will lie within three standard deviations above and below the mean (that is, a range of six standard deviations). The mean and the standard deviation together allow statisticians to distinguish one particular normal curve from another. Each time we specify a particular combination of mean and standard deviation a different distribution will be generated. Figure 7.2 shows three different distributions. Distributions A and B have the same mean but different standard deviations. Distributions A and C have the same standard deviation but different means. Distributions B and C depict two distributions that differ in respect of both.

Because the normal curve has a standard shape, it is possible to treat the area under the curve as representing total certainty that any observation will be encompassed by it. We can say, furthermore, that 50 per cent of the area is above the mean for that variable, and 50 per cent below. In other words there is a 50 per cent chance that any observation will be above (or below) the mean. This argument can be taken further so that we can calculate the area under the curve between the mean and one standard deviation. The area is, in fact, 34.1 per cent (see Figure 7.3). Thus just over two thirds or 68.2 per cent of the area is between plus one standard deviation and minus one standard deviation from the mean. Thus if the mean score of a set of cases is 20 with a standard deviation of 6, then just over two thirds of the area (and, by implication, of the observations) would be within 20 ± 6 or between 14 and 26. Figure 7.3 also shows that all but 4.6 per cent of the area lies between plus and minus two standard deviations. There are, in fact, tables of areas under the normal curve, so that if we wished to know how many standard deviations encompassed exactly 95 per cent of the area, we could look it up and discover that 1.96 standard deviations either side of the mean does so. This characteristic becomes very important when we move on to consider statistical inference.

Figure 7.2   *Three normal distributions with differing parameters*

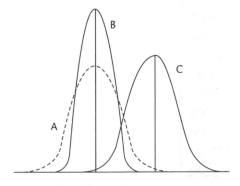

Figure 7.3   *The normal distribution*

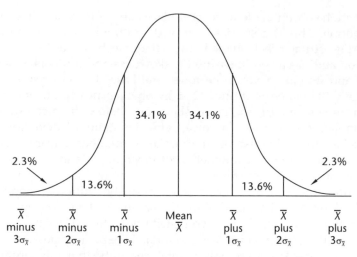

Percentile values

Percentiles are values of an interval-scaled variable that divide the ordered data into groups so that a certain percentage is above and another percentage is below. The median, described above, is, in fact, the 50th percentile. Quartiles (the 25th, 50th, and 75th percentiles) divide the observations into four groups of equal size. Table 7.5 shows the percentile vales in 10 equal groups plus the 25th, 50th and 75th percentiles. The middle 50% (that is, between the 25th and 75th quartile) is often called the inter-quartile range, which in this case lies between the ages of 10 and 14, so half of the respondents lie between these ages.

Table 7.5   *Percentile values for 'agebegan'*

At what age did you take up table tennis?		
N	Valid	120
	Missing	0
Percentiles	10	8.00
	20	10.00
	25	10.00
	30	10.00
	40	11.00
	50	12.00
	60	13.00
	70	14.00
	75	14.00
	80	15.00
	90	17.90

BIVARIATE DATA SUMMARY

We saw in Chapter 5 that to display the relationship between two interval variables we could plot a scattergram. Data sumary involves calculating a measure of association similar to those we calculated for crosstabulations. The good news is that there is only one measure that is universally used – Pearson's r, otherwise known as the correlation coefficient or the product-moment correlation coefficient. The bad news is that it is a bit more difficult to explain than the measures we have looked at so far. If you have access to SPSS then it can be calculated for you at the click of a mouse button. However, the point is to understand how the statistic is calculated and what it is telling you.

If the two variables are correlated, then high values on one variable are associated with high values on the other for a positive correlation and with low values for a negative one. The problem is that the two scales will have different averages, as measured by the arithmetic mean, and are likely in addition to be in different units (for example, one in years old and the other in Pound Sterling). To take account of the different averages, we can calculate by how much an observation for a particular case is above the mean of Y for variable Y and above the mean of X for variable X. If we then multiply the result we will get a large positive product. The same will happen if both are large negative figures. If we add all these products for all cases together, we will get a large sum. If, on the other hand, high values on one variable are associated with low values on the other, we will get a large negative sum. If there is little correlation, then positive and negative values will tend to offset one another. So, the sum we are calculating – the covariation in technical parlance – is an indication of the extent to which the two variables are correlated. The formula is:

$$\sum (X - \overline{X})(Y - \overline{Y})$$

If we divide this covariation by the number of cases, n, we get an average covariation called the covariance, which takes account of the fact that the mean of X and the mean of Y may be different. To take account of the differences in units, the covariance is divided by the standard deviation of X multiplied by the standard deviation of Y. This standardises the covariance. If we divide both the numerator and the denominator by n, the formula for r becomes:

$$r = \frac{\sum (X - \overline{X})(Y - \overline{Y})}{\sqrt{\left[\sum (X - \overline{X})^2\right]\left[\sum (Y - \overline{Y})^2\right]}}$$

where X and Y are actual scores, and $\overline{X}$ and $\overline{Y}$ are the mean of the X values and Y values respectively. Suppose four students (cases A, B, C and D) take two tests that are scored out of 10. The results are shown in Table 7.6. You can see that there is a tendency for those who perform well in Test X also perform well on test Y. The calculation of r for Table 7.6 is shown in Table 7.7.

The correlation coefficient, r, measures the amount of spread about an imaginary line, called a regression line, that goes through all the dots on a scattergram in such a way that the distances between all the points and the line are minimised. This is a 'best-fitting' line, which for the four students A–D is shown in Figure 7.4. The maximum value for r is 1.00, indicating a perfect correlation where all the points fall exactly on the regression line. A value of

Table 7.6   *Scores of A–D on two tests*

Individual	Test X	Test Y
A	0	1
B	6	2
C	6	4
D	8	5
Total	20	12

Table 7.7   *The calculation of r from Table 7.6*

	X	Y	$(X-\bar{X})$	$(Y-\bar{Y})$	$(X-\bar{X})(Y-\bar{Y})$	$(X-\bar{X})^2$	$(Y-\bar{Y})^2$
A	0	1	−5	−2	+10	25	4
B	6	2	+1	−1	−1	1	1
C	6	4	+1	+1	+1	1	1
D	8	5	+3	+2	+6	0	4
Total	20	12			16	36	10

$\bar{X} = 20/4 = 5$

$\bar{Y} = 12/4 = 3$

$r = \dfrac{16}{\sqrt{36(10)}} = 0.843$

$r = 0.84$, for example, would indicate that most observations are close to the line. A coefficient of $r = 0$ or nearly zero would mean that the line is no help in predicting X from Y or vice versa. Pearson's r can be negative and the regression line will have a negative slope. Pearson's r itself is a little difficult to interpret, but if we square the result to produce r^2 then we have what is often called the *coefficient of determination,* which gives the proportion of the variance on the Y observations that is accounted for or 'explained' by variations in X. Thus if

Figure 7.4   *Scattergram of X on Y*

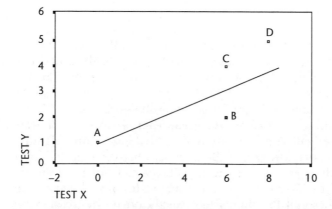

Table 7.8   *SPSS regression coefficients*

Coefficients^a

Model		Unstandardized Coefficients	
		B	Std. Error
1	(Constant)	.778	1.168
	VAR00001	.444	.200

a. Dependent Variable: VAR00002

$r = 0.84$ then r^2 is 0.71. This means that 71 per cent of the variance in Y is accounted for by the variance in X. If the value calculated for r^2 is very low or zero, do not assume, however, that there is no relationship between X and Y – it might be that the relationship is not linear but curvilinear. The best way to check is to draw or get SPSS to draw the scattergram.

The regression line may be described by a formula whose general form is:

$$Y = a + bX$$

where Y and X are values from the two interval variables and a and b are constants. The constant a indicates at what point the regression line cuts the vertical axis (it is the value of Y when X is zero), and b is the steepness of the slope of the line. In order actually to make a prediction of the value of Y from a particular value of X you would need to know what these constants are. The regression output from SPSS is shown in Table 7.8. The constant a is 0.778 and b is 0.444, so the full equation is:

$$Y = 0.778 + (0.444)X$$

This means that for any given value of X we can calculate what Y would be from the equation – and vice versa.

The correct use of correlation and regression depends on a number of conditions being met.

■ Both variables must be scaled, or assumed to be scaled, at the interval level.
■ Each case has been scaled on both variables.
■ The relationship between the variables is linear.
■ Where the statistics are to be used for the purposes of statistical inference, the variables should be approximately normal in distribution.

Correlation and regression

What is the difference, then, between correlation and regression? They are clearly related statistics, but they serve different purposes. Correlation is concerned with measuring the *strength* of the relationship between variables. It determines the extent to which the values of two or more interval variables covary. The square of the correlation coefficient measures how near on average each datapoint is to an hypothetical line that runs through the points in a way that minimises the distances between each datapoint and the line. The procedure makes no distinction between dependent and independent variables as both variables have equal status.

Regression, by contrast, helps the researcher to determine the *form* of the relationship. The objective is to be able to predict or estimate the value of one variable corresponding to a given value of the other. It is concerned with identifying the parameters of the regression so that it can be used to make such predictions. However, which variable is chosen as the dependent variable makes a difference to the regression line that is derived.

Spearman's rho

The calculation of Pearson's *r*, as we have just seen, makes a number of assumptions. If any of these assumptions do not hold, what can the researcher do? Suppose the relationship is clearly not linear, or we cannot or do not wish to assume interval scaling? An alternative is to use Spearman's rho, which was mentioned at the end of Chapter 6. This statistic is appropriate for situations where both scales are fully ranked with as many rankings as there are cases to be ranked. Spearman's original formulation took the difference in ranking on both scales for each case, squared the difference and summed all the differences. The formula that is normally given is:

$$\text{rho}(r_s) = 1 - \frac{6 \sum d^2}{n(n^2 - 1)}$$

where d is the difference in ranking on the two variables and n is the total number of cases. Sometimes the denominator is expressed as $n(n-1)(n+1)$ or as $n^3 - n$. This formula is fine as a computational aid when calculations are to be made by hand or by calculator, when there are relatively few cases and where there are no or few tied ranks. Tied ranks may emerge when the ranking is derived from original interval scores like a percentage in a class test and some cases have the same score. In this situation all the cases are given an average rank. So if three individuals occupy the 4th, 5th and 6th positions but have the same score, then they will be given an average rank of 5.

The computing formula is derived from Pearson's *r*, substituting ranks instead of metric values, using the formula:

$$r = \frac{\sum (X-)(Y - \overline{Y})}{\sqrt{\left[\sum (X - \overline{X})^2\right]\left[\sum (Y - \overline{Y})^2\right]}}$$

where X and Y are pairs of ranks on the two variables for each case. Where there are no tied ranks, Spearman's rho = Pearson's *r*. Where there are ties, rho begins to loose its accuracy, and adjustments have to be made to the formula which can get quite complex, so the Pearson formula is to be preferred. Where calculations are to be done using computer software, there is no advantage in using the hand-computation formula. In short, if you throw Spearman's rho and Pearson's *r* at the *same* ranked data, you will obtain an identical result (see Exercise question 4 at the end of this chapter).

Where the rankings are derived from interval data, then if we compute Spearman's rho on the ranked data and Pearson's r on the original interval data (instead of on the ranked data) there will still tend to be a general correspondence between the two measures. If, in fact, the distances between the metric scores are the same throughout both variables, then converting them to ranks and applying rho will produce an identical result. However, the interval values are generally not equally spaced and the statistics can be expected to diverge. If, for example, we take the two interval variables on our table tennis data, 'spend' and 'agebegan', and get SPSS to calculate both statistics, we obtain the result in Tables 7.9 and 7.10. Pearson's r is 0.808 and Spearman's rho is 0.779. The difference is very small and both would round off to 0.8.

Table 7.9   *SPSS Pearson correlation output*

Correlations

		At what age did you take up table tennis?	Approximately how much have you spent on table tennis in the last 6 months?
At what age did you take up table tennis?	Pearson Correlation	1.000	.808**
	Sig. (2-tailed)	.	.000
	N	120	120
Approximately how much have you spent on table tennis in the last 6 months?	Pearson Correlation	.808**	1.000
	Sig. (2-tailed)	.000	.
	N	120	120

**. Correlation is significant at the 0.01 level (2-tailed).

Table 7.10   *SPSS Spearman's rho output*

Correlations

			At what age did you take up table tennis?	Approximately how much have you spent on table tennis in the last 6 months?
Spearman's rho	At what age did you take up table tennis?	Correlation Coefficient	1.000	.779**
		Sig. (2-tailed)	.	.000
		N	120	120
	Approximately how much have you spent on table tennis in the last 6 months?	Correlation Coefficient	.779**	1.000
		Sig. (2-tailed)	.000	.
		N	120	120

**. Correlation is significant at the .01 level (2-tailed).

Figure 7.5　*A histogram for 'spend'*

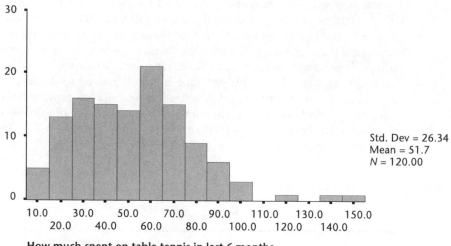

How much spent on table tennis in last 6 months

So what, then, is the advantage of Spearman's rho? Are there any circumstances in which it is the preferred statistic? Certainly if the data are already ranked, then both statistics will produce an identical result anyway. If the data are in interval form then the researcher can either calculate a Pearson's r directly, or use the interval data to create ranks and calculate Spearman's rho. Where the data in both scales are normally or fairly normally distributed with a central concentration, the ranks will be closer together at the centre than at the extremes. The value of rho can then be expected to be slightly less than that of r, as it is in the above example. Pearson, in fact, investigated the relationship between the two statistics and showed that where both variables are normally distributed, the maximum difference is approximately 0.02 and occurs when both r and rho are near 0.5. Figures 7.1 and 7.5 show that the variables 'agebegan' and 'spend' do have central concentrations although they are some way from being a normal distribution.

MULTIVARIATE PROCEDURES

Multivariate analysis allows for the analysis of three or more variables simultaneously. There are many different techniques and there are excellent books that cover them all such as by Hair *et al.* (1998). SPSS does not provide all the techniques, and just four techniques offered by SPSS will be briefly reviewed below. These are:

- multiple regression,
- factor analysis,
- cluster analysis,
- multidimensional scaling.

The following review is by no means comprehensive and is intended only to give you some idea of what these techniques entail.

Multiple regression

Multiple regression attempts to predict a single dependent variable from two or more independent variables and is an extension of bivariate regression. As we saw earlier, a linear regression line may be used to make predictions of a dependent variable from a single independent variable. The statistic r^2 indicates how 'good' that line is in making such predictions. In reality, not one but several variables are likely to affect the dependent variable. Thus the level of sales is affected not only by price, but by, for example, advertising expenditure, interest rates, and personal disposable income. The formula describing any regression line is, as we have seen above:

$$Y = a + bX$$

Multiple regression extends this to:

$$Y = a + +b_1X_1 + b_2X_2 + b_3X^3 \ldots + b_nX_n$$

where $X_1, X_2, X_3 \ldots X_n$ are the independent variables. The values $b_1, b_2, b_3, \ldots b_n$ indicate the rates of change in Y consequent upon a unit change in $X_1, X_2, X_3, \ldots X_n$. The calculation for each value of b is made with the degree of correlation between Y and the other variables held constant. As with the bivariate procedure, the value for r^2 indicates the percentage of variation in Y associated with the variation in the independent variables.

If, for example, we wanted to explain the amount spent on table tennis not by correlating with 'agebegan', but by looking at the extent to which the perceived importance of various aspect of playing table tennis explains this variable, we can use the SPSS linear regression procedure to produce the results in Table 7.11. The multiple r is 0.217 which is considerably lower than the regression of 'spend' on 'agebegan'. The constants in Table 7.12 can be used to complete the whole equation linking spend with the five predictor variables.

Factor analysis

While multiple regression is one of a number of 'dependence' methods that attempt to explain one or more dependent variables on the basis of two or more independent variables, factor analysis is an 'interdependence' method. These methods review the interdependence between variables or between respondents in order to generate an understanding of the underlying structure, and to create new variables or new groupings. Factor analysis recognises that when many

Table 7.11 *Multiple regression: 'Spend' regressed on 'Enjoyment', 'Social benefits', 'Competition', 'Relaxation' and 'Health and fitness'*

Model Summary

Model	R	R Square	Adjusted R Square	Std. Error of the Estimate
1	.217[a]	.047	.005	26.27

a. Predictors: (Constant), Enjoyment, Social benefits, Competition, Relaxation, Health and fitness

Table 7.12   *SPSS model constants for multiple regression*

Model		Unstandardized Coefficients	
		B	Std. Error
1	(Constant)	41.133	14.489
	Social benefits	-.325	2.382
	Competition	-1.219	2.676
	Relaxation	4.968	2.474
	Health and fitness	.142	2.462
	Enjoyment	-.168	2.493

variables are being measured some of them may be measuring different aspects of the same phenomenon and hence will be inter-related. It systematically reviews the correlation between each variable forming part of the analysis and all the other variables, and groups together those that are highly inter-correlated with one another, and not correlated with variables in another group. The groups identify 'factors' that are in effect 'higher order' variables. This helps to eliminate redundancy where, for example, two or more variables may be measuring the same construct. The factors themselves are not directly observable, but each variable has a 'factor loading' which is the correlation between the variable and the factor with which it is most closely associated. The effect, and advantage, of factor analysis, is to reduce a large number of variables to a more manageable set of factors that themselves are not correlated.

Factor analysis begins by calculating a correlation matrix – a table of the value of Pearson's *r* for each variable with each other variable. If there are, for example, just five variables, then the correlation matrix might look like that in Table 7.13. From visual inspection it is clear that variables 4 and 5 are highly correlated and both are negatively correlated with variable 3. Variables 1 and 2 are also correlated, but neither is correlated with variables 4 or 5. A factor analysis might produce a 'solution' like Table 7.14. Variables 3, 4 and 5 combine to define the first factor and the second factor is most highly correlated with variables 1 and 2.

There are problems associated with factor analysis. First, it is possible to generate several solutions from a set of variables. Second, a subjective decision needs to be made as to how many factors to accept. Third, the grouping has to make intuitive sense. Thus if variables 1–5 above were consumer reactions to a new product, then variables 4 and 5 might be two questions that tap the 'value-

Table 7.13   *A correlation matrix*

Variable	1	2	3	4	5
1	1.00	0.61	0.47	−0.02	−0.10
2		1.00	0.33	0.19	0.32
3			1.00	−0.83	−0.77
4				1.00	0.93
5					1.00

Table 7.14   *Factor loading on two factors*

Variable	Factor 1	Factor 2
1	−0.25	0.72
2	0.06	0.87
3	−0.94	0.33
4	0.94	0.21
5	0.95	0.26

for-money' factor, and variables 1–3 are different aspects of 'benefits-derived-from-use'. Factor analysis will always produce a solution; whether it is a good or helpful one is another matter. There may not, in fact, *be* any factors underlying the variables.

Cluster analysis

All scientific fields have a need to group or cluster objects, just as historians group events and botanists group plants. Marketing managers often need to group customers, for example, on the basis of the benefits they seek from buying a particular product or brand, or on the basis of their lifestyles. Any procedure for deriving such groupings is clearly crucial for market segmentation. Cluster analysis is a range of techniques for grouping cases (usually respondents to a survey) who have characteristics in common. Cases are placed into different clusters such that members of any cluster are more similar to each other in some way than they are to members in other clusters.

Two very different approaches are possible. One is based on taking individual cases and combining them on the basis of some measure of similarity, such as the degree of correlation between the cases on a number of variables. Each case is correlated with each other case in a correlation matrix. The pair of cases with the highest index of similarity is placed into a cluster. The pair with the next highest is formed into another cluster and so on. Each cluster is then averaged in terms of the index being used and combined again on the basis of the average similarities. The process continues until, eventually, all the cases are in one cluster.

The other approach is to begin with the total set of cases and divide them into sub-groups on a basis specified by the researcher. Thus the researcher may want a four-cluster solution of 1200 respondents on 10 variables. An iterative partitioning computer program might begin by setting up four equal-sized groups at random. The centre of each cluster on the 10 variables is then calculated and the distances between each of the 1200 respondents and the centres of the four groups is measured. On the basis of these distances, respondents are reassigned to the group with the nearest cluster centre. The new cluster centres are recalculated and the distances again measured, with a further reassignment taking place. This process is repeated until no further reassignments are needed.

Unfortunately, the different methods of cluster analysis can produce quite different solutions. Furthermore, cluster analysis, like factor analysis, *always* produces clusters, even when there are, in fact, no natural groupings in the data. The various techniques work by *imposing* a cluster structure on the data rather than allowing the structure to emerge from the analysis.

Multidimensional scaling

Multidimensional scaling (MDS) is used most often in marketing to identify the relative position of competing brands or shops as perceived by customers, and to uncover key dimensions underlying customers' evaluations. It seeks to infer underlying dimensions from a series of similarity or preference judgements provided by customers about objects within a given set. In a sense it does the reverse of cluster analysis: while the latter groups objects according to similarities on prespecified dimensions, MDS infers underlying evaluative dimensions from similarities or preferences indicated by customers. These data can be in the form of ranks (that is, categorical or 'non-metric'), so the technique is sometimes referred to as non-metric MDS, or in the form of numerical ratings.

Suppose a customer is given a set of six multiple chain stores (like Asda, Tesco, Sainsbury) and asked to say how similar each store is to the others. The customer is asked to compare pairs of stores, and then rank the pairs from most similar to least similar. With 6 stores there are $n(n-1)/2$ or 15 pairs. The ranks given by just one customer might look like those in Table 7.15. MDS, like cluster analysis, is an iterative process that can be carried out using one of several available computer programs. Such a program would generate a geometric configuration of stores so that the distances between pairs of stores are as consistent as possible with customer's similarity rankings, so that the pair of stores ranked 15th are furthest apart, the pair of stores ranked 14th next furthest, while the pair AD is the closest together. The objects are presented usually in two-dimensional space, as in Figure 7.6, which shows a two-dimensional configuration of the six stores in which the interstore distances are consistent with the rankings in Table 7.15.

It is necessary to know, however, what the two dimensions represent. Labelling them is a subjective process and involves inspecting the relative position of the objects along each dimension and inferring what the dimension is most likely to represent on the basis of prior knowledge about the objects

Figure 7.6   *A multidimensional map based on ranking in Table 7.15*

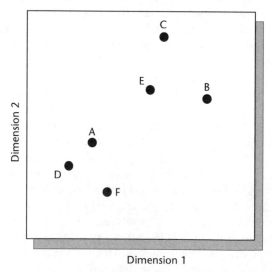

Table 7.15   Similarity rankings of six multiples

Multiple	A	B	C	D	E	F
A		12	11	1	7	3
B			5	15	4	10
C				13	6	14
D					9	2
E						8

themselves. Looking at the first dimension, we might notice that the stores D and A offer the lowest prices, and C and B the highest. So dimension one could be price. Looking at dimension two vertically, we may observe that store C has a large product range and store F a limited product range, with the others in between. So, dimension two could be product variety. It is possible, of course, that somebody else looking at the same diagram may see other dimensions. However, it is possible to infer that this customer implicitly used price and product variety as the key criteria for comparing the six stores. Other customers may, of course, have other perceptions, resulting in a totally different multidimensional map. Where the maps from customer to customer differ greatly, making global inferences may be difficult. In such a situation the researcher may attempt to identify segments of customers with fairly similar multidimensional maps, perhaps using appropriate cluster analysis techniques.

USING SPSS

There are two ways of obtaining univariate statistics for interval variables in SPSS. One is to use the Analyze/Descriptive Statistics/Descriptives procedure and the other is to use Analyze/Descriptive Statistics/Frequencies. The former just gives a quick summary that includes the minimum and maximum scores and the mean and standard deviation. The latter offers all these plus the measures that are described above. They are to be found by clicking on the Statistics button on the Frequencies dialog box. So, access the *tabten.sav* file, select Analyze/Descriptive Statistics/Frequencies and then click on the Statistics box. You should obtain the Frequencies:Statistics dialog box as illustrated in Figure 7.7. Just put a tick in the box against the statistics you want by clicking with the left mouse button. By clicking with the right mouse button you will get a quick explanation of each statistic. To impose a normal curve on an interval variable, select Graphs/ Histogram and tick the Display normal curve box. For bivariate analysis of two metric variables select Statistics/Correlate/Bivariate, put two interval-scaled variables into the Variables box, for example, 'spend' and 'agebegan'. Under Correlation Coefficients you will find the Pearson box already ticked. If you want Spearman's rho as well just tick that box and click on OK. The outputs are illustrated in Tables 7.9 and 7.10. Notice that in both outputs the bottom line is a mirror image of the top line. Clearly each variable correlates with itself perfectly with a value of 1.000. The correlation coefficient between the two variables is 0.808. The Spearman's rho equivalent is 0.779. If you were to enter more variables in the Variables box you would get a series of bivariate correlations for each combination of variables.

Figure 7.7 *The SPSS 'Frequencies:Statistics' dialog box*

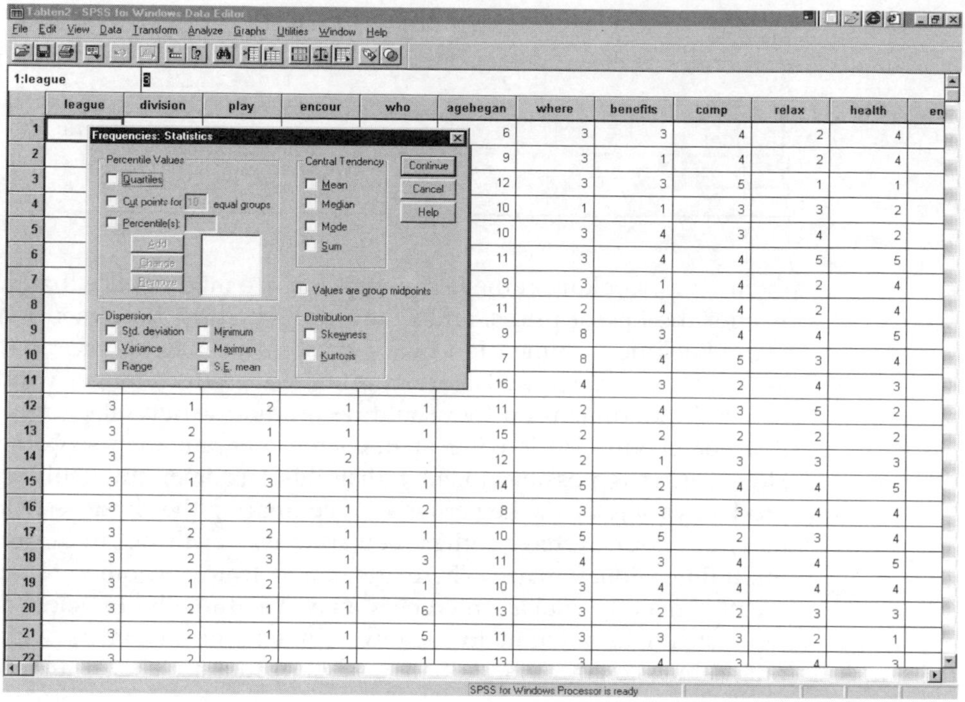

To obtain a regression analysis, select Analyze/Regression/Linear. Notice that you now have to make a selection of dependent and independent variables. The dependent variable goes along the *Y*-axis. It is the one we are trying to predict. You can have one or more than one independent variable if you wish to undertake multiple regression. In discussing the linear relationship between *X* and *Y* we speak of the regression of *Y* on *X*. Let's assume that the amount spent on table tennis is the dependent variable and that the age at which they began is the independent variable. (It does not make a lot of sense to consider 'agebegan' as the dependent variable – it has already happened!). Put these into the appropriate boxes and click on OK. You now get four tables. The first table (see

Table 7.16 *SPSS regression output – variables entered*

Variables Entered/Removed[b]

Model	Variables Entered	Variables Removed	Method
1	At what age did you take up table tennis?[a]	.	Enter

a. All requested variables entered.

b. Dependent Variable: How much spent on table tennis in last 6 months

Table 7.17   *SPSS regression output – model summary*

Model Summary

Model	R	R Square	Adjusted R Square	Std. Error of the Estimate
1	.808[a]	.652	.649	15.60

a. Predictors: (Constant), At what age did you take up table tennis?

Table 7.16) tells you what variables have been entered as independent variables and what the dependent variable is. The next table is an analysis of variance, which we will ignore until Chapter 10. The third table in a model summary, which gives the values for Pearson's r (0.808) and r^2, which is 0.652 (see Table 7.17). This is the amount of variation in 'spend' that can be explained by the regression of 'spend' on 'agebegan'. If the data relate to a small sample, then r^2 gives a biased estimate of r^2 for the population from which the sample was drawn. The adjusted r is an unbiased estimate provided by adjusting the equation for r^2 for the number of values that were used in the original calculation. For large samples, the difference is very small. The standard error of the estimate you can ignore for the moment.

In the fourth table, the unstandardised coefficients under B give the constants a and b in the equation $Y = a + bX$ (see Table 7.18). So the regression of 'spend' on 'agebegan' provides:

$$Y = -2.691 + (4.253)X$$

So, for somebody aged 20, for example, we can predict from the equation that he or she will have spent £82 on table tennis in the last six months. If you review Figure 5.6 you can see this from the scattergram.

Factor analysis is available on SPSS under Analyze/Data Reduction/Factor. The variables to be used in the analysis are just moved across into the Variables box. The data in the *tabten* file, however, are not suitable for factor analysis. Furthermore, the SPSS output requires some understanding of the process to be able to interpret it. Have a look at Hair *et al.* (1998), Chapter 3.

Cluster analysis is under Analyze/Classify/K-means cluster. Again, the variables to be included are put into the Variables box, but you need to specify in advance how many clusters you want. See Hair *et al.* (1998), Chapter 9. Multidimensional scaling is available under Analyze/Scale/Multidimensional scaling. (See Hair *et al.* (1998), Chapter 10.)

Table 7.18   *SPSS coefficients*

Model		Unstandardized Coefficients		Standardized Coefficients	t	Sig.
		B	Std. Error	Beta		
1	(Constant)	-2.691	3.928		-.685	.495
	At what age did you take up table tennis?	4.253	.286	.808	14.871	.000

SUMMARY

As for categorical variables, data summary for interval variables may be univariate, bivariate or multivariate. Univariate measures include a range of measures of central tendency, dispersion and distribution shape plus the calculation of percentile values. Under distribution shape the idea of a normal distribution was introduced.

Bivariate data reduction involves the related but separate processes of correlation and regression. The Pearson correlation coefficient measures the strength of the degree of correlation between two interval-scaled variables, while regression focuses on the form of the relationship. It facilitates the prediction of the values of one variable from given values on the other. The parallels and contrasts between Spearman's rho and Pearson's r were then explained.

Multivariate procedures include multiple regression, factor analysis, cluster analysis and multidimesional scaling. There are many other multivariate procedures, but these are the ones provided by SPSS.

Finally we looked at how to use SPSS to obtain all the procedures for use on interval variables that were explained in the Chapter.

Exercises

1. Use SPSS to generate measures of dispersion for the variable 'spend' and interpret the results. Now look at measures of distribution shape. Is the distribution normal?
2. Look at a table of areas under the normal curve in any statistics book and determine what z-score includes 99 per cent of the area.
3. Open a new SPSS file and enter the data from Table 7.6. Now obtain the Pearson's correlation coefficient using **Analyze/Correlate/Bivariate** and reaffirm the calculation for Table 7.7.
4. Using the equation for the data in Table 7.6, $Y = 0.778 + (0.444)X$, calculate what Y will be when $X = 6$. How does that compare with the actual values of Y when $X = 6$?
5. Using the same data from Table 7.6, use SPSS to calculate Spearman's rho. How does this compare with Pearson's r

Points for discussion

1. Is the use of statistics summarising central tendency, dispersion, distribution shape and percentiles on discrete interval variables appropriate?
2. Is the mode of any value as a statistic?
3. Is Spearman's rho of any value as a statistic?

Further reading

Bryman, A. and Cramer, D. (1999) *Quantitative Data Analysis with SPSS Release 8 for Windows*, London, Routledge.

Chapters 8–11 cover bivariate and multivariate procedures for interval data in rather more detail than is attempted here.

Hair, J., Anderson, R., Tatham, R. and Black, W. (1998) *Multivariate Data Analysis*, 5th edn, London, Prentice Hall International.

A very thorough and detailed explanation of all multivariate procedures. A good book to dip into when you need to look up a particular technique, but not for those who crack up at the sight of statistical formulae.

chapter 8

Sampling and the Concept of Error

INTRODUCTION

Chapter 2 explained that survey data arise from the process of keeping systematic records of responses to questions or information-giving tasks addressed to respondents. Sometimes the number of potential respondents is very large and it may be necessary to take a sample rather than to try to study them all. This chapter considers when it is necessary or advisable to take samples; it then turns to sample design and the kinds of error that arise from the sampling process.

WHEN WE NEED TO TAKE SAMPLES

It is not always necessary for the survey researcher to take a sample. Sometimes, the set of respondents that are the focus of the researcher's attention, the 'population', is sufficiently limited in number for him or her to study them all, that is, to take a 'census'. Thus the members of a particular community that is to be studied may not total more (or many more) than the researcher decides is an adequate number for the purpose of analysis – or has the time or resources to cover.

More usually, however, the population of interest is far greater than the survey researcher can handle. In this situation it will be necessary to select a subset of cases and to use these to draw conclusions about the population from which they were drawn. Sampling, however, adds problems additional to those of measurement, scaling and survey design and execution considered in Chapters 2 and 3. There is, for example, always the danger that the sample the researcher has drawn is an unrepresentative one and it may be necessary to decide whether statements or hypotheses established for the sample can be generalised to the population.

Despite these drawbacks, sampling may, in fact, still be preferable where contacting every person would be feasible, but nevertheless difficult, slow or too expensive. Attempts to contact every individual may, in any event, not be totally successful, and the researcher may end up with an incomplete census. This may be less representative than a carefully drawn sample. Researching a small sample carefully may, in fact, result in greater accuracy than either a very large sample or a complete census, since the problems associated with handling a large number of interviewers and a large number of questionnaires may create errors of a greater magnitude than those arising from the sampling process. However, the researcher will need to bear in mind the guidelines suggested on pp. 201–3 for minimum sample sizes for deciding how 'small' a sample can be.

SAMPLE SELECTION

A lot of confusion about sampling arises because while any survey necessarily involves a population of cases, some or most of whom act as individual respondents, what the researcher actually samples may not be those individuals, but households, clubs, groups, organisations, businesses, geographical areas or some other kind of unit. Thus, in order to interview head teachers in schools, the researcher may actually sample schools or local authority areas; to telephone marketing managers, the researcher may sample business units. These units we can refer to as 'sampling units'. Sampling units will correspond with cases where individuals are being sampled in order to address questionnaires to them. In other situations the sampling units will be entities quite different from the individuals to whom questions are to be addressed. We can now use the term 'unit' to mean whatever entity is being sampled.

There are two rather different bases on which the researcher may make his or her selection of units:

■ purposive,
■ representative.

Purposive samples are generated when the selection of units is made by the researcher using his or her own judgement. The selection may be made on the basis of contacting those units that are easiest to access, those that are deemed to be the most important, those that reflect a variety or extremes, or those that are typical. A researcher may, for example, select those organisations in which he or she already has contacts, or those that are within travelling distance. If the study is of retailers and electronic data are not available, then a sample of retailers may need to be taken; but some have much higher turnovers than others. So, the researcher may deliberately choose all the major multiples, and then make a purposive selection of the remainder based on turnover, type of shop and location. The researcher may choose units on the basis that each one is an example of every type of entity that the researcher wishes to cover. Sometimes the researcher may pick extreme units; for example all the most marketing-oriented companies may be selected in order to look at the extent to which or the manner in which they use marketing planning procedures. Finally, units may be chosen because they are 'typical'. Thus particular towns, cities or areas may be chosen because they have typical or average populations, or industrial, institutional and social structures.

Purposive samples are used, quite legitimately, for research that is exploratory, qualitative or indeed experimental where the focus is on understanding situations, generating ideas or evaluating social situations, products, ideas for products, advertising or ideas for advertising. Purposive sampling, however, is not normally appropriate for survey research, since the purpose of such surveys is to use the results from them to generalise about the population of units or cases from which the sample was drawn.

Representative samples, by contrast, are chosen in such a way that they attempt to reproduce the structure and features of the population of units from which the sample was drawn, so that they are a microcosm of the entire set of units. They are used primarily for quantitative analysis, either to make estimates of the size or frequency of a population characteristic, or to measure and test the extent to which the characteristics of units or cases are related together in the population. Ideally, the results obtained from the sample should be broadly the same as those that would have been obtained had the whole population of units been studied.

Warning

The researcher may be interested in studying the units that are sampled, but in a survey the information will necessarily be obtained from individuals. The bottom line is that questions can be addressed only to individuals. These individuals may be asked about themselves or about the entities of which they are members (or both). Thus a study of, say, 200 companies may be made on the basis of information generated by addressing questions to company directors.

The selection of units to create a representative sample is usually made using one of three main techniques:

- randomisation,
- systematic selection,
- interviewer selection.

Randomised selection is the selection by chance, using a technique that is independent of human judgement, from a complete list of the population of units which is to be sampled (the 'sampling frame'). Sampling techniques entail using some form of lottery, like taking names out of a hat, using tables of random numbers to select numbered units, or relying on computerised random procedures.

Systematic selection creates a rule that determines the selection of the units, thereby removing (or largely removing) human judgement. This may mean taking every nth name from a list at N/n intervals where N is the population size and n is the sample size. If, for example, the researcher wants a sample of 100 from a list of 1000 names he or she can pick every 10th name. In principle the starting name should be a name between the first and the ninth name picked at random. Suppose, using a pack of cards, we just pull out a card at random and it is a six (of whatever suit). The names selected will then be the 6th, 16th, 26th and so on. This gives each name in the list at the outset an equal probability of being selected at random and is independent of the judgement of the researcher, who might otherwise tend to pick out certain types of case. Another form of systematic sampling is to take every nth house along a street and follow some rule about the selection of streets.

Interviewer selection may be used for sampling individuals as respondents and clearly it will involve human judgement, but this judgement will normally be limited in a number of ways, often in combination, by restricting:

- the numbers of types of people to be chosen – that is, interviewers are given quotas, for example, of so many men and women, so many of different age groups,
- the time of day at which interviews may take place – for example, allowing no interviews of males before 5 p.m. to get a cross-section of men in employment, or observing customers in pubs and bars at specific times of the day,
- the area in which the interviewer may make his or her selection – for example to particular streets or other locations.

SAMPLE DESIGN

Sample design is an integral part of the overall research design. The quality of the sample has a significant impact on the overall quality of the research, but designing an appropriate sample is seldom easy, partly because many factors need to be taken into account and partly because – particularly for country-wide samples – the design may need to be both complex and sophisticated.

Most textbooks on marketing or social research make a basic distinction between random (or probability) samples and non-random (or non-probability) samples. The former use techniques of selection (like randomisation or systematic selection) that are independent of human judgement and which produce a known and non-zero probability that any one particular unit from the population of units will be included in the sample. Consequently, it is possible to apply the laws of chance (probability theory) to undertake a statistical evaluation of sampling error, enabling the researcher to assess how likely the sample is to be unrepresentative and by how much. Different types of random sample will typically include simple random samples, stratified samples, cluster samples, multi-stage samples and multi-phase samples. Non-random samples arise where human judgement is involved in the selection process making it impossible to apply any systematic scientific model that could be used to assess the degree of sampling error. Such samples typically include quota samples, convenience samples and judgemental samples.

The problem with this 'shopping list' type of approach is that most samples are, in practice, a mixture of different elements, and it is seldom possible to classify any particular sample uniquely into one of the categories. Furthermore, there are varying degrees of 'independence' from human judgement, so the distinction is not always as clearcut as the theory suggests. Moreover, neither practitioners nor theorists agree amongst themselves as to which particular sample selection procedures count as 'random'.

What statisticians do tend to agree (if not insist) upon is that the 'theory' of statistical inference (which is explained in Chapters 9 and 10) is based on the assumption that the kind of sample drawn is a simple random one. Such samples use either randomised or systematic selection techniques (and some purists would argue that systematic procedures are not strictly 'random', but only an approximation) from a complete list of the population of units, giving all units to be sampled an *equal* chance of being selected. Thus if we select a sample of 300 names from a list of 3000 students at a university, then each student has a one-in-ten chance of being selected.

However, in practice, simple random samples are seldom used because:

- they require a sampling frame for the total population of units to be sampled – this could mean taking random selections from lists containing maybe 40 million people, perhaps on a regular basis,
- if face-to-face interviewing is to be carried out (or even questionnaires or diaries left personally for respondent completion) the interviews would be scattered throughout the length and breadth of the geographical area to be sampled, and interviewers would have a considerable amount of travelling to do,
- the resulting samples may still not accurately reflect the structure of the population of units in respect of a number of variables whose incidence or size is already known – in other words, simple random samples do not utilise data that are already available on the population structure.

Departures from simple random sampling are a result of the application of one or more of three main procedures that are used in the design of samples:

- stratification,
- clustering,
- imposing quotas.

Stratification

Stratification is a procedure that utilises information already contained in sampling frames to construct a sample that is guaranteed to be representative in respect of that information. Thus if a list of individuals contains information on the sex of each person, then the proportion of males to females is known. Suppose it is a list of members of a golf club, and 60 per cent are male. We can then ensure that 60 per cent of our sample is male. Thus if we wanted a sample of 100 members, we could select sixty men and forty women at random (using either randomised or systematic techniques). If the list also contained data on age, and we knew that 30 per cent of members are aged 16–30, we could select 30 individuals from this age group (again at random) and the appropriate numbers from other age groups. If we stratified by sex *and* age together, then our

30 individuals aged 16–30 could be selected on the basis of 60 per cent (that is, 18) men and 40 per cent (12) women. Provided the proportions in the sample are the same as the proportions in the population (usually called 'proportional stratification') then the resulting sample is likely to be *more* accurate and representative than the simple random sample because some of the sources of variation have been eliminated. However, it does require an accurate sampling frame and one that contains information on the factors we want to use for stratification.

Sometimes the stratification is disproportionate. Suppose our golf club contained only 10 per cent women and we wanted to be able to compare the views of the women with those of the men on the facilities provided to members. A proportionately stratified sample of 100 would give only 10 women – not enough on which to base an analysis of responses to a questionnaire – so we might select 50 women and 50 men, that is, deliberately over-sample the women. This would enable us to make our comparisons, but if we wanted to estimate the extent of certain views or characteristics overall, then the answers of the men would have to be upweighted and the answers of the women downweighted to their original proportions.

Clustering

Clustering is used where interviewing takes place face-to-face. It makes sense for each interviewer's respondents or potential respondents to be geographically concentrated in order to minimise travel time. Accordingly, it is normal to cluster interviewing in limited geographical areas. This is normally achieved by selecting (usually at random) a fixed number of 'sampling points' and allocating one interviewer to each. These will usually be parliamentary constituencies, electoral wards, polling districts or postcode districts or sectors. The sampling points are usually carefully chosen in such a way that they are a representative cross-section of types of area. Normally the selection of sampling points will be stratified by a number of variables. This is possible because, while there may be no lists of individual respondents that contain data on variables that can be used for stratification, there *will* be lists of polling districts or whatever area is to be used as a sampling point, and there will usually be plenty of information about each.

While the effect of stratification is to reduce errors arising from the sampling process, the effect of clustering is to increase it. How much it will do so depends on how 'tight' clustering is. For small-area clusters the error will be greater than for larger areas. In practice, the reduction in error due to stratification is very limited since it is usually only the selection of sampling points that is stratified, not the selection of individuals or households within them. Accordingly, the departure from simple random sampling brought about by the stratified selection of clusters has the overall effect of increasing the sampling error.

Imposing quotas

Imposing quotas can take a number of forms. In some situations, respondents are selected from a list at random, but interviewers are then asked to fill quotas from these lists. Such a procedure might be called 'random sampling with quotas', but the imposition of quotas will increase the sampling error since substitutes are, in effect, being allowed. The main context, however, in which quotas are imposed is for quota samples in which the interviewer decides who to approach in the street.

Quota sampling is generally regarded by statisticians and textbooks on market and social research as 'non-probability' or 'non-random' sampling. This is mainly because the final selection of respondents is made by the interviewer, so human judgement enters into the selection process. The interviewer, instead of being issued with a pre-selected list of names and addresses, is given an assignment in the form of a quota. This might, for example, require the interviewer to find, usually at a fixed sampling point, 20 adults aged 16 and over:

- 10 of them female,
- 10 aged 45 or over and 10 aged 16–45,
- 8 in social class ABC1,
- 12 in social class C2DE.

In this case, sex, age and social class would be described as the 'quota controls'. These controls may be interlaced so that individuals who combine these characteristics need to be located and persuaded to participate in the survey. While this ensures that, for example, not all 10 under 45s are in social class ABC1, the interlacing can get quite complicated and independent quotas are often applied. The selection of which variables to use as quota controls depends on which variables the researcher thinks are most strongly associated with the variables being estimated or tested. The usual quotas are on sex, age and social class, because these are associated with many other characteristics, behaviours and attitudes. However, for some products, like double-glazing, type of property or tenancy may be more relevant.

SAMPLING IN PRACTICE

The kind of sampling used in practice will depend, in the first instance, on whether respondents are to be approached via the telephone, through the post, face-to-face or via the Internet. Since telephone directories provide a complete sampling frame for telephone interviews, clustering is not required and there seems little point in using other than systematic random sampling from the listed names. The only decision is whether there should be prior stratification (for example, by region) and whether there should be any imposition of quotas as the telephoning proceeds. This would amount to random sampling with quotas. For postal surveys the telephone directories will leave out non-telephone households, so the Post Office Postcode Address File would be a more appropriate sampling frame. These sampling frames are described below. Again, clustering is not required and the imposition of quotas is not possible since this requires information on the quota variables at the point of initial contact.

It is for face-to-face interviewing that a real choice needs to be made between random sampling and quota sampling. In both cases there is likely to be clustering into sampling points to minimise interviewer travelling time. In practice, random sampling means that interviewers are given lists of names and addresses and they have to make systematic efforts to obtain interviews with the individuals listed taking no substitutes. The main advantage of random sampling is its accuracy. Compared with sampling techniques that are not strictly random, random samples:

- minimise bias in the selection procedure,
- minimise the variability between samples,
- will, with a measurable degree of error, reproduce *all* the characteristics of the population from which the sample was drawn, not just those selected as quota controls,
- will, where samples are drawn at regular intervals, reflect any changes that are taking place in the population,
- allow probability theory to be applied to calculate the chances that the sample result was not a random sampling fluctuation.

There are, however, disadvantages to random samples:

- they are slower and more expensive than non-random techniques,
- they need a sampling frame,
- the sample achieved will almost certainly be smaller than the sample drawn.

Surveys using quota samples can often complete fieldwork in two to three days: for random samples it is likely to be two to three weeks. This can be important when quick result are needed. Random samples are, furthermore, an expensive process in terms of administration and interviewer costs. The sample drawing procedures can be quite complex, while interviewers may be instructed to make at least three callbacks in the evenings or at weekends before recording a 'non-contact'. This all adds to the cost. Random samples can in fact easily be twice the cost of quota samples of the same size. However, some statisticians argue that, because such samples are more accurate, it is more cost-effective (in terms of accuracy per £1 spent on fieldwork) to design a smaller, high quality random sample than a larger quota sample.

Random samples need a sampling frame, that is, a complete list of the population that is to be sampled (normally within selected sampling points). Frame errors were considered earlier on pp. 52–4. Two frames commonly used to obtain names and addresses of potential respondents in the UK are:

- the Registers of Electors,
- the Post Office Postcode Address File.

The Registers of Electors have been the standard sampling frame for decades, but there are problems with them. They are completed every October and published the following February, so are already four months out of date. They contain the names and addresses of all British subjects aged 18 and over who are entitled to vote and are registered. No information about age and sex of the person is available (other than first names). Any study that takes 'adults' to mean 16 and over will require special procedures to obtain a sample of 16–18 year olds. Also, many of the 18 year olds will be missing from the lists; so will people who are not entitled to vote (for example, non British subjects), or who are not registered. While the Registers are readily accessible, their validity is constantly affected by deaths and population movements. Up to 12 per cent of electors are no longer at their registered address by the time the Registers come up for renewal. Non registrations almost certainly became higher while the Poll Tax was in operation.

The Postcode Address File covers some 22 million addresses in 1.5 million postcodes within 8900 sectors within 2700 districts within 120 postcode areas. The file tends to be more complete and more up-to-date than the Registers of Electors, and is good for sampling households in several stages. However, for sampling individuals it is necessary to have some procedure for selecting individuals within a household. The postcodes are often used in association with geodemographics (these were explained in the suggestion box on p. 26).

Other kinds of sampling frame include:

■ membership lists of clubs, associations, societies or other kinds of organisation,
■ registers of various kinds, for example the Kompass Directory of companies,
■ frames that have been constructed from market intelligence or from surveys that have been carried out on a regular basis.

One 'solution' to an inadequate sampling frame is to redefine the population of cases being studied. Thus it is known that certain kinds of people are missing from the Registers of Electors. If the problem is ignored, then the survey population is being redefined as only those addresses appearing in the Registers. A sample that uses the telephone directories can define its population as all telephone subscribers.

Perhaps the most serious drawback of random samples, however, arises from the fact that there is always a degree of non-response. There will always *be* non-response whatever method of selection is used, and at least the response rate is known for random samples. However, it does mean that the sample which is drawn (the target sample) is seldom the sample which is achieved. For interview surveys the response rate will typically be 60–70 per cent of the sample drawn. Provided those not responding are not significantly different in key respects from those who do, the size of the achieved sample may simply have to be lived with, and the response rate reported as part of the results (non-response was considered in some detail on pp. 56–9).

By contrast with random sampling, the key feature of quota sampling in practice is that it is the interviewer who makes the final selection in the street or in the shopping centre. Unlike stratified samples where a random selection is made in advance of the data collection process according to defined proportions within strata, in quota sampling the characteristics to be used for quotas are not known in advance and the interviewer needs to establish these. A typical approach will be to address a person who looks likely to meet quota requirements as follows: 'Good morning, my name is [name of interviewer] from [name of research agency]. We are looking for men aged 30–49 who have a driving licence to answer a few questions about motoring. Do you fit into that category?'

The key advantages of quota samples are that they:

■ are quicker, cheaper and relatively simple to administer than random samples,
■ they do not require a sampling frame,
■ the sample size and sample composition in terms of the quota controls is always achieved.

The speed of quota sampling is derived from two sources. First, if in-home quotas are used then no callbacks are required; and if street quotas are used, there is no travelling time between interviews. Second, the procedures for drawing the samples are very simple and there is no need to give interviewers lists of names and addresses. In terms of cost per interview, quota samples thus work out a lot cheaper. Furthermore, no sampling frame is required – however, data on the structure of the population being sampled are needed in order to be able to set the size of the quotas. Since each interviewer continues until his or her quotas of sexes, ages and social classes are filled, the exact size and basic structure of the sample can be determined in advance.

There are, however, a number of disadvantages:

- there is considerable potential for bias,
- there is more variability between samples,
- the application of probability theory to such samples is questionable,
- they impose a structure on the sample.

Bias arises from two main sources: the interviewer and the high (and generally unrecorded) level of non-response. It is normally left to the interviewer how he or she goes about finding respondents who meet quota requirements in the sampling point. This leaves open the possibility of the interviewer avoiding certain types of locations or types of people, and for there to be systematic differences between one interviewer and another. Thus one interviewer may consciously or unconsciously avoid approaching people in groups, while another may avoid people who look like they are in a hurry.

It is, furthermore, often forgotten that there is considerable non-response when either street or in-home quotas are used. On the surface, there is no problem of non-response since all quotas are filled, or mostly filled. However, this is only because the non-response is undeclared and, effectively, substitution is being allowed. People who cannot be contacted or who refuse at the first attempt are excluded. The effective response rate in quota sampling is unknown, but certainly huge. The average random sample survey achieves a response rate of only about 25 per cent at first calls. This is boosted by subsequent callbacks to 60–80 per cent. So quota samples, at best, probably have an effective response rate of 25–30 per cent.

Work on actual surveys suggests that even good quality quota samples produce at least twice as much variability from one sample to another as do random samples. The implication, according to some researchers, is that estimates made or inferences deduced from quota samples need to be adjusted to take this extra variability into account. Such adjustments, in the form of a design factor, are explained in Chapter 12. Others will argue that, because quota sampling is non-random, then the application of statistical inference (which is considered in the next chapter) to such samples is not legitimate, since the probability of inclusion in the sample for any one case is unknown. In practice, researchers often treat quota samples as an *approximation* of random samples and will apply such techniques, frequently without making any adjustment in recognition of the fact that the sample is not a simple random one.

The structure imposed on the sample by the quotas will have been derived from data that reflect the population of cases as a whole. This, in turn, means that these quotas will not reflect the different composition of the sampling points, nor any changes that have taken place since the original data were collected. Thus social classes A and B may be over-represented in a sampling point in a depressed mining village, and under-represented in expensive, fashionable areas. It can even be difficult to fill some quotas in some of the sampling points.

SAMPLING ERRORS

Whatever kind of sample is taken and whatever the sample size (the topic of sample size is taken up in detail on pp. 201–3) there will always be error arising from the sampling process. The extent of such error may be defined as the difference between a sample result, and the result that would have been achieved by undertaking a complete census using identical procedures. Such errors arise because particular types of sampling units or cases are under-represented or over- represented in the sample compared with the population as a whole. If, for example, there is under or over-representation of the sexes, ages or social classes of individuals, it will affect the measurements (and, more importantly, the estimates made from them) of a large number of variables. Lack of representation in the appropriate quantities may be a product of two factors:

- systematic error (or bias),
- random error (or variance).

Systematic error

Bias arises when the sampling procedures used bring about over or under representation of particular types of unit in the sample that is mostly in the same direction. This may happen because:

- the selection procedures are not random,
- non-respondents are not a cross-section of the population,
- the selection is made from a list that does not cover the population, or uses a procedure that excludes certain groups (see Chapter 3 on frame error).

If the selection procedures are not random then it means that human judgement has entered into the selection process. For example, interviewers may be asked to choose respondents at some geographical location or to select households in specified streets. The result is likely to be that certain kinds of people or households or organisations are excluded from the sample. Thus choosing respondents in a shopping centre will miss out people who seldom or never go shopping; the selection of households by an interviewer may result in the omission of flats at the tops of stairs.

Non-response was considered in Chapter 3 (pp. 56–9) and is a problem for both censuses and samples. For censuses non-response means that the enumeration will be incomplete. If large numbers are missing, it would be inappropriate to treat those successfully contacted as a representative 'sample'. For samples, it means that estimates made from the sample will be biased if non-respondents are not themselves representative of the population. If they are representative, then non-response is not so much of a problem; but it may still mean that analyses are made on the basis of too small a sample.

Whatever the reason for the systematic error, the effect will be that all samples that could be drawn from a population will tend to result in the same direction of over- or under-representation. The average of all these samples, then, will not be the same as the real population average or proportion. Thus if we took lots of samples using a procedure that tended to omit working mothers with young children, then all the samples will manifest such under-representation rather than some over-representing them and some under-representing them so that the average of all samples was very close to the real population proportion.

Systematic errors cannot be reduced simply by increasing the sample size. If certain kinds of people are not being selected, cannot be contacted or are not responding, it will not be 'solved' by taking a bigger sample. Indeed, some kinds of errors will increase with more interviewers, more questionnaires and greater data processing requirements. All the researcher can do is minimise the likelihood of bias by using appropriate sample designs. Biases for some variables can be checked, for example against Census data or data from other sources. Sometimes attempts are made to discover the characteristics of non-responders, as was explained in Chapter 3 (p. 58).

Warning

Do not confuse systematic error with systematic sampling that was referred to on p. 141. Systematic sampling, in fact, is used to *eliminate* systematic error!

Random error

If we take a number of random, unbiased samples from the same population there will almost certainly be a degree of fluctuation from one sample to another. Over a large number of samples such errors will tend to cancel out, so that the average of such samples will be close to the real population value. However, we usually take only one sample, and even a sample that has used unbiased selection procedures will seldom be exactly representative of the population from which it was drawn. Each sample will, in short, exhibit a degree of error.

Warning

Such error is often called 'sampling error', but it would be clearer to think of it as 'random error' to distinguish it from bias (which some statisticians and some textbooks, confusingly, categorise as 'non-sampling' error).

Unlike bias, which affects the general sample composition and relates to each variable being measured in unknown ways, random error will differ from variable to variable. The reason for this is that the extent of such error will depend on two factors:

- The size of the sample – the bigger the sample, the less the random sampling error, (but by a declining amount),
- The variability in the population for that particular variable – a sample used to estimate a variable that varies widely in the population will show more random sampling error than for a variable that does not.

These two factors are used as a basis for calculating the likely degree of variability in a sample of a given size for a particular variable. This, in turn, is used as an input for establishing with a specified probability the range of accuracy of sample estimates, or that sample findings are only random sampling fluctuations from a population of cases in which the findings are untrue. These calculations are explained in the next chapter.

THE CONCEPT OF ERROR

If you look up 'error' in the index of any statistics book or a book on social or market research, it is unlikely that you will find any discussion of what 'error' actually means. You might find a reference to 'type I' and 'type II' errors. You might find that the term 'error' arises in the context of establishing the reliability and validity of measurements, and that a valid measure is (apparently) error-free. Do not believe it! Errors in measurement are, in fact, only a fraction of the errors that can arise in survey research and a 'valid' measure certainly does *not* mean that it is free from errors.

A conceptual definition of 'error' such as you would find in a dictionary would probably refer to the idea of a 'mistake' or 'inaccuracy'. There is an implied difference, or discrepancy, between an observation and some 'true' or 'real' value. Unfortunately, to gauge the extent of such errors we would need to know what this 'true' or 'real' value is. In most situations, of course, we do not, and if we did we would certainly not need to concern ourselves with measurement or scaling at all!

There are, however, some circumstances where researchers take measurements that, after a period of time, may be compared with more accurate data. Thus consumer panels take measures of panellists' purchases on a brand-by-brand basis over a period of, say, four weeks and this is used to estimate regional or national purchases of these brands. Eventually, these estimates may be summed over the year and compared with actual sales. This provides a quite accurate gauge of the extent of measurement error and this may then be used to adjust or recalibrate future estimates. In other situations, it may be possible to calculate a probability that the amount of error is no greater than a given magnitude. This is true for random sampling error, but, as we shall see, this type of error accounts for a tiny proportion of errors that can arise in survey research.

It is far more likely, however, that there is no way of actually knowing what the 'true' value is; there may even be some debate over whether or not a 'true' value even exists. Individual perceptions, beliefs, attitudes and even knowledge change all the time. The proportions of the population holding particular opinions will change rapidly and this certainly raises questions about the existence of a true value, even at one arbitrarily chosen moment of time. While the belief in a 'true' value independent of the measuring instrument must be particularly weak in the area of individual perceptions, similar weaknesses also beset measures of concepts like unemployment, poverty, health, housing – in fact, anything related to the human condition. Therefore there may be no 'real' or 'true' level of unemployment or poverty independent of the particular definitions used and measures deployed in their assessment.

If we accept this argument, it may be inappropriate to talk about 'error' at all, but instead we should review the 'quality' of the measurement process (indeed perhaps of the whole research process). We might, for example, wish to evaluate measurements as 'good', 'adequate' or 'poor', but we could realistically do so only on the basis of the fitness of those measurements for the purposes for which they were intended. If, for example, a manufacturer only wants relative sizes of various markets to decide on which ones to focus marketing efforts, then rough estimates of sales may be adequate. However, if the objective is to prepare accurate sales forecasts, then rough estimates will no longer be satisfactory. In short, measures that are good for one purpose may be poor for another.

In the final analysis, all the researcher can do is take measurements very carefully, bearing in mind all the potential sources of error.

TOTAL SURVEY ERROR

Any research that is based on addressing questions to people and recording their answers risks error resulting from measurement and from scaling (see Chapter 2), from survey design and execution (see Chapter 3) and from any inadequacies of sampling. Total survey error is the addition of all these sources of error, both sampling and non-sampling. It is difficult to estimate what the total survey error is in any one survey, and it will tend to vary from question to question. What is certainly true is that the error that results from random sampling fluctuations – which is the only kind of error that is taken into account when statistical inference is being used – accounts for only a very small proportion of the total survey error. Assael and Keon (1982) for example, estimate that it is perhaps only about 5 per cent. For a full discussion see Kish (1965) or Churchill (1999).

Errors of various kinds can always be reduced by spending more money, for example, on more interviewer training and supervision, on random sampling techniques, on pilot testing or on getting a higher response rate. However, the reduction in error has to be traded off against the extra cost involved. Furthermore, errors are often interrelated so that attempts to reduce one kind of error may actually increase another, for example, minimising the non-response errors by persuading more reluctant respondents may well increase response error. Non-sampling errors tend to be pervasive, not well-behaved and do not decrease – indeed may increase – with the size of the sample. It is sometimes even difficult to see whether they cause under or over estimation of population characteristics. There is, in addition, the paradox that the more efficient the sample design is in controlling random sampling fluctuations, the more important in proportion become bias and non-sampling errors.

While errors arising from sampling may be clearly classified into random or systematic, non-sampling errors may well be some combination of randomness and bias. Thus mistakes made by interviewers *may* tend to cancel out, but alternatively may result in systematic error. This means not only that the magnitude of such errors is often unknown, but also it is often hard to see whether they cause under- or over-representation of the population values.

As yet there is no comprehensive theory for assessing the impact of error other than for random sampling error. This is hardly surprising given the complex nature of surveys and the multiple opportunities for error. What has become known as 'total survey design' is the attempt to control total error bearing in mind all sources of error. This involves assessing the level of error associated with different procedures and choosing that combination that will minimise total error of estimates made within the resources of the survey. The procedure, however, assumes that total error and total cost models are available and that good information to put in them can be obtained. Contact rates, refusal rates, response rates, missing data, edit failure rates, consistency checks, and re-interviewing are just some of the methods used to detect errors. Setting up the parameters of total error models would involve introducing experimental procedures into the survey process that allow for the determination of the size of the impact of a particular error source on total error estimates. Unfortunately, all this takes considerable time and additional expense which many, if not most, researchers are unwilling to face. The temptation must be to fall back on the familiar practice of utilising probability theory to measure the likely impact of random sampling error. Readers and users of survey findings are interested in the substantive results, not in technical qualifications, warnings and limitations.

There is a considerable literature on ways of calculating errors of various kinds (see Lessler and Kalsbeek, 1992, for a review). However, the calculations can get quite complex and most formulae assume interval data, taking the 'mean square error' as the key dependent variable which is explained by a range of sources of bias plus random error. In practice, researchers are more likely to focus on ways of minimising the likelihood of error arising in the first place by adopting strategies and procedures to control its occurrence.

CONTROLLING ERROR

Survey researchers should make all reasonable attempts, within the limits imposed by cost and time constraints, to minimise, or at least measure the impact or make some estimate of, non-sampling errors and of bias in the sampling procedure. To minimise response errors researchers would be well advised to:

- pilot-test questionnaires in order to check for misunderstandings of questions,
- analyse tendencies to overclaim or underclaim for certain kinds of individual behaviour, for example, the tendency to underclaim the consumption of alcohol, or to overclaim television watching,
- use 'aided-recall' techniques (prompted lists) to help respondents remember products that they may have purchased and forgotten about, or radio programmes that they forgot they had listened to,
- use questioning techniques that minimise the effort respondents need to make.

To minimise interviewer error, researchers should:

- set rigorous training standards for interviewers,
- monitor the process of interviewing by doing 'backchecks' – calling or telephoning respondents who have already been interviewed to check that the interview was carried out properly, or sending supervisors to accompany interviewers on a regular sample basis,
- make statistical analyses of questionnaire errors to identify interviewers who may need retraining or reminding of particular points.

To minimise errors resulting from non-response several procedures need to be considered:

- for interview surveys interviewers may be asked to make a specified number of callbacks if the respondent was not at home on the first call. Three or four such callbacks may be made, ideally at different times and days of the week,
- interviewers may make an appointment by telephone with the respondent,
- self-completed questionnaires may be left where no contact has been made,
- monetary incentives or gifts may sometimes help to improve the response rate,
- interviewers may get a 'foot-in-the-door' by having respondents comply with some small request before presenting them with the larger survey,
- non-respondents to a postal survey may be sent interviewers to persuade respondents to complete the questionnaire, or they may be sent further reminders.

Processing errors will be minimised by careful editing and checking of the questionnaires in addition to the use of data entry validation procedures (see Chapter 3, pp. 61–2). Sampling bias will be minimised by using carefully-constructed sample designs that use random procedures wherever possible, or by imposing restrictions on interviewer choices where it is not. These sample designs were described earlier. Biases will still remain, however, and sometimes these are known. Thus it may be known that there are too many women in the sample, or too few men aged 20–24, compared with known population proportions. It is possible to make corrections to the data to adjust for these biases by 'weighting' them. (For an explanation and a worked example of weighting see Kent, 1999, pp. 90–2.)

One form of error that cannot be controlled (although it may be influenced by adjusting the size of the sample) is random error. However, it is possible for such error to calculate, using probability theory, what are the chances that the error will be of a certain magnitude. Such calculations fall under the general title of statistical inference and Chapters 9 and 10 take up this topic first for categorical and then for interval variables.

SUMMARY

Where it is not feasible, economic or practical to study every unit or case for the purpose of undertaking any particular piece of research, a selection will have to be made. This may be done on a purposive or on a representative basis. Purposive samples are selections made by the researcher and are used mainly for exploratory or for qualitative research; representative samples are chosen by randomised or systematic techniques, or by an interviewer following certain rules, and are used for quantitative research where the objective is either to estimate the size or frequency of characteristics or the relationships between them in the population of units or cases from which the sample was drawn.

In designing samples, the researcher will almost certainly want to make use of procedures for stratification, clustering or imposing quotas. Clustering is needed only where face-to-face interviews are to be conducted. The selection of clusters to use as sampling points is nearly always on a random basis, but is usually combined with stratification. The final selection of respondents may be random or quota, and both procedures have their strengths and limitations. For telephone and postal surveys no clustering is required and there is no need to use interviewer selection, but where the sampling frame used to get telephone numbers or postal addresses is felt to be inadequate, quotas may be imposed, even if the selection from the list was random. Whether this procedure counts as a 'random' sample is an issue that will either be hotly debated or send people to sleep!

The errors that arise when taking samples are a combination of those errors that might happen irrespective of the procedures used for selecting cases and will occur even when census studies are made, and those errors that arise from the over- or under-representation of types of case when sample selections are made. Sampling errors include both bias (systematic error) and variance (random error). Statistical measures based on probability theory that are used to estimate 'sampling error' in fact refer only to variance, and, strictly speaking, only to those samples where random selection of the final cases is made. Variance, furthermore, accounts for only a very small proportion of total survey error.

Exercises

Carefully define the relevant population for the following projects. Decide whether sampling is necessary and if so suggest an appropriate sample design:

■ A manufacturer of domestic lawnmowers in Scotland wants to know the proportion of households that own various types of lawnmower.
■ A hospital administrator wants to find out if the single parents working in the hospital have a higher rate of absenteeism than parents who are not single.
■ A company is about to launch a new product which is a vibrating massage cushion for use by motorists. The manufacturer wants to know what kinds of motorist are likely to consider purchasing the product.

Points for further discussion

1. Given the kinds of error that can arise when taking samples, is it better to go for census operations wherever possible?
2. Are purposive samples really 'samples' at all?
3. Why are quota samples so popular when they clearly produce more error?

Further reading

Churchill, G. (1999) *Marketing Research: Methodological Foundations*, 7th edn, Fort Worth, Texas, The Dryden Press.
See Chapter 12 on non-sampling error.
Kish, L. (1965) *Survey Sampling*. New York, John Wiley.
See Chapter 13, 'Biases and Nonsampling Errors'

References

Assael, H. and Keon, J. (1982) 'Nonsampling versus sampling errors in survey research', *Journal of Marketing*, Vol. 46, Spring, pp. 114–23.
Lessler, J. and Kalsbeek, W. (1992) *Nonsampling Errors in Surveys*, New York, John Wiley and Sons.

chapter 9

Making Inferences from Samples: Categorical Variables

INTRODUCTION

We saw in Chapter 8 that there are many situations faced by social and market researchers where the number of units or cases to be investigated is very large and it is not feasible to study them all, so a sample is taken. The sample is then analysed in detail using the procedures that have been described in Chapters 4–7 to produce tables, charts and summary measures. It would, of course, be possible to leave the analysis there and imply or assume that the results are likely to be typical of the total population of units from which the sample was drawn. However, the researcher is sometimes interested in making precise quantitative statements about the population based on the evidence from the sample. As was explained in the previous chapter, errors are likely to arise when this is done. Two kinds of error were mentioned: systematic error and random error. Both are selection errors and result in the over- or under-representation of certain types of units in a particular sample compared with the population. The difference between them is that over a large number of samples, the random errors will tend to cancel one another out, but the systematic errors will not. Systematic errors are often referred to as 'bias' and all samples taken will tend to over- or under-represent certain types of units or cases in the same way. This means that while the average of all possible samples will be identical to the true population value where the error is random, where there is bias, this will not be so.

Since random errors are, in the long run, self-cancelling it is possible to calculate the probability that, for any one *individual* sample, errors will be of a certain size. Such a calculation is not possible for bias. Another name for a random sample is a 'probability' sample. It means that the probability that any one particular unit will be selected from the population is known and that probability theory can be used to calculate the chances that errors will be of a certain magnitude. There are, however, two rather different ways in which such a theory may be deployed. In one situation the researcher may have little idea of the summary measure for the population (often called a population 'parameter'), so the sample is used to make an estimate of it. In the other situation, the researcher may feel that he or she knows the value of the parameter and the sample statistics are used to test an hypothesis to this effect.

ESTIMATION

Estimation is the process of using the value of a statistic derived from a sample to estimate the value of a corresponding population parameter. If the sample taken is a random one and there are no other sources of error, this estimate should be reasonably close. However, since the sample statistic is unlikely to be *exactly* the same as the parent population, statistical inference is used to attach a degree of uncertainty to this process.

Any statement we make about the population of cases should have two properties: it should be precise and it should be correct. If we took a random sample of adult consumers and found that 46 per cent purchased a chocolate bar in the last seven days, we could just say that the per cent in the population of adult consumers is just the same. This statement is very precise and is called a *point estimate*. Point estimates, however, are seldom likely to be correct. It would be very unusual for the value found in the sample to be exactly the same as the actual value in the population. As an alternative, we could say that the percentage of the population who purchased a chocolate bar in the last seven days is between zero and 100 per cent. This statement is undoubtedly correct, but not very precise. A statement of this kind is called an *interval estimate*. To be more precise we could say that the per cent who purchased a chocolate bar in the last seven days is between 42 and 50 per cent (that is, 4 per cent either side of the sample result). There is still a risk, however, that this statement is wrong. To make it correct as well as relatively precise we need to calculate the probability that the statement is correct. This is where statistical inference comes in.

A concept basic to all statistical inference is the *sampling distribution*. Imagine that we take lots of samples of a given size and calculate a particular statistic for each sample, say, the proportion who purchased a chocolate bar in the last seven days. If the real proportion in the population is, for example, 46 per cent, we may take a sample and obtain a proportion of 47 per cent. Another may come out as 45 per cent. In fact, most sample results will cluster around 46 per cent with relatively few producing 'rogue' results of, say, 39 per cent. The tendency for this to happen will decline as the sample gets larger and increase as it gets smaller.

Figure 9.1   *A sampling distribution of sample size n*

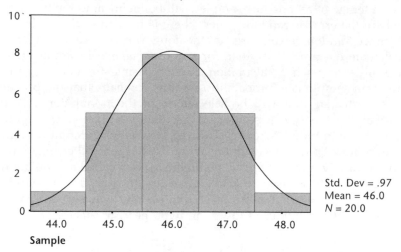

If we plot the results as a distribution, we might obtain something like Figure 9.1. If we in fact took every conceivable sample of size *n* from a population and plotted the results we would obtain a *normal* distribution like the one imposed on Figure 9.1 by SPSS. In practice we would not, of course, actually do this, but the distribution can be derived statistically by calculating a theoretical sampling distribution.

The normal distribution, as we saw in Chapter 7, has a number of interesting characteristics. One of these is that we can calculate what proportion of the observations lie between specified values of the standard deviation. Thus 95 per cent of the area lies between plus and minus 1.96 standard deviations. Each sampling distribution will have its own standard deviation called the *standard error*. Since taking samples will result in less variation about the population parameter than picking one case, the standard error will be less than the standard deviation for the population. In fact we divide by the square root of the sample size, so that we halve error in a sample of four, it is one third in a sample of nine, one fifth in a sample of 25 and so on. For proportions, it can be shown (using binomial theory, which we will not go into here) that the standard deviation of the sampling distribution (the standard error of the proportion) is given by:

$$\frac{\sqrt{p(1-p)}}{n}$$

where *p* is the proportion possessing the characteristic. In constructing an interval estimate, the first thing we need to do is decide on the confidence level for our estimate, that is, we have to decide how often we want to be correct that our interval will in fact contain the population parameter in question. If, for example, we want to be 95 per cent sure that our interval contains the population parameter, then we need to know how many standard errors enclose 95 per cent of the area in a normal distribution. We saw earlier that this will be 1.96 standard errors. (Do not forget that the standard error is the standard deviation for the sampling distribution.)

Thus if a sample of 300 found that 40 per cent had purchased brand A in the last week, then we can be 95 per cent confident that the real population proportion lies between:

$$0.4 \pm 1.96\sqrt{\frac{(0.4(0.6)}{300}} = 0.4 \pm 1.96(0.028)$$
$$= 0.4 \pm 0.06$$

that is between 0.34 and 0.46 (34 and 46 per cent, or 6 per cent error).

For a given sample size the larger the proportion that report a given characteristics (up to 50 per cent) the greater will be the sampling error. For example, if only 1 per cent of a random sample of 300 said they had purchased a particular brand, the error will be roughly plus or minus 1 per cent at the 95 per cent level of confidence, that is:

$$1.96\sqrt{\frac{(0.01)(0.99)}{300}} = 0.01$$

Thus we can be 95 per cent certain that the true result lies between zero and 2 per cent (or one per cent error). If 50 per cent said they had made such a purchase, the error will be plus or minus 5.7 per cent at the 95 per cent level, that is:

$$1.96\sqrt{\frac{(0.5)(0.5)}{300}} = 0.057$$

Thus we can be 95 per cent certain that the true result lies between 44.3 and 55.7 per cent (or 5.7 per cent error). A larger sample would mean that the standard error of both of these results would be lower.

When interpreting the confidence interval, remember that the particular interval you have constructed is only one of many possible intervals based on different samples. So, if you *say* you are 95 per cent confident that the real population parameter lies between the intervals you have constructed, appreciate that what you *really* mean is that 95 per cent of all possible intervals constructed in this way will include the parameter concerned (and thus the particular interval involved has a 95 per cent chance of being one of them).

Warning

Bear in mind when constructing interval estimates that you are assuming that the sample is a simple random sample, that the sample is 30 or more in size, that there is no bias in the selection procedure, and that there is no non-sampling error. We saw at the end of Chapter 8 that perhaps only 5 per cent of total survey error consists of random error. This means that, in practice, the true values are in fact more likely to lie *outside* the interval estimates than inside them. In the physical sciences, Youden (1972) listed 15 estimates of the average distance between the earth and the sun obtained over the period 1895–1961. Each estimated value was, in fact, outside the limits of the one immediately preceding it. In the socio-economic field, Williams and Goodman (1971) found that where estimates were made of numbers of telephones, subsequent observed true values were covered by the 95 per cent confidence limits only about 80 per cent of the time. In short, in the absence of any assessment of bias, or reassurance that there is no or little bias or other sources of non-sampling error, all confidence intervals need to be approached with extreme caution.

TESTING HYPOTHESES FOR STATISTICAL SIGNIFICANCE

Where researchers feel that they know the value of a parameter, they may want to take a sample to test whether or not their feeling, hunch or hypothesis is correct. Put more formally, researchers will calculate the probability that the result derived from the sample did, in fact, come from a population in which the hypothesis is true. Hypotheses may be of many different kinds, as we shall see in Chapter 11, but for the purpose of testing hypotheses for statistical significance, it is convenient to distinguish hypotheses according to whether they refer to one, two or more than two variables. Univariate hypotheses make statements about one variable, or several variables that are unrelated, for example, 'the group is predominantly male, exclusively from social classes A, B and C1, with a mean age of 33 years'. There is no implied relationship between sex, social class and age. Bivariate hypotheses relate just two variables together. Some may not spell out the nature of the relationship involved, for example, 'Variable A is related to (associated with, correlated with) Variable B'. Others may specify or imply some degree of influence, causality or determination, for example, 'Variable A is a major factor giving rise to Variable B', or 'Variable A is a cause (or *the* cause) of Variable B'. Multivariate hypotheses specify relationships between three or more variables. Again, these may or may not specify or imply the nature of those relationships. The process of establishing causality is taken up in Chapter 11.

So, in this chapter we can think about testing univariate, bivariate and multivariate hypotheses where the variables embodied within them are categorical. There are, of course, many different ways in which hypotheses can be tested, but in the context where a random sample has been drawn, researchers may be interested to know whether it is likely that the result achieved in the sample is a 'real' result or whether it is likely that it is a product of random sampling fluctuations. The word 'likely' gets interpreted more specifically to refer to the precise probabilities involved. Thus a researcher may want to be 95 per cent certain that the result is a 'real' one (which is the mirror image of saying that there are fewer than 5 chances in 100 that it was a result of random sampling fluctuations). Let us begin by looking at how to test univariate hypotheses that refer to one categorical variable.

Univariate hypotheses

A researcher may have reason to believe – on the basis of a deduction from theory, or on the basis of past research or personal experience – that 70 per cent of a population of cases possess a particular characteristic (for example, that 70 per cent of women in the UK object to advertising of highly personal products on television). If a sample of 100 cases found that 60 possessed this characteristic, could this proportion of responses in the sample easily have been obtained from a population in which the real proportion is in fact 70 per cent? The statement or prediction that is made about the population of cases in advance is usually called the *null hypothesis*. 'Null' means empty of significance, void or containing nothing. For univariate statements the null hypothesis is not really 'null' in this sense. It is rather a statement we are assuming is true of the population from which the sample was drawn.

As with estimation, a sampling distribution of the test statistic is used. However, unlike estimation, where we use the sample result to estimate the standard error, in testing the null hypothesis *we assume that the null hypothesis is true* and use the predicted proportion to estimate the standard error that would exist if the null hypothesis is true. In the previous example, if the null hypothesis is true, then the standard error of the proportion is:

$$\sigma p = \sqrt{\frac{p(1-p)}{n}} = \sqrt{\frac{(0.7(0.3)}{100}} = 0.046$$

This implies that 95 per cent of all samples of size 100 will produce results that vary between:

$0.7 \pm 1.96(0.046)$ or between 61% and 79%

Since the original sample result was 60 per cent, it lies outside this range and so is unlikely to have come from a population in which $p = 0.7$. In other words, random error is an unlikely explanation of the difference between the sample result of 60 per cent and the predicted 70 per cent. It is worth noting that we cannot conclude from the sample result that the real proportion is 60 per cent, but only that it probably did not come from a population in which the null hypothesis is true.

Why, it may be asked, did we not simply use the sample result for estimation purposes rather than going to the trouble of setting up a null hypothesis prior to the analysis? The answer is that if we have a theory, a principle or a wealth of experience that we think allows us to make a prediction, then it is this prediction we want to test. If we wanted, for example, to compare the results of two or more pieces of research, then it is their support or questioning of the theory or principle or experience that we want to compare. Calculating confidence intervals does not test the hypothesis because the results could be consistent with a large number of hypotheses or predictions.

For univariate categorical data, besides tests for proportions there are also tests for 'goodness-of-fit' for which the Chi-square statistic may be used. (The calculation of this statistic was explained in Chapter 6, p. 110.) Suppose a company has two brands of a product and these are measured for preference in a survey of 100 respondents. The results suggest that 60 prefer brand A and 40 brand B. If we wished to test the null hypothesis that there is equal preference for the brands, then, in theory, we would expect 50 to prefer brand A and 50 brand B. The difference between the observed and expected frequencies is 10, so Chi-square is:

$$\chi^2 = \sum \frac{(fo - fe)^2}{fe}$$
$$= \frac{10^2}{50} + \frac{10^2}{50} = 4$$

Like all other statistics we could, in principle, calculate Chi-square for a large number of samples and plot their distribution. This would be a sampling distribution of Chi-square. This distribution, however, is not a single probability curve, but a family of curves. These vary according to the number of observations that can be varied without changing the constraints or assumptions associated

Table 9.1   *Critical values of Chi-square*

Probability Degrees of freedom	0.05	0.01	0.001
1	3.841	6.635	10.827
2	5.991	9.210	13.815
3	7.815	11.341	16.268

with a numerical system. Thus if our sample is 100 then any number between 1 and 100 may prefer brand A. Once it is discovered that 60 prefer brand A then, by definition 40 (100 − 60) prefer brand B. In short, there is only one 'degree of freedom' – only one figure is free to vary. The probability of obtaining Chi-square values of a given magnitude can be looked up in a table of critical values for Chi-square. A simplified table is illustrated in Table 9.1. This shows, for example, that the value of 3.841 will not be exceeded more than 5 per cent of the time in a random sample with one degree of freedom. A value of 6.635 will not be exceeded more than one per cent of the time. With more degrees of freedom, values rise. We can conclude that the sample result of Chi square = 4 was unlikely to have occurred with a probability greater than $p = 0.05$ since 4 > 3.841. So, at the five per cent level we could reject the null hypothesis and conclude that the difference between the sample result and our expectation was unlikely to have been a result of random sampling fluctuations. However, if we had chosen the one per cent level of confidence, then the null hypothesis would have been accepted since the critical value is 6.635.

Suggestion

Notice that the table of critical values for Chi-square gives the values for selected probability levels – 0.05, 0.01, 0.001. The output from SPSS, however, gives the *actual* level of probability involved. This is usually called the p-value, and it is the probability of getting a sample value as extreme as or more extreme than the one we actually get, if the null hypothesis were true. In other words it is the probability of obtaining in a random sample a statistic like Chi-square, that is as far, or even further, away from the null hypothesis value of Chi-square = zero. The p-value is normally used in the following way. If it is *less* than the significance level chosen for the test (for example, 0.05) then the null hypothesis is rejected and we accept the result as statistically significant. If it is *more* than the significance level then we have to accept the null hypothesis and conclude that the result could have come from a population in which the null hypothesis is true.

The p-value provides a bit more information on how far down in the significance region a result lies. Articles in scientific journals often discuss their results in terms of these values. They make statements like $p < 0.05$ or $p < 0.01$. Unlike critical values, which are specific to the particular test concerned, p-values represent a kind of 'common currency' across which the results of different tests maybe compared. In this context it could be argued that it is better to report the actual p-values (for example, $p = 0.016$) rather than to use the conventional cut-off points, for example, $p < 0.05$. This would allow readers to form their own judgements about the significance of the result and the strength of the evidence against the null hypothesis. Different people may, for example, feel that different levels of significance are appropriate.

Bivariate hypotheses

Statistical inference for bivariate categorical data takes a rather different form. It is usual to test the null hypothesis that there is *no* association in the population from which the sample was drawn. If the null hypothesis can be rejected, then we can conclude that the sample result was unlikely to have come from a population in which the null hypothesis is true and that there is, indeed, some association.

If we are going to use the null hypothesis of no association then the obvious basis for such a calculation is departure from independence. The statistic Chi-square, you will recall, is based on the difference between observed frequencies and the frequencies that would be expected if there were independence between the two variables. This is the same notion as the null hypothesis of no association.

The top part of Table 9.2 shows a crosstabulation of the perceived importance of the social benefits of playing table tennis by age groups which have been recoded from 'agenow' into two categories of 34 and under, and 35 plus. The lower part of Table 9.2 shows the value of Chi-square, the number of degrees of freedom in the table, the statistical significance of the achieved value of Chi-square (the p-value), plus Cramer's V. The value of Chi-square is 9.6.

Warning

Note that it is called **Pearson Chi-Square**, which is unfortunate, because it sometimes gets confused with Pearson's correlation coefficient, which is a totally different statistic.

The table has four degrees of freedom and the result is just statistically significant at 0.049. This means that there are fewer than 5 chances in 100 (or less than 0.05) that the value of Chi-square derived could have arisen as a result of random

Table 9.2   *Importance of social benefits by age groups*

Count

		Social benefits					Total
		Unimportant	Fairly unimportant	Neither unimportant nor important	Fairly important	Very important	
Age groups	Under 35	10	12	28	19	5	74
	35 plus	1	6	13	18	8	46
Total		11	18	41	37	13	120

	Value	df	Asymp. Sig. (2-sided)
Pearson Chi-Square	9.558[a]	4	.049
Cramer's V	.282		
N of Valid Cases	120		

a. 2 cells (20.0%) have expected count less than 5. The minimum expected count is 4.22.

sampling fluctuations. We can therefore reject the null hypothesis of no association (or independence) and accept that there does appear to be a connection between age and perceived importance of the social benefits of playing the game. You can see by looking at the table that it is the younger group who are saying that it is unimportant or fairly unimportant. Cramer's V for this table is 0.282, which shows that the degree of association is in fact quite small.

Warning

Beware that the categories of nominal variables are sometimes described in textbooks on statistics as 'groups', or even as 'samples'. Thus when the variable is binary, it may be described as a 'two-sample' situation. The use of Chi-square on crosstabulated data may be referred to as the 'two sample Chi-square test' where the independent variable is binary and each category is seen as a different sample or sub-group, or as the 'k-sample Chi-square test' where the independent variable has three or more categories, that is to say it is nominal. Thus a relationship or association between sex of respondent and purchase of Brand X can be expressed alternatively as a difference in brand purchasing between the sexes. The statistical tests available may then be labelled 'two-sample' tests or described as 'making comparisons'. Relationships, according to this approach, arise only when we can talk about directionality – positive and negative relationships. This means that the data have to be at least ordinal. However, we will continue to think of crosstabulations involving binary or nominal scales as illustrating the relationship between the variables concerned.

Multivariate hypotheses

For categorical data it is usual to restrict tests against the null hypothesis to univariate or bivariate statements. An overall test for 3-way and n-way crosstabulations requires loglinear analysis, which is available on SPSS under Analyze/Loglinear. See Dibb and Farhangmehr (1994) for a discussion of loglinear analysis.

STATISTICAL INFERENCE AND BIVARIATE DATA SUMMARIES

These two procedures are closely related together yet they perform very different functions. A lot of problems in student projects and dissertations arise through a failure to understand what these different functions are. Statistical inference is concerned with the connection between a sample result and the corresponding value in the population from which the sample was drawn. It is trying to infer things about the population from evidence in the sample. Bivariate data summary, by contrast, utilises descriptive statistics to pick out features in a dataset whether these are a sample from a wider population, whether they constitute the entire population or are the result of an attempt to reach the entire population. Thus measures of association like Cramer's V evaluate the strength of the relationship between two variables in the data we have before us.

It may help if you are clear about how the two procedures are related. If a researcher takes a random sample, it will be true that the stronger the relationship between the two variables – as measured by a particular coefficient – the more likely it is to be statistically significant. In other words, high values of Cramer's V, for example, are unlikely to have come from a population in which there is no association between the two variables. We saw in Table 9.2, for example, that a Cramer's V of 0.282 was only just significant at the 0.05 level (having a p-value of 0.049). This gives some idea of the value of V that separates significant and non-significant results. However, this cut-off point cannot be applied throughout the research. This is because the significance of any one particular result will depend on the number of cases used in the calculation and on the size of the crosstabulation. We saw in Chapter 2 that the number of cases used in a given calculation does not necessarily equal the size of the sample and may well vary from table to table. This will affect the value of Chi-square. Basically, if you double the number of cases, you will double the size of Chi-square for a table that shows basically the same pattern of association. The size of the table, furthermore, affects the number of degrees of freedom, which, as was seen from Table 9.1, determines the critical value of Chi-square. In short, simply because a Cramer's V of 0.282 is statistically significant on one table in a piece of research does not mean that it is on another.

Take another look at Table 9.2. This is the SPSS output derived from checking the **Phi and Cramer's V** tick box in the **Crosstabs:Statistics** dialog box. The value of V is 0.282, which is a fairly small degree of association. In the column headed **Approx.Sig.(2-sided)**, SPSS is giving you the approximate level of statistical significance (the p-value), which is 0.049. This means that there are 4.9 chances in 100 that the achieved value of Chi-square (on which Cramer's V is based, and which Table 9.2 shows to be 9.558) could have arisen as a result of random sampling fluctuations. This is less than the 0.05 level normally demanded as a level of confidence and the result will be described as 'statistically significant'. So, a 'statistically significant' result does *not* mean that there is a high degree of association. It simply means that the result probably cannot be explained away as a result of random sampling fluctuations – more technically, that the sample result was unlikely to have come from a population in which there is in fact no association.

All statistical inference makes two crucial and key assumptions:

- the result being tested comes from a sample that was selected at random,
- no other source of error other than random sampling error is being taken into account.

If the sample taken by the researcher was not selected by random methods (for example it was a convenience sample or a quota sample) then it would seem rather pointless to be fine-tuning our application of probability theory which is based on having a probability sample. We also saw in Chapter 8 that random sampling fluctuation (where there *is* a random sample), furthermore, accounts for perhaps only 5 per cent of total survey error. When we come to consider what is often referred to as 'the significance test controversy' in the next chapter we shall see that many researchers will, despite having a non-random sample or a sample selected by random methods but where there was a very poor response rate, still apply statistical inference. This may be a harmless, if futile, pastime, but it becomes potentially harmful and misleading if researchers *rely* on finding 'significant' results without further analysis.

USING SPSS

Unfortunately, one thing that SPSS cannot do at present is calculate the standard error of the proportion for you (or the corresponding confidence intervals). However, for univariate hypotheses, SPSS will undertake what it calls a *Binomial Test* for the difference between a sample proportion and an hypothesised proportion. Select Analyze/Nonparametric Tests/Binomial. This produces the Binomial Test dialog box. The test proportion default is 0.50, but this can be changed to any other hypothesised value. The result gives a p-value that is one-tailed for any specified proportion and two-tailed for the default value of 0.05. The terms one-tailed and two-tailed are explained in the next chapter.

There are two ways of obtaining Chi-square in SPSS. One way is to check the tick-box against Chi-square on the Crosstabs:Statistics dialog box (select Analyze/ Descriptive Statistics/Crosstabs/Statistics). Table 9.3 shows, in the top part, a crosstabulation of division played by whether or not somebody else in the household plays table tennis. It is worth noting that the fourth division has been added into the third division so that there are no cells with an expected frequency of less than 5. The lower part shows the SPSS output. The value for Chi-square is 1.056, which, clearly, is not significant. In fact there are 59 chances in 100 that such a value for Chi-square could arise as a result of random sampling fluctuations.

The other way to obtain Chi-square is by selecting Analyze/Nonparametric Tests/ Chi-square. This enables you to use Chi-square as a goodness-of-fit test. If, for example, you put the variable 'division' into the Test Variable List box, the default

Table 9.3   *Division played in by whether anybody else in the household plays*

Count

		Does anybody else in your household play table tennis?		Total
		Yes	No	
Division	First	19	19	38
	Second	17	24	41
	Third or fourth	16	25	41
Total		52	68	120

Chi-Square Tests

	Value	df	Asymp. Sig. (2-sided)
Pearson Chi-Square	1.056[a]	2	.590
N of Valid Cases	120		

a. 0 cells (.0%) have expected count less than 5. The minimum expected count is 16.47.

Table 9.4   *A 'goodness-of-fit' test using Chi-square*

In which division do you compete?

	Observed N	Expected N	Residual
First	38	30.0	8.0
Second	41	30.0	11.0
Third	36	30.0	6.0
Fourth	5	30.0	-25.0
Total	120		

Test Statistics

	In which division do you compete
Chi-Square[a]	28.200
df	3
Asymp. Sig.	.000

a. 0 cells (.0%) have expected frequencies less than 5.
The minimum expected cell frequency is 30.0.

for expected values will be that they are equal for all categories. The output is shown in Table 9.4. The top portion shows that the expected values for each category of division is 30 (that is, they are all equal), the calculated Chi-square is 28.2, which with three degrees of freedom is statistically significant. The researcher can, however, specify his or her own expected values and Chi-square will take all the differences between observed and expected values and derive Chi-square in the manner explained in Chapter 6.

SUMMARY

Statistical inference for categorical variables may involve either estimation or testing hypotheses. Estimation is used when the researcher has little idea of the population proportion possessing a characteristic and is using the sample to estimate it. The researcher can attach confidence intervals to such estimates by calculating the standard error of the proportion and deciding on a confidence level, which in the social sciences is commonly 95 per cent, but in some situations may be 99 per cent. The standard error of the proportion can be calculated only for binary variables where a case either does or does not possess a characteristic. Where a variable is not binary then it is possible to use 'goodness-of-fit' tests which calculate the probability that the set of values

Summary continued

departs from some specified expectation or distribution. Chi-square may be used for this purpose. An alternative 'goodness-of-fit' test is the Kolmogorov–Smirnoff (K–S) test, which is particularly useful for testing whether observed values may have come from a normally distributed population. This is to be found in SPSS under **Analyze/Nonparametric Tests/Sample K-S**. The data can then be compared with one of four distributions including the normal distribution. Estimation is normally used only at the univariate level, that is, one variable at a time. Statisticians do not normally try to estimate the degree of association between two or more variables from evidence from the sample.

Where the researcher feels that he or she does know the value of a parameter at the univariate level, then this value can be taken as a 'null' hypotheses and the probability may be calculated on the chance that a sample result did indeed come from a population of cases with that value. At the bivariate level it is usual to take zero association as the null hypothesis and calculate the probability that the sample result did or did not come from a population in which the null hypotheses of no association is true. The statistic Chi-square is normally used for this purpose.

Exercises

1. Take the three examples of confidence intervals that are calculated on p. 159 and calculate what the intervals would have been had the sample size been 1000.
2. A random sample of 500 was used to estimate what proportion of households in a particular area owned a microwave oven.
   (a) Calculate the standard error of the proportion for each of three results:
      (i) 250
      (ii) 100
      (iii) 20
   (b) Calculate the confidence interval for the 95 per cent level of confidence for each of these results.
3. The brand manager for Brand X, on the basis of past studies, hypothesises that 10 per cent of the target market purchases his brand. A simple random sample of 1200 individuals recorded that 96 people had purchased Brand X in the last four weeks. Test the manager's hypothesis at the 95 per cent level of confidence.
4. Recreate Table 9.3 using SPSS on the *tabten.sav* file and ask for Cramer's V. What can you conclude from the result?

Points for discussion

1. If random sampling accounts for only about 5 per cent of total survey error, and statistical inference relates only to such errors, what is the value of statistical inference?
2. Why is it important in the context of testing results against the null hypothesis to decide on the level of confidence in advance of conducting the test?
3. If a researcher sets up a null hypothesis in advance and decides on a level of confidence, why does he or she not simply calculate confidence intervals on the results of the survey rather than assuming that the null hypothesis is true?

Further reading

Bowers, D. (1997) *Statistics Further from Scratch: An Introduction for Health Care Professionals*, John Wiley and Sons, Chichester.
This is the follow-up to Bowers (1996) – it covers statistical inference. Have a look at Chapter 3 on estimating the population proportion and Chapter 5 on Hypothesis-testing: Nominal Variables.

References

Dibb, S. and Farhangmehr, M. (1994) 'Loglinear Analysis in Marketing', *Journal of Targeting, Measurement and Analysis for Marketing,* Vol. 2, No. 2, pp. 153–68.
Williams, W. and Goodman, M. (1971) 'A Simple Method for the Construction of Empirical Confidence Limits for Economic Forecasts', *Journal of the American Statistical Association*, Vol. 6, pp. 752–4.
Youden, W. (1972) 'Enduring Values', *Technometrics*, Vol. 14, No. 1, pp. 1–10.

chapter 10

Making Inferences from Samples: Interval Variables

Learning objectives

This chapter will help you to make inferences about a population of units or cases where your data are interval and arise from a survey whose respondents are a random sample. In particular it will help you to:

- construct interval estimates for population means,
- test the statistical significance of univariate and bivariate hypotheses,
- use SPSS to generate the confidence intervals and use analysis of variance,
- appreciate the key arguments in the significance test controversy.

INTRODUCTION

We saw in Chapter 9 that statistical inference involves two processes: estimation and testing hypotheses. The procedures for both were explained for situations where the data are categorical. In this chapter we turn to parallel calculations needed when the data are interval.

ESTIMATION

The good news is that most of the concepts you require for statistical inference for interval data have already been explained in the context of categorical data. More good news is that SPSS will do all the calculations for you. The bad news is that we need a whole new battery of statistics that are called 'parametric' statistics that use the mean and the standard deviation as the key parameters for all variables. It was explained in the previous chapter that the sampling distribution for any statistic has its own standard deviation called the standard error. If we are concerned, for example, with estimating a population mean, then we need the standard error of the mean. This is the standard deviation of the sampling distribution we would derive by plotting the means for all possible samples of a given size. We can calculate the standard error of the mean by taking:

$$\frac{\sigma}{\sqrt{n}}$$

where σ is the standard deviation of the population and n is the sample size.

Thus the standard error increases with an increase in the standard deviation for the population, and decreases with an increase in sample size, but as the square root of the sample size. Where the standard deviation for the population is unknown – which is usually the situation – the standard deviation found for the sample variable (s) is taken as an estimate of the population standard deviation. In this case we need what is called an 'unbiased' estimate which divides the sample standard deviation by the square root not of n, but $n - 1$:

$$\frac{s}{\sqrt{n-1}}$$

Thus if the mean score of a sample of 60 cases is 20 with a standard deviation of 6, then we can be 95 per cent certain that the real population mean lies between the achieved sample mean plus or minus 1.96 standard errors, that is:

$$20 \pm 1.96\left(\frac{6}{\sqrt{60-1}}\right)$$

or between 18.5 and 21.5. Subtracting one from the sample size makes a meaningful difference only if the sample is quite small. Some statisticians will argue that if the standard deviation of the population is unknown we should use not the normal distribution but what is called the t distribution. For samples over 30 or so, however, this makes very little difference. SPSS will calculate confidence intervals for you. How this is done will be explained later in the chapter.

TESTING THE NULL HYPOTHESIS

Univariate hypotheses

If a researcher suggests a univariate hypothesis about an interval value then it is possible to use the standard error of the mean to test for the statistical significance of such hypotheses. Suppose we hypothesise that the mean age at which people take up table tennis is 15 years old. The results from the table tennis survey show a mean age of 12.8 and a standard deviation of 5 years. *If* the null hypothesis is true (that is, the mean age is actually 15), then 95 per cent of samples will produce means in the range:

$$15 + 1.96(\frac{5}{\sqrt{120-1}}) = 15 \pm 0.9 \quad \text{or} \quad 14.1-15.9$$

Since 12.8 is outside this range, there is sufficient evidence from the sample to *reject* the null hypothesis at the 95 per cent level. This implies that the sample result probably did *not* come from a population of cases in which the null hypothesis is true.

Whenever we reject a null hypothesis, the conclusion we accept is usually called the 'alternative' or the 'research' hypothesis. Note that there may be different alternatives:

- the population mean is not 15,
- the population mean is greater than 15,
- the population mean is less than 15.

Figure 10.1   *Critical regions: two-tail test*

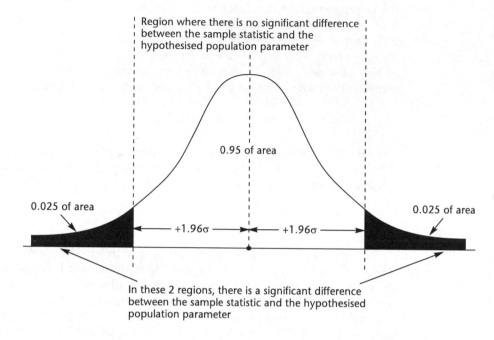

Region where there is no significant difference between the sample statistic and the hypothesised population parameter

0.95 of area

0.025 of area

0.025 of area

← +1.96σ →   ← +1.96σ →

In these 2 regions, there is a significant difference between the sample statistic and the hypothesised population parameter

In the first situation, we have little idea in rejecting the null hypothesis whether the real mean is above or below 15. The 5 per cent area of the normal distribution outside the hypothesised interval could be at either end of the distribution as in Figure 10.1. If we divide the two tails into 2.5 per cent each, then 2.5 per cent of the area is above 1.96 standard deviations and 2.5 per cent below minus 1.96 standard deviations. Suppose, however, that we were interested only in whether the mean is below 15. All the 5 per cent of the area needs to be in the left tail, as in Figure 10.2. Here, 5 per cent of the area lies below 1.645 standard deviations, so we could have constructed our interval as:

$$15 - 1.645 \frac{5}{\sqrt{120 - 1}} = 14.25$$

In other words, if the null hypothesis is true, fewer than 5 per cent of samples will give mean ages below 14.25 years. Clearly, we would still reject the null hypothesis that the mean is 15 if the sample result is 12.8, but by a slightly greater margin. The alternative hypothesis, however, is no longer that the population mean is not 15, but that it is *less* than 15. In the first situation we have constructed what is usually called a 'two-tailed' test and in the second situation a 'one-tailed' test.

Warning

Where p-values are being reported, then it is necessary to accompany p-value information with whether they relate to one or two-tailed tests.

Figure 10.2   *Critical region: one-tail test*

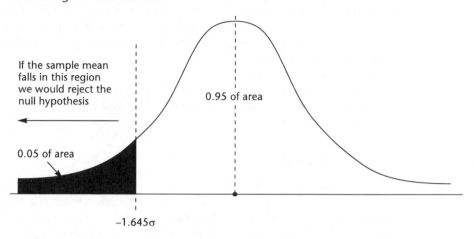

If the sample mean
falls in this region
we would reject the
null hypothesis

0.95 of area

0.05 of area

−1.645σ

Suppose, alternatively, that the researcher had hypothesised that the mean age at which table tennis players begin is 12, then, if this is the case, 95 per cent of samples would have produced results within the range 12 ± 0.9 or 11.1 − 12.9. Since 12.8 lies within this range there is now insufficient evidence to reject the null hypothesis. Note that, although a statistician will now say that, in this result, the null hypothesis is 'accepted', this does not prove that the null hypothesis is true. The result does not, for example, prove that the population mean is 12, only that from the sample evidence we cannot say that it is not 12. Furthermore, there is still a 5 per cent probability that we might have accepted a null hypothesis that is, in fact, false. So, remember that if we say we 'accept' the null hypothesis – which appears to be the standard terminology – we actually mean that we cannot reject it. We have to behave as though the null hypothesis still stands.

An alternative way of undertaking tests of significance is to construct what is sometimes called a z-test. The result is exactly the same, but the procedure is a little different. Instead of constructing intervals under the assumption that the null hypothesis is true, we calculate differences between the sample statistic and the hypothesised population parameter in terms of standardised units. In this sample, then, the difference between the sample mean and the hypothesised mean and divide by the standard error:

$$z = \frac{X - \mu}{s/\sqrt{120 - 1}} = \frac{15 - 12.8}{5/\sqrt{120 - 1}} = 4.8$$

In a two-tailed test, the critical value of z at $p \leq 0.05$ is 1.96 and for a one-tailed test is 1.645. Since 4.8 is greater than either of these figures, we can reject the null hypothesis.

The rhetoric of conventional statisticians insists that the level of confidence (or alpha value – 0.05, 0.01 or 0.001) be established *in advance* of the test and that the null hypothesis is then subsequently accepted or rejected. To decide on the confidence level after the results have been seen is generally regarded as not a legitimate practice since this amounts, in effect, to testing the hypothesis on the same data that suggested it in the first place. However, as we saw in the previous chapter, modern computer programs do not give a decision, but the probability of obtaining a test statistic as extreme or more extreme than the one actually obtained. This is the p-value. While reporting the p-value provides more information on how far down in the significance region a particular result lies than does simply accepting or rejecting a result, such a procedure may nevertheless compromise the idea of setting up the test criteria in advance. If a researcher produces a lot of results without prior hypotheses, then simply looking for significant results will probably involve picking out all or most of the sampling accidents.

Bivariate hypotheses

There are many situations in social and market research where the researcher has, or assumes that he or she has, an interval dependent variable, like the results of deploying rating scales, and wants to check whether there is any relationship between the mean scores of these results and various types or categories of respondents in a survey. Do the men have the same mean scores as the women? Do those who grew up in a single-parent family give different average responses to those who grew up in families where both parents were together? The researcher has, in short, an interval dependent variable and one or more categorical independent variables. As was explained in the previous chapter, the categories may be described as 'groups' or 'samples' and the researcher will ask whether or not differences discovered among survey respondents between various groups (or samples) arose from a population in which there is, in fact, no difference (or whether, in short, the result is statistically significant). In this situation, researchers will use a statistical procedure called analysis of variance (or ANOVA for short). The first section below explains ANOVA in some detail and shows how this can be accomplished using SPSS.

In other situations, researchers may have the results of two or more interval variables and will wish to know whether the degree of correlation between them is statistically significant. Chapter 7 explained that the strength of these relationships is measured using the Pearson correlation coefficient. The question that arises, however, is whether in a random sample discovered correlations are or are not likely to be the result of random sampling fluctuations; that is, whether or not they come from a population in which the null hypothesis of no correlation is true. The use of SPSS to undertake this analysis is explained in a later section.

Comparing means: the analysis of variance

The statistical significance of differences in interval values between binary or nominally scaled categories is usually measured by using analysis of variance (ANOVA). If, for example, we measure satisfaction scores using rating scales and assume the scoring system to be interval, then we might find that, on average, the males score differently from the females. Provided that males and females were chosen at random, then the question arises: can the difference in the scores be explained by random sampling variation, or does it represent a 'real' difference, that is, the sample result was unlikely to have arisen from a population in which there are no differences?

ANOVA assumes, then, that the dependent variable is interval and the independent variable is binary or nominal, that is, represents different groups or categories of respondents. What we are comparing is the *average* (mean) differences between the groups. However, there will be variations in individual scores within groups as well as differences between groups. The logic of ANOVA is that it compares the variance of scores between the groups with the variance within the groups. If the variance between groups is larger, we conclude that the groups differ; if not, we conclude that the results are not statistically significant.

The steps involved are as follows:

1. Calculate the mean score of each group.
2. Calculate to what extent individual scores within the groups vary around the group mean (this is done by calculating the variance – the standard deviation squared).
3. Calculate the overall mean for all the groups, that is, the whole sample.
4. Calculate how much group means vary about the overall mean.

These steps enable us to derive two quantities: the between group variance and the within group variance. The ratio between the two is called the F-ratio, calculated by dividing the between group variance by the within group variance. When F is large, between group variance is significantly greater than within group and there are 'significant' differences between the groups. To determine whether the ratio is sufficiently large we need to compare it with a critical value derived from a table of the distribution of F.

When there is only one basis for classifying groups, then it is called 'one-way' ANOVA. A special case of this is when the independent variable is binary, that is, there are only two groups. This makes it identical to what is called a 't-test'. 'Two-way' ANOVA is used when the groups are classified in two ways, for example by sex and employment status, that is, there are two independent variables.

In the table tennis data, the average score for the perceived importance of the social benefits of playing the game is 3.19. This assumes, of course, that the allocated scores of 1–5 represent 'equal' distances of amounts of importance and that we can, accordingly, sensibly treat this variable as scaled at the interval level. Suppose, however, that the researcher wants to compare the average score of those households where somebody else plays the game and those households where there is nobody else. The average scores of the two groups are shown in Table 10.1. From this you can see that the mean score of those who have others in

Table 10.1   *Mean importance of social benefits by presence of other household players*

Social benefits

Does anybody else in your household play table tennis?	Mean	N	Std. Deviation
Yes	3.23	52	1.10
No	3.16	68	1.13
Total	3.19	120	1.11

Table 10.2   ANOVA of perceived importance of social benefits by whether anybody else in the household plays table tennis

ANOVA

Social benefits

	Sum of Squares	df	Mean Square	F	Sig.
Between Groups	.140	1	.140	.113	.737
Within Groups	146.451	118	1.241		
Total	146.592	119			

the household who play is higher at 3.23 than for those who have no others in the household who play (3.16). The question now arises as to whether this difference could have arisen as a result of random sampling fluctuation or represents a 'real' difference. The null hypothesis is that there is no difference in the population from which the sample was drawn. Can this hypothesis be rejected from evidence in the sample? The SPSS results of an analysis of variance are shown in Table 10.2. The F-ratio is 0.113 and the p-value is 0.737. This means that in 100 random samples, over 73 of them would produce an F-ratio as large as this anyway as a result of random sampling fluctuations, so the difference is not statistically significant. From Table 10.2, if you divide the mean square for between groups (0.14) by the mean square for within groups (1.241) you should obtain the F-ratio. The same procedure can be used if there are more than two groups to be compared.

ANOVA was developed for use mainly in experimental set-ups where the differences being tested are between experimental groups and control groups. To use ANOVA properly, four key conditions need to be met:

■ the respondents whose results are being compared must be a random sample,
■ the scores of the dependent variables must be continuous interval and normally distributed within each group,
■ the variance within the groups must be approximately equal,
■ the groups or categories must be 'independent' samples.

The last term requires some explanation. Recall that the categories of binary or nominal variables are sometimes called 'groups' or 'samples'. So, in comparing the results, for example, of male and female respondents, we have two 'samples', one sample of males and another of females. Strictly-speaking, these samples should be 'treatments', that is, randomly allocated to groups. Thus a researcher may decide to compare the crop yields of fields that have been randomly allocated to the use and non-use of genetically modified seeds. We cannot, of course, randomly allocate individuals to their sex, but provided the selection of respondents has been made randomly, we can consider this to be the equivalent of two separate samples of males and females even though in reality they are from the same sample of respondents. The samples are 'independent' in the sense that the scores of the males and the scores of the females are independent of one another. This might not be the case if, for example, the males and females involved were married couples and so their attitudes to a whole range of things may well be related.

ANOVA is, in fact, a family of related but different procedures. They all have in common that they involve comparing means, but which particular technique is appropriate depends on two things. First, it depends on how many independent variables there are, thus 'one-way' ANOVA has one independent variable, 'two-way' ANOVA has two independent variables and so on. Second, it depends on whether the means being compared are for different respondents (SPSS calls these 'independent' samples) or whether they are means derived from the same respondents, for example scores on two tests taken by all subjects. SPSS calls these 'repeated' measures (or, in the case of the t-test, a 'paired samples' t-test in which the scores of the same respondents are compared on two interval variables). In Version 9.0 of SPSS, differences between means, t-tests and one-way ANOVA for independent samples are in the Analyze/Compare Means menu. All other procedures are under the Analyze/General Linear Model menu.

Many researchers use ANOVA on the results of surveys even though it is very difficult to meet all the conditions necessary for its use. Samples are often not random or not entirely random or random with very poor response rates, the distribution of scores within groups may not be normal and the variances may not be even approximately equal. The use of ANOVA on rating scales like Likert scales may be dubious if the variables cannot be considered to be approximately scaled at equal intervals. Remember that ANOVA depends on statistical inference. The end result of any analysis is always a p-value. Like all techniques that use probability theory, it takes account *only* of random sampling fluctuations, not any other source of error.

The only exception to this is the statistic Eta, which is a descriptive statistic for situations where the independent variable is nominal and the dependent variable is interval. Eta-squared is sometimes known as the *correlation ratio* and it can be interpreted as the proportion of the total variability in the dependent variable that can be accounted for by knowing the categories of the independent variable. The statistic takes the variance (the square of the standard deviation) of the dependent variable as an index of error in using the mean of the variable to make a prediction for each case. This is then compared with the variance in each subgroup of the independent variable. If the variables are associated, the variance within each subgroup will be less than the overall variance. The correlation ratio is then:

$$\eta^2 = \frac{\text{original variance} - \text{within-group variance}}{\text{original variance}}$$

The correlation ratio (η^2 or Eta squared) is always positive and ranges from zero to one. It is an asymmetric measure and is an index of the degree to which scores on a metric scale can be predicted from categories on a binary or nominal scale.

Eta is available both on the SPSS Statistics:Crosstabs procedure and on the Analyze/Compare Means/Means/Options procedure. It is only for bivariate situations where the dependent variable is interval and the independent variable is binary or nominal. It is thus related to one-way ANOVA for independent samples. Eta is not a commonly used statistic, perhaps because of the limitations of the situations in which it may be used; perhaps because it seems unglamorous compared with the sophistication of ANOVA.

The statistical significance of correlation

Have a look back at Table 7.9, which shows the SPSS output for the Pearson correlation coefficient, which is 0.808. Just below is the level of significance, indicated as 0.000. This is the p-value and it shows that the result is statistically significant even at the 0.001 level (since 0.000 is even lower than this!). SPSS has, in fact, looked up the result for you in a table of critical values. Remember that the p-value needs to be less than 0.05 if the result is to be statistically significant at the 95 per cent level. If it is, then you can reject the null hypothesis that there is no association between the two variables (or, more correctly that the result came from a population in which the null hypothesis is true). The test is usually a two-tailed test: this assumes that the test is non-directional and that there was no expectation as to the sign of the population value, positive or negative. Like all significance tests, the result is always sensitive to the size of the sample. Thus, for a sample of 30, the Pearson correlation needs to be greater than 0.36 to be significant at the 0.05 level. For a sample of 100 it needs to be larger than 0.2 and for a sample of 1000 larger than 0.062. In short, statistically significant results for large samples do not imply that the degree of correlation is large.

THE SIGNIFICANCE TEST CONTROVERSY

Most textbooks on statistics pay a great deal of attention to statistical inference and in particular to the process they usually refer to as 'hypotheses testing'. Remember that this does *not* amount to testing our ideas against the data we have generated from our research. (How this is done will be considered in Chapter 11.) For the moment, however, it is important to be clear about the role and value of significance tests in survey research. Significance tests would be better described as 'tests against the null hypothesis'. Thus they calculate the probability that the null hypothesis is true in a population from which a random probability sample has been drawn. These tests take into account only random sampling error, not bias or non-sampling error arising, for example, from non-response or interviewer mistakes. As we saw earlier in Chapter 8, random sampling error accounts for maybe 5 per cent of total survey error, so in rejecting the null hypothesis and accepting the alternative hypothesis, we are really saying, 'ignoring all other kinds of error except random sampling error, we can be 95 per cent sure that we are making the correct decision from evidence from our sample'.

Assuming that we have made the right decision, what have we accepted? We have accepted either:

- a **non-directional hypothesis** – for example, the mean age is not 32 years, or there is an association between two variables,
- a **directional hypotheses** – for example, the mean age is higher than 32 years, or there is a positive association between two variables.

Bear in mind, however, that 'positive' or 'negative' do not really apply when binary or nominal variables are involved. Instead, we need to specify what combination of categories tend to be found together, for example, it is the men rather than the women who tent to say 'yes' to a particular survey question.

In accepting the alternative hypothesis we are not saying anything about the magnitudes involved. If we accept that the mean age is greater than 59 years, we cannot say by how much greater. If we accept that there *is* an association between two variables, we are saying nothing about the strength of that association. For a two-by-two table, for example with one degree of freedom, the critical value of Chi-square is 3.841 at the 0.05 level of probability, so any Chi-square value greater than this will lead us to reject the null hypothesis. However, as will be explained in Chapter 12, sample sizes need to be at least 100 even for a very simple quantitative analysis. Cramer's V (or Phi) when Chi-square $= 3.841$ will be $\sqrt{[3.841/100]} = 0.196$. This is a very small degree of association. To the researcher, this is more likely to be of value as a negative finding (the degree of association is very small) rather than as a positive finding (the association is statistically significant). With larger samples, even smaller values of Cramer's V can be significant, so for a sample of 1000, a $V = 0.06$ will be statistically significant for a two-by-two table at the 0.05 level.

In short, with samples of 100 or more, almost *any* association large enough to attract the attention if the researcher will, by definition, always be statistically significant. For larger tables, the critical value for Chi-square is, of course, much higher. Thus a five by four table has $4 * 3 = 12$ degrees of freedom. The critical value at $p = 0.05$ is 21. For a sample of 100 this will give a Cramer's V of 0.46. But, of course, with 20 cells a sample of 100 will be far too small. A sample of 500 would be more appropriate (giving marginals averaging 100), but then Cramer's V will be $\sqrt{[21/500]} = 0.21$ – again, very small. In short, a 'statistically significant' result is not necessarily an important or interesting finding. When large samples are taken in survey research, tests against the null hypothesis are of limited value. They do give the researcher some feel for the levels of association that may safely be ignored. However, results for which random sampling error is an unlikely explanation, need to be taken as the starting point for further analysis. They should never be accepted as the 'findings' of the research.

A further limitation of tests of significance is that because they depend on a selected critical value (and, more often than not, arbitrarily selected, or just accepting the traditional 0.05 level) it means that there is a non-zero probability of getting it wrong anyway. Now if we look at 100 tables and pick out five that are 'significant' at the 0.05 level, then we are probably just picking out the five accidents we would expect anyway. In effect, the hypotheses have just been tested on the same data that suggested them in the first place. This is why it is so important, if tests of significance are going to be used, that hypotheses are set up in advance. If we pick out tables from the data, then to test any hypotheses that arise, we really need to test them on another dataset from another survey.

The whole edifice of significance testing depends on random samples. Indeed, as such tests are commonly applied, they assume *simple* random sampling. But a lot of research is based on sampling procedures that have non-random elements involved in the selection of sampling units or cases. Some procedures, like judgemental sampling and quota sampling are certainly not random and the potential for bias is considerable. Some practitioners will, nevertheless, argue that the resulting sample is an *approximation* of a random sample and that tests against the null hypothesis will somehow tell researchers something they would otherwise not know. Purists will argue that non-probability samples cannot be an appropriate basis for using probability theory. Remember, furthermore, that even in random samples there will always be some degree – and in many surveys a large degree – of non-response and quite possibly other failings in the sampling frame and data collection methods, so the presentation of 'significant' results as 'findings' is almost certainly misleading whether the sample was random or not.

Tests of significance may appear to be 'scientific', giving clear conclusions, but the choice of critical value is, nevertheless, a subjective one, as is the choice between alternative tests where these are available. Furthermore, the statements we can legitimately make from statistical inference are so circumscribed that they are of limited value anyway, and in consequence are liable to misinterpretation. Thus to say that we 'accept' the null hypothesis can be misleading unless we appreciate that all we can really say is that there is probably ($p = 0.05$) insufficient evidence in the sample to reject it since the result obtained could have been the product of random sampling fluctuations.

Criticism of statistical inference is certainly not new. Over 40 years ago Selvin (1957) argued that tests of statistical significance are generally inapplicable in non-experimental research where the influence of antecedent variables is not taken into account as it is in the design of an experiment. In survey research, 'significant' results are reported without reference to other conditions or possible influences. All too often, 'significant' results are seen as the final evidence instead of merely the beginning of a further analysis into results that need some kind of explanation.

Some researchers have even conducted tests of significance on total populations on the basis that such a population may still represent a sample of some wider, hypothetical and infinite universe. The issue, however, is not always clearcut. If the researcher selects all the employees in an organisation, then this is a census and the researcher should have no reason for concern about sampling error. However, if a researcher interviews all residents in streets selected at random in a particular city, then is this a census of the streets concerned, is it a 'sample' of the population of the city, a sample of all people living in cities in a given area, or is it a sample of the entire population at large? Some researchers will argue that, since the streets were selected by probability methods, then randomness was involved and that tests of significance are appropriate. Technically, however, it is a random sample of streets, not of households or individuals, and to conduct a test of significance, for example on the relationship between household size and income would be meaningless. The idea that we can study the operation of sampling error when there is no real sample is wishful thinking.

So, if statistical inference is of limited value in non-experimental research, what is the alternative? Certainly, the more informed use of bivariate and multivariate descriptive techniques (data summary) would yield better analyses than relying on tests of significance in circumstances where they are dubious. More attention could be paid to the potential sources of bias in a dataset, and some attempt could be made to determine the effects of such bias. More careful and sophisticated measurement procedures would pay higher returns on the quality of research than assuming that we have a perfect random sample, and a focus on measuring the reliability and validity of measurement scales would be more informative than concluding that we can or cannot reject a null hypothesis.

As will be explained in the next chapter, tests of significance do not, in fact, constitute a test of our theories against the data derived from the research. At best, in carefully selected samples, they enable us to take into account the possible effects of random sampling error. So, how *do* we test our ideas against the data? This is a topic to which we return in Chapter 11.

USING SPSS

SPSS provides confidence intervals for interval data under Analyze/Descriptive Statistics/Explore. This gives you the Explore dialog box. Put the variable 'agebegan' in the Dependent List and click on OK. You should obtain the table illustrated in Table 10.3. This provides many different statistical summaries, but the confidence interval for the mean at the 95 per cent level is 11.9–13.7. This implies that we can be 95 per cent sure that the real population mean age lies between 11.9 and 13.7 years. If you click on the Statistics box you can change the level of confidence, for example to the 99 per cent level and the intervals become 11.6–14.0. All these statistics can be split by a number of factors, for example sex of respondent, in which case you get separate tables for each. Just put the variable in the Factor List box.

Analysis of variance is to be found under Analyze/Compare Means. The top sub-menu, Means, calculates subgroup means and related univariate statistics. Put the variable whose means you want to compare into the top Dependent List box and the variable to form the subgroups into the Independent List box. Do not forget that this needs to be a categorical variable. The default table gives you the mean for each subgroup, the frequency in each group and the standard deviation (see Table 10.1) If you click on the Options box you can choose from a vast selection of statistics to put into the tables. Under Statistics for First Layer you can select to have an ANOVA table and the Eta statistic.

Table 10.3   Using SPSS 'Explore' to generate confidence intervals

Descriptives

			Statistic	Std. Error
At what age did you take up table tennis?	Mean		12.80	0.46
	95% Confidence	Lower bound	11.90	
	Interval for mean	Upper bound	13.70	
	5% Trimmed Mean		12.19	
	Median		12.00	
	Variance		25.018	
	Std. Deviation		5.00	
	Minimum		6	
	Maximum		43	
	Range		37	
	Interquartile Range		4.00	
	Skewness		2.869	0.221
	Kurtosis		12.575	0.438

The other sub-menu of interest here is the One-Way ANOVA. In the One-Way ANOVA dialog box again you need to put the interval dependent variable into the Dependent List box and the variable forming the groups goes under Factor. You can only have one factor and it needs to be categorical to form the groups. Table 10.2 was produced in this way. If the factor variable is binary, you will obtain the same result as an independent samples t-test. If you want more than a one-way ANOVA for independent samples, you will need the Analyze/General Linear Model procedure. This, however, can get quite complex. If you want more details, consult Bryman and Cramer (1999), Chapter 9, but remember the conditions that need to be met before such procedures can be properly used.

SUMMARY

As for categorical variables, statistical inference for interval variables may entail either estimation or hypothesis-testing. The estimation of interval variables usually entails estimating average scores or mean values. The standard error of the mean is used to calculate confidence intervals. SPSS can be used to calculate the upper and lower intervals. Testing univariate hypotheses may be accomplished in one of two ways. Either the null hypothesis is assumed to be true and the intervals under this assumption are calculated to see if it includes the sample result, or a z-test is constructed. In neither case can SPSS be used to make these calculations.

Testing bivariate hypotheses may involve two rather different procedures. One involves testing the statistical significance of differences between mean values where these values may clearly be seen as dependent variables and where the independent variables are categorical. If the independent variable is binary, a t-test is commonly used. If the comparison is for separate respondents who are independent of one another then this produces a result similar to the analysis of variance (ANOVA) for independent samples which may be used for any number of categories. SPSS offers a large range of procedures for the analysis of variance. If the categories are ordinal, then it is possible to simply ignore the ordinality and treat them as nominal. An alternative is to use special procedures for ordinal data like the sign test, the Wilcoxon Signed-ranks Test, or the Mann-Whitney Rank Sum Test. For an explanation of these tests see Bowers (1997). For how to use them in SPSS see Bryman and Cramer (1999).

The other bivariate procedure establishes the statistical significance of two or more interval variables that have been correlated. When SPSS (and other computer packages) is used, the end-product of all tests of significance is the calculation of a p-value. This needs to be below 0.05 to be statistically significant at the 95 per cent level, and below 0.01 to be statistically significant at the 99 per cent level.

Exercises

1. Use SPSS to produce the 95 per cent and 99 per cent confidence intervals for the variable 'spend' on the table tennis data.
2. Suppose you hypothesise that the mean age at which people begin playing table tennis is 12 and that your sample result is 12.8. Construct a z-test to see if you get the same result as on p. 173.
3. From the table tennis data, use SPSS to conduct an independent samples t-test for perceived importance of the social benefits of playing by whether or not anybody else in the household plays and compare your results with Table 10.2, which was derived from the one-way ANOVA procedure.
4. Obtain an ANOVA table which is identical to Table 10.2, but using the **Analyze/Compare Means/Means/Options** procedure. How would you interpret the result of Eta and Eta Squared?

Points for discussion

1. Is statistical inference ineffective for analysing the results of social and market research surveys?
2. If statistical inference is not ineffective, in what contexts should it be used?

Further reading

Bowers, D. (1997) *Statistics Further from Scratch: An Introduction for Health Care Professionals*, Chichester, John Wiley and Sons.
    Have a look at Chapter 2 on estimating the population mean and Chapter 7 on Hypothesis Tests: Metric Variable.
Bryman, A. and Cramer, D. (1999) *Quantitative Data Analysis with SPSS Release 8 for Windows*, London, Routledge.
    See Chapter 6 on sampling and statistical significance and Chapter 7, which looks at exploring differences between scores on two variables and covers analysis of variance.
Foster, J. (2000) *Data Analysis Using SPSS for Windows, Versions 8.0-10.0*, 2nd edn, London, Sage.
    See Chapter 16 on parametric statistical tests comparing means. This chapter takes you through all the SPSS ANOVA procedures. It may well be more detailed than you want, but it is helpful if you do need to use ANOVA.
Selvin, H. C. (1957) 'A critique of tests of significance in survey research', *American Sociological Review*, Vol. 22, pp. 519–27.
    This is the seminal article on the so-called significance controversy. It is still as relevant today as it was in 1957.

chapter 11

Evaluating Hypotheses and Explaining Relationships

INTRODUCTION

Chapters 9 and 10 showed how hypotheses can be tested for their statistical significance in situations where the respondents selected for the research were chosen randomly. The procedure involves calculating the probability that the sample result did in fact come from a population in which the null hypothesis is true. Testing for statistical significance, however, is only one of many ways in which researchers can judge their hypotheses. It is a way, furthermore, that is appropriate only when random samples are involved. This chapter considers other ways and other criteria against which hypotheses may be judged; it then goes on to outline how discovered relationships between variables may be explained.

WHAT IS AN 'HYPOTHESIS'?

In a dictionary sense, an hypothesis is a proposition assumed for the sake of argument; a supposition to be proved or disproved by reference to facts; a provisional explanation of something. In the sciences generally, an hypothesis is any formal statement that a researcher makes about one or more variables that are the focus of the research, but which is as yet untested. 'Formal' means that the statement is purposefully constructed and signalled explicitly as an 'hypothesis' or a 'proposition' in the report of the results. Once an hypothesis has been tested, it becomes a research 'finding', even if the data do not support or fully support the statement.

Hypotheses may take many forms and we can classify them in several different ways. One basis was suggested in Chapter 9 namely to distinguish hypotheses according to whether they are univariate (they refer to one single variable or several variables that are not specifically related together), they are bivariate (they relate two variables together), or they are multivariate (they relate more than two variables).

Another basis on which to classify hypotheses is whether or not bivariate or multivariate hypotheses specify or imply any direction of influence of one variable upon another. Some hypotheses – let us call them 'relational' hypotheses – simply state that certain variables are related, but do not spell out the nature of the relationship involved, for example, 'Variable A is related to (associated with, correlated with) Variable B'. Others may specify or imply some degree of influence, causality or determination, for example, 'Variable A is a major factor giving rise to Variable B', or 'Variable A is a cause (or the cause) of Variable B'. Sometimes influence or causality is implied, but the direction of influence may operate both ways, for example 'Variable A and Variable B are mutually interdependent'.

Textbooks and research articles often make a great play of the distinction between 'research' and 'null' hypotheses. (We looked at null hypotheses in Chapters 9 and 10.) The null hypothesis is a statement made by the researcher about a population of cases from which a random sample has been drawn; a statement which, furthermore, the researcher hopes on the basis of evidence from the sample to reject. It will thus often be formulated in such a way that its rejection enables the researcher to accept the alternative or research hypothesis, which is the hypothesis that the researcher wishes to substantiate. The process involves calculating a probability that the results obtained from the sample could have come from a population in which the null hypothesis is true. If this is unlikely at a specified level of confidence the null hypothesis is rejected and the research hypotheses is accepted. The research hypothesis is, in short, the mirror image of the null hypothesis. For example, if the null hypothesis states that there is no association between two variables in the population from which the sample is drawn, and evidence from the sample suggests that this hypothesis should be rejected, then the researcher can accept that there *is* such an association.

Unfortunately, it is not always possible to formulate our null hypotheses in such a way that their rejection leads us to accept what the research is trying to demonstrate. If the researcher wishes to demonstrate that there is a *high* level of association between two variables, then ideally the null hypothesis should state that there is not a high level. However, even if we can agree as to what counts as 'high' (for example, a Cramer's V of not less than 0.7), current statistical theory based on departure from independence is geared towards having a null hypothesis that there is no association. As we saw in the last chapter, rejecting this hypothesis certainly does *not* mean that the association is high. In fact for samples of 400 a Cramer's V as low as 0.1 will still be statistically significant if the table is a two-by-two with one degree of freedom.

SHOULD HYPOTHESES BE STATED IN ADVANCE OF UNDERTAKING THE RESEARCH?

In principle, hypotheses should be set up *in advance* of undertaking the data collection process. Generalisations that emerge *after* looking at data already collected are empirical generalisations that should not be 'tested' on the same data that suggested them in the first place. These may, however, be used as hypotheses for future research and tested on other data.

There are a number of advantages in stating hypotheses in advance. Such a procedure:

■ forces researchers to think systematically about what they intend to investigate,

■ helps to focus the research so that, for example, it is clear that the key objective of the research is to evaluate or test those hypotheses,

■ clarifies what crosstabulations are needed, or what correlations or regressions should be carried out where hypotheses are bivariate or multivariate,

■ makes the presentation of the findings look far more 'scientific' and will be appreciated by supervisors, examiners or reviewers of articles that are submitted for publication.

There might be some debate about whether you should set up the hypotheses before collecting data, or after the data are collected, but before the analysis begins. If the survey is to be preceded by an exploratory piece of qualitative research, then it would seem sensible to argue that hypotheses will be developed after the exploratory research has been carried out, but before the survey begins. The best advice, really, is as soon as you can – the earlier the better. It makes all subsequent activity much more focused.

In practice, however, hypotheses often begin to emerge or become more refined or precise as researchers analyse their data matrices. Usually, researchers at least start out with 'hunches' or feelings about what variables they wish to study and what patterns in the way they relate together may be present. When patterns do emerge, then formal hypotheses may be spelled out and focused on more specifically in subsequent analysis. Instead of either beginning with the data or beginning with hypotheses, the research moves backwards and forwards between hunch or expectation and the data. The processes of induction and deduction are used in alternation; hypotheses are reworked in the light of empirical findings.

In writing up the results of research, however, researchers will normally spell out their hypotheses in advance of presenting the data, giving at least the impression that they were formulated in advance of data collection. Philosophers of science will tend to see such a practice as unethical, unscientific and unacceptable. Researchers, on the other hand, who need their work published and who cannot wait to carry out another study, will argue that it is a matter of style of presentation. What can be said is that provided the hypotheses are clearly related to earlier literature or research findings then they *could* have been developed in advance, and therefore have a rationale for being positioned in the report of the research before the description of the research findings.

However, it sometimes happens that researchers do not wish to prejudge what they expect to see in the data, or they have little idea about what hypotheses may be formulated. In this situation they will collect their data first and then analyse the data in every conceivable way to see if patterns emerge. This approach has been referred to as 'data dredging' and is considered in some detail in the next chapter.

EVALUATING HYPOTHESES

Evaluating hypothesis is really about studying the relationship between our ideas or concepts (the theory) and the data arising from our research. It involves the twin processes of theory-building and theory testing. Unfortunately, books on the philosophy of science or on the logic of empirical inquiry debate endlessly on whether or not hypotheses can ever be conclusively proven or disproven, while books on research methods see hypothesis evaluation and testing purely in terms of testing the null hypothesis for statistical significance. In practice, researchers simply want to compare the data they have generated with the ideas with which they began. This involves a number of fairly distinct stages:

■ translating the objectives of the research into hypotheses that can be tested,
■ designing and filling a data matrix,
■ undertaking univariate display and summary of all the variables,
■ determining whether any data transformations may be needed,
■ undertaking bivariate and multivariate display and summary of the relationships implied by the stated hypotheses,
■ checking the results for random sampling error using statistical inference, if appropriate,
■ comparing the results with the original hypotheses,
■ analysing and explaining the relationships between variables.

Translating the objectives of the research into hypotheses that can be tested is something that researchers find quite tricky. A piece of research may, for example, have the objective of studying how attitudes to the advertising of cigarettes are affected by lifestyle. This is not a statement that can be tested – it is only outlining what is being looked at. We could, however, formulate the following hypotheses:

H_1 Positive attitudes towards the banning of all cigarette advertising is related to participation in sport.
H_2 Positive attitudes towards the banning of all cigarette advertising is related to party political activity.
H_3 Positive attitudes towards the banning of all cigarette advertising is related to concern for 'green' issues.

Designing and filling the data matrix was explained in detail in Part I. The procedures for analysing survey data have been explained in Part II, except for the process by which results may be compared with the original hypotheses and attempting to explain why the findings are as they are.

Comparing the results of a survey with the original hypotheses involves making some difficult decisions, for example, deciding what size of differences, what degrees of association or what levels or correlation count as 'confirmation' of the hypothesis. There are no rules or guidelines for this activity since what counts as a 'high' association in one piece of research may be relatively 'low' in another. A lot depends on the survey analysis objectives, particularly the research orientation. Thus for descriptive research the problem hardly arises since no hypotheses are stated in advance and the results are simply reported. For investigative research the actual level of association between the stated variables is critical, while for causal research the level of association after the relationships has been tested and controlled for other potentially prior confounding variables assumes a greater significance. To report statistically significant results as 'findings' is misleading since, as already explained, this does not mean that the degree of association or correlation is at all high. It would be common – and sensible – to report what are the highest levels of association in that particular piece of research, so the results are comparative. In one piece of research the highest level may be around 0.3 and in another 0.5 or more. It still, however, enables the researcher to say what variables are *most* strongly associated.

Having reviewed the magnitude of discovered patterns of relationships between variables, the last stage is to analyse and explain the patterns involved. It is to this topic that we now turn.

ANALYSING AND EXPLAINING RELATIONSHIPS BETWEEN VARIABLES

What is an 'explanation'?

To 'explain' in a dictionary sense can mean many things: to make plain, comprehensible or intelligible; to unfold and illustrate the meaning of; to expound, elucidate or remove obscurity from; to account for, offer reasons for or a cause of; to give sense or meaning to something. This variety of meaning is mirrored in social and market research. To some researchers, an explanation of research findings means establishing causal connections between measured variables, and the 'success' of the undertaking is judged by the extent to which the correct procedures have been followed and a number of criteria have been met. What these procedures entail is 'explained' below.

To other researchers, establishing causality is only describing ways in which variables may be connected. It does not enable us to understand why this is so. From this perspective, an explanation is something that provides understanding or removes puzzlement in a audience. It will typically make reference to means and ends, to motives and reasons, or intentions and dispositions. Its 'success' is judged by the extent to which the audience is satisfied with the level of understanding communicated.

Yet another perspective on explanation will see it as the discovery of an underlying process – a dialectic. This is a process of change that contains its own dynamic and which often arises from a conflict or tension between opposing forces or inherent contradictions. Understanding the internal dynamics of the family, social groups, society in general, an organisation, a market system, a distribution channel or an entire mode of production goes beyond establishing causes or satisfying an audience to something much deeper and more fundamental – the ultimate 'truth'.

The answer to the question, then, concerning, 'What is an "explanation"?' is that it depends on who you ask. The three approaches mentioned above are reviewed in more detail below. Remember, however, that these three certainly do not exhaust the list of different approaches to explanation. When a statistician, for example, talks about 'explanation', he or she probably means that the statistical variance in a dependent variable is accounted for by the variance in one or more independent variables.

Causal analysis

It is difficult for social scientists to avoid the notion of causality, and this has certainly been the dominant mode of 'explanation'. It fits with our own experience of connections between events. But what is 'causality' and how do we establish it?

Causal analysis is concerned with the ways in which some events or circumstances can produce or bring about others. The presumed causes are the 'independent' variables and the effects are the 'dependent' ones. Evidence for such causality comes from three main sources.

■ While the existence of a correlation or association is no proof of cause, it *is* a necessary precondition, and its absence would demonstrate that no causality is present.
■ The independent variable must precede the dependent variable in time, that is, the causes must come first and the effects afterwards.
■ The apparent relationship between the variables must not be spurious, that is, a result of their joint relationship with other prior variables.

Establishing each of these is, however, problematic. In a literal sense, to establish that Variable A 'causes' Variable B, it is necessary that there is a perfect association between the two variables – otherwise other factors are involved and we have to say that Variable A is *a* cause (amongst others) of Variable B. Measures of correlation or measures of association are, however, in practice seldom perfect, that is, coefficients seldom approach unity. If we accept a 'high' correlation or association as evidence, we have to make a decision about what counts as 'high'. Statisticians often assume that a measure that is 'statistically significant' *does* exist. However, this really only means that, for random samples, it is unlikely to have come from a population of cases in which there is no association. If we calculate a coefficient of correlation between two variables that works out at, say, 0.23 and which, because it was based on a large sample, is 'statistically significant', does this mean we have fulfilled the first criterion for establishing causality? Probably not.

Establishing the temporal sequence between variables can be even more difficult. For some variables it is not easy to say at what point of time they 'happen'. They may be states or conditions that exist for periods of time. Exactly at what point of time a customer becomes 'brand loyal' may be difficult to determine. Much social and market research, furthermore, is cross-sectional, (that is, measurements are taken at one moment of time) in which case it is impossible to say which variables preceded or followed others in time.

The testing of relationships for lack of spuriousness can be more complex still. There are at least three forms of spurious interpretation.

- The association is a result of a joint relationship with an extraneous variable. Thus there may be a correlation between essay grades and examination performance. One is not the 'cause' of the other; rather they are both the outcome of some prior combination of ability and work effort.
- The two variables apparently associated are in fact components of a wider system. Thus certain toilet-training techniques for babies and the use of public libraries may correlate. Again, one does not 'cause' the other, but both are components of a 'middle-class' style of life.
- The relationship between two variables may not be totally spurious, but indirect or conditional. Thus other variables may intervene or one of the variables may be influenced by factors other than the variables with which it is being correlated.

The investigation of spurious relationships may to some extent be carried out in a statistical manner. If the variables concerned are categorical then three-way crosstabulation is appropriate. The method essentially involves looking at what happens to the association between two variables when another is introduced. Thus there may be a degree of association between Variable A and Variable B. If a 'control' variable, Variable C, is introduced, then supposing Variable C has two categories C_a and C_b, then the researcher examines what happens to the association between A and B when C_a is true and compares it with what happens when C_b is true.

Look at Table 11.1. This is a bivariate crosstabulation of income, crudely divided into 'low' and 'high' and type of wine consumed, again crudely divided into 'cheap' and 'expensive'. Only the per cent 'cheap' is shown on the table. The table shows that 88 per cent of those with low income bought cheap wine compared with only 34 per cent of those with high incomes. An hypothesis of the form:

H_1 Those individuals with high disposable income are less likely to purchase cheap wines.

would have been confirmed by the data. However, suppose the researcher felt that patterns of wine consumption are likely to be influenced by age; that older people are less likely to buy cheaper wines (and to have higher incomes). Table 11.2 shows the relationship controlled by age, again crudely divided into an older age group of 35 and over and a younger group of 18–34. Both in the older and in the younger age groups the relationship between type of wine consumed and income still holds. Whatever the age group, those with lower incomes tend to buy cheap wine.

Table 11.1   *Type of wine consumed by income*

	Income	
	Low	High
% who buy cheap wine	88	34

Table 11.2   *Wine consumed by income, controlling for age*

| | Age 18–34 | | Age 35+ | |
	Low income	High income	Low income	High income
% who buy cheap wine	86	34	89	32

Table 11.3   *Wine consumed by income, controlling for social class*

| | Non-manual | | Manual | |
	Low income	High income	Low income	High income
% who buy cheap wine	33	33	85	85

So H$_1$ still stands, but let us now assume that the researcher, being the kind of sceptical scientist he or she is meant to be, suspects that social class may have something to do with it. Table 11.3 shows the relationship between income and type of wine consumer controlled this time by social class, crudely distinguished into non-manual and manual groups. The relationship between income and wine consumption has now 'disappeared'. Irrespective of income, those non-manually employed are less likely to buy cheap wines. The explanation may be that suggested in Figure 11.1. Those non-manually employed are *both* likely to have higher incomes *and* are more likely to drink more expensive wines, so the original relationship may be spurious.

Ideally, the researcher should undertake three-way analyses for every factor that could conceivably affect the relationship between the hypothesised variables. In practice this is often not done and researchers are often tempted to draw causal inferences from the occurrence of reasonably high measures of association or correlation between two variables.

Some philosophers argue that causal analysis is itself inadequate as a form of explanation. Some would argue that the notion of cause is itself an abstract concept – it is a 'black box', a mystical concept. Establishing association, temporal sequence and lack of spuriousness is evidence of causality – but not *proof*. That can never be established. Some philosophers have doubted that cause inheres in the nature of things. Scientists can always observe that Variable *A* is always associated with Variable *B* – but we cannot observe what binds them together.

Figure 11.1   *A 'spurious' relationship*

Is there, then, such a thing as a 'causal explanation'? Is it not a contradiction in terms – an oxymoron? If we accept that explanation is the provision of understanding to an audience, then whatever an audience accepts as providing such understanding, counts as an 'explanation'. From this perspective, cause *is* explanatory, but only to those who accept a largely positivistic natural science view of the world.

Providing understanding

Understanding is something whose function is to resolve puzzlement in an audience. This, however, *may* mean establishing a connection between beliefs, motives and actions, that is, we try to understand why somebody, or some group or organisation, did something. Another form of understanding, which is usually referred to as 'teleological', involves explaining events in terms of purpose. In other words we say: 'The purpose of *A* is to produce *B*', or '*A* exists in order to achieve *B*'. This may be focused at the group or social level – that certain social structures arise to meet the needs of society, or at the individual level – 'I did this in order to'. People must think in teleological terms if they are to be held responsible for their actions. Such forms of 'explanation' can be psychologically satisfying, but are ultimately difficult to prove, test or justify. Max Weber, one of the founding fathers of sociology, tried to establish the method of constructing 'ideal-types' so that we could understand more easily the relationship between means and ends. 'Functional' analysis, which also uses teleological relationships, looks at the relationship of the parts of a system to the whole – the parts are there 'because' they perform some function for the system or the system's purpose. Other devices that researchers might use to facilitate understanding include the use of such literary devices as drawing analogies between situations with which audiences might be familiar and the situation the researcher is attempting to explain. Thus the way in which the various 'parts' of society interrelate may be 'explained' by saying that it is 'like' a human body with arms, legs and so on.

Dialectical analysis

The idea of looking for underlying processes goes back a long way, probably to Plato, but its classic formulation was in the hands of Hegel. Hegel believed that a dialectic is a process in which for every proposition (a thesis) there is an alternative (an antithesis) which, ultimately, forms the basis of a new synthesis – hence the process of change. Karl Marx used the notion of dialectical materialism in which any form of economic development contains the seeds of its own destruction. Thus in capitalism there are inherent contradictions that eventually will result in the overthrow of the capitalist system. Dialectical analysis, however, is not necessarily a deterministic approach to knowledge. It is possible to intervene to change the course of history once the internal, underlying dynamics have been revealed and understood.

For Hegel and Marx a dialectic entailed a final point of arrival. For contemporary writers – who would certainly not think of themselves as 'Hegelians' or 'Marxists' – the approach signifies more a pathway, an underlying process in which things will progress, develop or change in particular ways if left to themselves. The product life cycle thesis used by marketers can be considered in this light.

The problem with this form of explanation is that it is untestable in the way that causal analysis may be subjected to empirical validation, and, furthermore, it may not necessarily relate to demonstrable ways in which social actors perceive their own realities, as with the attempt to provide understanding.

SUMMARY

An hypotheses is any formal statement that a researcher makes about one or more variables that are the focus of the research and which is as yet untested. In principle, hypotheses should be set up in advance of data collection, but in practice may emerge while data are being analysed. Hypotheses may be univariate, bivariate or multivariate. They may, in addition, be relational or causal, and they may be null hypotheses or research hypotheses. Testing hypotheses involves a number of steps, only one of which entails testing hypotheses for statistical significance.

Once hypotheses are established they usually need to be subjected to further analysis to demonstrate that the hypothesised relationships still hold when controlled for other factors. Such a procedure, while it may just be establishing the robustness of the findings, may also be seen as part of the process of establishing causal connections between variables. Whether or not this, in turn, counts as providing an 'explanation' will depend on the perspective adopted by the researcher. Resolving puzzlement in an audience or discovering an internal dialectic may be seen as other perspectives on what is meant by the term 'explanation'.

Exercises

1. Look at the questionnaire that relates to the table tennis study and suggest three bivariate hypotheses that you think might help to explain what sorts of people are more likely to play the game.
2. Using SPSS, crosstabulate the variables for each hypothesis in Exercise 1 and try controlling each bivariate analysis for another variable by using the layering facility. Ask for the statistic Cramer's V for all of your tables and compare the values of V for the bivariate and then the controlled tables. How would you interpret the results?
3. Again taking the three bivariate hypotheses you developed in Exercise 1, outline what you would need to do to establish some causal connection between the variables.

Points for discussion

1. If causality is difficult, if not impossible, to establish with any degree of certainty and if, furthermore, there is no such thing as an 'ultimate' or 'final' explanation, is it appropriate for researchers to talk about 'explaining' results at all?
2. If a 'successful' explanation is one that resolves puzzlement in an audience, does that imply that there should be a range of different explanations to suit different audiences?

Further reading

Following up any of the topics outlined in this chapter in the published literature is not an easy task because:

■ anything on 'hypothesis testing' will invariably be about establishing statistical significance,
■ anything about explanation in methodology books will be about establishing causality,
■ anything on the nature of explanation will be heavily philosophical in nature.

However, try one of the following books:

Blalock, H. M. (1961, 1964) *Causal Inferences in Nonexperimental Research*, The University of North Carolina Press, USA.
Hughes, J. (1980) *The Philosophy of Social Research*, London, Longman.

Analysing Survey Data

Knowing How to Handle Your Data

Introduction to Part III

Part II was all about choosing the right data analysis techniques. Knowing what techniques to apply, however, does not answer some of the 'hands on' problems that researches frequently face, for example, what to do when answers to some of the questions are missing, or understanding the different ways in which summated rating scales can be analysed.

Chapter 12 reviews a number of issues that might arise when handling your data matrix in practice and offers suggestions about the kinds of things you can actually do with your data. Some of the questions in survey questionnaires, however, are open-ended and they may require separate consideration. Chapter 13 looks at when such questions are appropriate and reviews two key approaches to incorporating the results into your research report.

chapter 12

Handling Your Data Matrix

INTRODUCTION

Despite knowing all the procedures explained in Part II, there will still be many questions that researchers, and students doing projects in particular, are likely to ask, and which are seldom mentioned in any of the literature available. Such questions will include things like, 'Can I upgrade the level of measurement achieved by some of my variables?', 'How do I decide what crosstabulations to run on SPSS?', 'How many cases do I really need?', 'What happens if I don't have as many cases as I had hoped?', 'How do I analyse the data from summated rating scales?', 'What do I do with the "don't know" answers?', 'What do I do with values that are missing?', 'How do I handle questions where respondents can choose more than one response category?, 'What happens if my sample is not really random – can I still test hypotheses?', 'Can I do all this using SPSS?'.

This chapter addresses all these issues. The suggestions made, however, should not be taken as the 'final word'; rather they are based on the answers the author has given to a large number of students over the years and which appear to have helped their understanding or even solved their problems. The chapter is really all about the 'nitty gritty' of survey analysis – getting your 'hands dirty' with the data before you.

UPGRADING AND DOWNGRADING SCALES

Researchers sometimes upgrade the level of measurement achieved by some of their scales in order to apply the more sophisticated statistical techniques that thereby become available. The most usual transformation is for sets of ordered categories to be upgraded to interval scales. There are two main ways in which this may be accomplished. The researcher may allocate numerical scores to ordinal categories, and then treat the scores as if they referred to metric quantities. Thus the level of interest in a television programme may be recorded on a 5-point scale:

	Allocate score
Extremely interesting	5
Very interesting	4
Fairly interesting	3
Not very interesting	2
Not at all interesting	1

A score is allocated to each individual response as shown and the total for all respondents can be added up and divided by the number of respondents to give an average score. This process, however, assumes that the 'distances' between each point on the scale are equal so that, for example, the distance between 'very interesting' and 'fairly interesting' is the 'same' as the distance between 'fairly interesting' and 'not very interesting'. Such an assumption may seem reasonable in this example. It also tends to be reasonable for Likert items where respondents are being asked about their degree of agreement or disagreement with a number of statements. However, for levels of satisfaction, where a set of categories like 'very satisfied', 'fairly satisfied' and 'dissatisfied' have been used, this assumption is suspect since the 'distance' between 'dissatisfied' and 'fairly satisfied' is probably much greater than the 'distance' between 'fairly satisfied' and 'very satisfied'. In any event, it would be unwise to treat total scores in any absolute sense. However, for measuring change, for example from one week to the next, then changes in the average scores *are* likely to reflect real changes in people's level of interest. Error, provided it is constant, does not affect measures of change.

Suggestion

When using SPSS remember that the scores you allocate must be entered as values using the **Define Variable/Labels** procedure. Make sure that you enter the categories in order and that 1 is the 'low' end and 5 or whatever is the highest score is at the 'high' end. You can then use either **Analyze/Descriptive Statistics/Frequencies** or **Analyze/Descriptive Statistics/Descriptives** to obtain a mean score for each variable.

The other way to create interval scales is to define categories of an ordinal scale in numerical terms. Thus a distinction between 'small', 'medium' and 'large' organisations is only an ordinal distinction. However, if the researcher defined 'small' organisations as having fewer than 50 employees, 'medium' as having between 50 and 200 employees, and 'large' as having over 200 employees then a discrete interval scale has been created, the 'metric' in this case being size measured by the number of employees. With a larger number of categories, more precisely defined, with upper and lower limits, it becomes possible to calculate an average size. This procedure is fine provided there is accurate information, for example in the previous situation, on the number of employees in each organisation of interest.

By creating (or assuming the creation of) interval scales, the researcher can now, for example, add up and then calculate average scores, calculate standard deviations, and use the variables in ways that were explained in Chapters 5, 7 and 10, which review tables, charts, data summaries and making inferences from samples for interval variables. In particular, multivariate procedures like multiple regression and factor analysis become possible.

Warning

Multivariate procedures are only as good as the data that have been entered and if the assumptions about equal intervals are unwarranted, then this will be another case of GIGO (garbage in, garbage out).

There are some circumstances when a researcher may downgrade a scale and treat it as if it were at a lower level. Thus an interval scale may be treated as a ranked scale by ignoring the distances between categories. A class test out of 100 may be used to create ranks of first, second, third and so on. This may be undertaken by the researcher either because he or she feels that the assumptions of the original metric are unwarranted, or because the variable is to be correlated with another ranked scale and the researcher wants to apply Spearman's rho, which requires two ranked scales. Interval scales can be ranked in SPSS using Transform/Rank Cases.

Another example of downgrading is when a researcher wishes to crosstabulate a nominal with an ordinal scale. An appropriate measure of association may be chosen that treats both variables as nominal (for example Cramer's V, see pp. 109–12), thereby ignoring the ordering of the categories in one of the variables. A more extreme example is when a researcher takes a continuous interval scale like age and groups respondents into a binary scale of 'old' and 'young' or into an ordinal scale of 'old', 'middle aged' and 'young'. This may be undertaken if the researcher wishes to crosstabulate age with another binary, nominal or ordinal variable, for example, 'purchased' and 'did not purchase' Brand B in the last seven days. The age split would normally be done in a way that creates two (or three or more as required) roughly equal groups. The SPSS procedure Transform/Compute can be used to create a new variable grouped in this way. This procedure is explained at the end of this chapter.

DATA DREDGING

'Dredging' normally means casting a net or other mechanical device to trawl whatever is on the sea bottom. In the context of data analysis it is a metaphor for a process of 'trawling' a dataset without specific hypotheses to test, or perhaps even without hunches or specific issues to pursue. In its most extreme form the data are explored in every conceivable way to see what patterns emerge. Researchers may, for example, crosstabulate every variable by every other variable in the dataset in order to see which ones produce the strongest associations. This can rapidly produce a lot of tables. In the table tennis survey there are 30 variables. If we were to crosstabulate each variable by each other variable, we would produce $(30 * 29)/2$ or 435 tables. Many of the tables would not, of course, be particularly helpful, but some relationships that we might not have expected may well emerge. As a deliberate strategy, however, it is not a particularly efficient one. It also raises the issue of how the researcher decided what variables to include in the questionnaire in the first place if he or she had no idea of what patterns he or she was wishing to study.

A little less extreme are situations where there is a single dependent variable, for example voting behaviour, and the researcher examines all possible bivariate relationships between this and all conceivable independent variables. Only those deemed to be statistically significant or which meet some other criteria appear in the published report of the findings, all others having been discarded. Another possibility is that instead of investigating all of a predetermined set, the researcher works in a more haphazard fashion, pursuing those ideas that come to mind.

Data dredging is an inductive process that may produce empirical generalisations from the ground up. It is often seen to be reprehensible, producing 'logically suspect' results (Alt and Brighton, 1981). It is an admission that researchers do not know what they are looking for. However, some patterns *are* discovered by chance, and dredging may turn out to be a fruitful way of producing new insights. It is important to recognise, however, that all the various data dredging procedures are exploratory, and the same data cannot be used to 'test' hypotheses that were derived from such data. This is because, by definition, the variables or findings retained have been selected and that affects subsequent probabilities that it was a 'chance' result. The only valid course of action is to use different data for testing the derived model that has been dredged from the first set of data. This need not necessarily involve a new sample or a new piece of research. The initial sample might be split using randomised methods into two parts for this purpose.

This argument, of course, only applies where the data represent a random sample, where all other sources of error are being ignored, and the 'test' being applied relates to statistical inference. If statistical inference is not being applied then the researcher can just report the findings using descriptive statistics, even if such findings emerged from data dredging. In a sense the research will still be exploratory and not conclusive, and it is likely that the researcher will suggest that further research is required before it is possible to have a degree of confidence in the findings.

HOW MANY CASES ARE NEEDED AND WHAT SIZE OF SAMPLE SHOULD BE TAKEN?

It may seem strange to pose these as separate (although related) questions. However, remember from Chapter 2 that there may well be a difference between:

■ the size of sample attempted or drawn from a list,
■ the number of questionnaires returned,
■ the number of usable returns.

It is the number of usable returns that is entered into the data matrix and which will form the basis for any analysis. The minimum number of cases you need in your data matrix depends on the kind of analysis you intend to perform.

For any kind of quantitative analysis a minimum of 100 cases are needed even to be able to calculate simple percentages for each variable. If, as is so often the case, analyses need to be performed on sub-groups, then the smallest subgroup must contain sufficient cases for reliable estimates to be achieved. If the variables are to be crosstabulated then much larger samples will be required. As a general rule, the number of cases should be 100 multiplied by the number of columns (or rows) that are to be used as a basis for percentage calculations. So for two-by-two table, the minimum sample size should be 200. For a two-by-three table where the three categories are to be used as a basis for percentaging, then a sample size of 300 is required and so on. Most market research agencies, for example, will need to do a series of breakdowns for clients and will tend to take samples of at least 1000. Few samples for *ad hoc* research will be much above 3000, but where the research is continuous and based on separate samples it may be possible to accumulate samples of 30 000 or more over the course of a year.

For student projects, obtaining the ideal number of cases may just not be feasible. He or she may, for example, wish to crosstabulate a number of variables, each of which has five categories. This would require 500 cases, which may well be beyond student capabilities or resources. Compromise is needed. About 200 cases would possibly just about allow for sensible interpretation, although some caution about interpreting the statistical results would be advisable. Serious thought, however, should be given to the possibility of collapsing the number of categories to three or even two. A further consideration to bear in mind is that if there are variables in the dataset for which there are no answers recorded for some of the cases (we will be considering what to do with missing values in a moment), then there really need to be more cases in the matrix to allow for adequate numbers of cases on each of the variables that are to be used in the analysis.

To obtain the desired or the minimum number of cases needed for a survey, it is often advisable to pick a sample that is greater than that number to allow for non-response and non-usable returns. If it is to be a random sample from a list, then the response rate for a postal survey is typically 20–30 per cent. If 200 cases are needed for analysis purposes, then 1000 questionnaires should be sent out. The response rate for an interview survey is usually considerably larger, say, 70 per cent. Even then, about 290–300 cases will need to be drawn as a sample. Where quota sampling is used, then the researcher can carry on until the required number is reached. However, some allowance may still need be made for the likely number of non-usable returns.

Textbooks tend to take a statistical approach to sample size that calculates the size of sample needed in order to achieve a specified degree of sampling error and a minimum level of accuracy. The problem with such calculations is that they assume that the researcher is able to specify an acceptable level of sampling error in advance of undertaking the research. This is usually impossible, particularly since errors will vary from variable to variable. Such calculations also fail to take into account very practical issues such as that larger samples will cost more and will take more time to complete. There may well be a limit to the size of sample that can be afforded or is practicable. Furthermore, how large a sample is needed also depends on the variability of the population characteristics and on the purpose of the research. The more the characteristics vary the larger the sample will need to be. Furthermore, if the purpose of the research is accurate assessment of quantitative variables then larger samples will again be required. If the purpose is to generate ideas for new products then a small sample of product category users may well be sufficient.

The notion of minimum sample size needs to be seen in relation to the declining 'payoff' of increasing sample size in terms of accuracy. For example, for categorical variables, if we use the 95 per cent level of confidence and take the maximum variability between proportions of 50:50, then the percentage sampling error can be seen from Table 12.1. Thus the 13.9 per cent given for a sample size of 50 is derived from:

$$1.96\sqrt{\frac{(0.5)(0.5)}{50}} = 0.139$$

Doubling the sample size from 50 to 100 reduces the per cent error from 13.9 to 9.8, a 4.1 per cent reduction. However, doubling sample size from 5000 to 10 000 only improves the situation from 1.4 per cent to 1.0 per cent, a 0.4 per cent reduction.

In some cases, the sample constitutes a significant proportion of the population from which the sample was drawn. Where the sample exceeds about 10 per cent of the population, then statisticians like Kish (1965) have argued that a finite population correction factor should be applied to the standard error calculation.

Table 12.1   *Percentage sampling errors: maximum variability at 50:50*

Sample size	95% level of confidence	99% level of confidence
50	13.9	18.2
100	9.8	12.9
200	6.9	9.1
400	4.9	6.4
500	4.4	5.7
1000	3.1	4.1
5000	1.4	1.8
10 000	1.0	1.3

This is defined as:

$$\sqrt{1 - \frac{n}{N}}$$

so that at 10 per cent, a sample of 100 out of 1000 would give a finite population correction of:

$$\sqrt{1 - \frac{100}{1000}} = 0.95$$

so that the error above is reduced to $(0.139)(0.95) = 13.2$. At 50 per cent (a sample of 500 in this example) it would become $(0.139)(0.71)$ or 9.8 per cent. If the entire population is included, the correction factor becomes zero and the standard error becomes zero.

STRATEGIES FOR COPING WITH RELATIVELY FEW CASES

If the number of usable returns from a survey is fewer than the ideal minimum number, then the first strategy of the researcher must be to use the Recode procedure on SPSS to create variables with fewer categories. If the number of cases is between 100 and 150 or so then variables should be made binary wherever possible. This means that most crosstabulations will be two-by-two tables. Where the variables are interval then this problem does not rise. Thus it is possible to calculate a correlation coefficient between two interval variables with just 3 or 4 cases. No survey researcher, however, is likely to have so few in number and a set of 100 cases will be ample.

Sometimes students protest that in the particular industry they are studying there *are* only 70 firms, so they cannot obtain more than this number. In reality, of course there will never be 100 per cent response, so there will almost certainly be fewer than this number to analyse. This means that any crosstabulations will be difficult to interpret. There will be very small frequencies in most of the cells and some cells may be empty. Furthermore, most measures of association, such as Cramer's V, will behave in an unreliable way in such circumstances. If you only have 30 or 40 cases, there is very little you can do by way of quantitative analysis. In this situation, you should give serious thought to changing your style of research and maybe undertake qualitative research instead. If you have 60 or 70 cases, then you can report univariate findings, but tentatively and with full recognition that the results are only indicative and not conclusive. Bivariate analysis on such small numbers, unless for interval variables, is unlikely to produce any 'findings' of value.

STRATEGIES FOR ANALYSING SUMMATED RATING SCALES

In Chapter 2 summated rating scales were explained. In this section we will look at how data from such scales can be analysed. In the table tennis survey, respondents were asked how satisfied they were with various elements of table tennis in Northern Ireland. These include practice facilities, competition facilities, administration, coaching opportunities and competitions. Answers were recorded into a 5-point rating scale from 'unsatisfied' to 'very satisfied'. The first stage in any analysis will be to review the raw frequencies (SPSS calls these the 'count') and the relative frequencies or percentages for each level of satisfaction for each of the five variables. Table 12.2 shows an output from SPSS using the Analyze/Custom Tables/Basic Tables procedure. The Basic Tables dialog box is explained at the end of this chapter. Table 12.2 gives an overall picture of the numbers and proportions responding in each of the categories. There are a lot of data here to take in, so each variable could be summarised by calculating the average score for each of the items, as Table 12.3. From this we can see that the overall satisfaction with the competitions is quite high compared with the other elements, while satisfaction with coaching opportunities is relatively low. This was not evident from Table 12.2.

Table 12.3, however, does not give an overall evaluation of all the elements added together. This is what a summated rating scale will do. Using the Transform/Compute facility on SPSS to create a new variable, 'totalsat', Table 12.4 shows the overall average satisfaction score, and that score broken down by sex

Table 12.2   *Satisfaction with various elements of playing table tennis*

		Count	Col %
Practice facilities	Unsatisfied	23	19.2
	Fairly unsatisfied	27	22.5
	Neither unsatisfied or satisfied	43	35.8
	Fairly satisfied	21	17.5
	Very satisfied	6	5.0
Group Total		120	100.0
Competition facilities	Unsatisfied	7	5.8
	Fairly unsatisfied	26	21.7
	Neither unsatisfied or satisfied	53	44.2
	Fairly satisfied	29	24.2
	Very satisfied	5	4.2
Group Total		120	100.0
Administration	Unsatisfied	17	14.2
	Fairly unsatisfied	27	22.5
	Neither unsatisfied or satisfied	54	45.0
	Fairly satisfied	18	15.0
	Very satisfied	4	3.3
Group Total		120	100.0
Coaching opportunities	Unsatisfied	26	21.7
	Fairly unsatisfied	34	28.3
	Neither unsatisfied or satisfied	43	35.8
	Fairly satisfied	15	12.5
	Very satisfied	2	1.7
Group Total		120	100.0
Competitions	Unsatisfied	9	7.5
	Fairly unsatisfied	16	13.3
	Neither unsatisfied or satisfied	40	33.3
	Fairly satisfied	37	30.8
	Very satisfied	18	15.0
Group Total		120	100.0

Table 12.3   *Mean satisfaction score for elements of playing table tennis*

	Mean
Practice facilities	2.67
Competition facilities	2.99
Administration	2.71
Coaching opportunities	2.44
Competitions	3.33

Table 12.4   *Total satisfaction scores by sex of player*

TOTALSAT

What sex are you?	Mean	N
Male	2.8447	103
Female	2.7176	17
Total	2.8267	120

of player using the Analyze/Compare Means procedure. You can see that the overall score for the men is a little higher than that of the women. It would then even be possible to do an independent samples t-test on the difference to show, for example, that the difference is not statistically significant.

Given that 'totalsat' is being treated as an interval variable, it would be possible to draw a scattergram of the relationship between this and both 'agebegan' and 'spend'. These are shown in Figures 12.1 and 12.2. As you can see, there is little point in getting SPSS to calculate a measure of correlation – there clearly *is* no pattern. Overall satisfaction does not appear to be related to either the age at which people began or how much they spent on the game in the last six months.

Figure 12.1   *A scattergram of 'agebegan' by total satisfaction score*

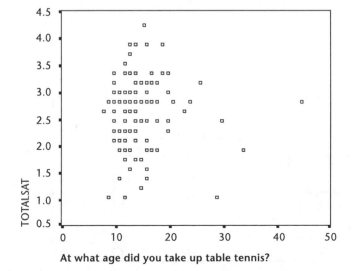

Figure 12.2 *A scattergram of 'spend' by total satisfaction score*

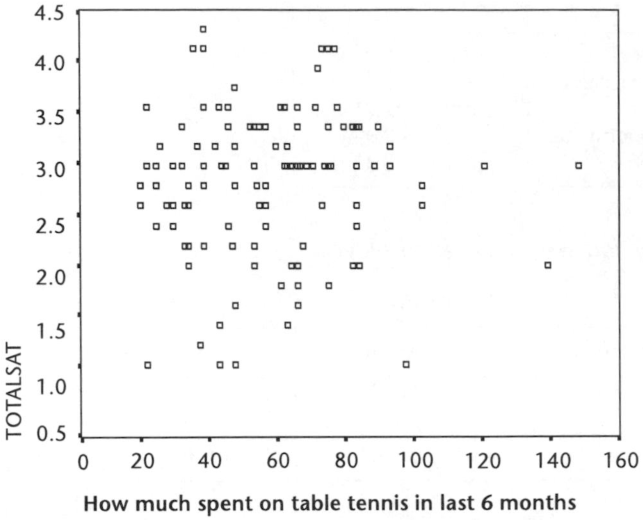

How much spent on table tennis in last 6 months

Remember, however, that negative findings like these are as useful as positive ones.

It would, of course, be possible to compare the mean satisfaction scores for any subgroup in the sample. However, this may hide patterns in the ways the different levels of satisfaction vary with some other variable. It would, instead, be possible to crosstabulate each of the items making up the overall scale separately against, for example, whether there is anybody else in the household who plays the game. Table 12.5 shows this for 'practice facilities'. The table is a little difficult to interpret because there are too many categories and too small frequencies in the cells. If we use the Recode facility to regroup the satisfaction categories into 'satisfied', 'neither' and 'unsatisfied', we obtain Table 12.6. It begins to look as though those players who have somebody else in the household who plays are less likely to be satisfied with practice facilities. However, the pattern is very

Table 12.5 *Satisfaction with practice facilities by whether anybody else in the household plays table tennis*

Count

		Does anybody else in your household play table tennis?		
		Yes	No	Total
Practice facilities	Unsatisfied	13	10	23
	Fairly unsatisfied	11	16	27
	Neither unsatisfied nor satisfied	18	25	43
	Fairly satisfied	8	13	21
	Very satisfied	2	4	6
Total		52	68	120

Table 12.6   *Satisfaction with practice facilities by whether anybody else in the household plays table tennis*

Count

		Does anybody else in your household play table tennis?		
		Yes	No	Total
Satisfaction with practice facilities	Unsatisfied	24	26	50
	Neither	18	25	43
	Satisfied	10	17	27
Total		52	68	120

	Value	Approx. Sig.
Cramer's V	0.087	0.632

small (Cramer's V is only 0.087) and the result is not statistically significant ($p = 0.632$, which is certainly a lot greater than 0.05!). The remaining elements can be checked out in this way.

Notice from Table 12.2 that over a third of all respondents for each of the five elements gave a 'neither unsatisfied nor satisfied' rating. On the argument that this category may well contain many people who checked this category because they did not really have an opinion or did not want to think about it rather then deliberately giving it a middle score, it would be possible to modify the analysis in different ways. One possibility is to treat this category as a missing value and exclude it from the analysis. This would have the effect, for example, of making Table 12.6 a two-by-two table, as shown in Table 12.7. This makes the pattern a

Table 12.7   *Satisfaction with practice facilities by whether anybody else in the household plays, excluding 'neither' category*

Count

		Does anybody else in your household play table tennis?		
		Yes	No	Total
Satisfaction with practice facilities	Unsatisfied	24	26	50
	Satisfied	10	17	27
Total		34	43	77

	Value	Approx. Sig.
Cramer's V	0.105	0.355
Number of Valid Cases	77	

little clearer and the value of Cramer's V has risen, although not by enough to make it statistically significant. This, however, is partly because the number of valid cases has now dropped to 77.

Reducing the number of cases deployed in an analysis in this way does, then, have its drawbacks. Another possibility would be to add the 'neither' category into either the 'satisfied' or the 'unsatisfied' categories. However, in this situation, there is no clear rationale for performing either of these modifications. Both actions would have the effect of creating one category much larger than the other and, furthermore, creating categories that do not make a lot of sense like 'satisfied and no opinion' versus 'unsatisfied' (or 'satisfied' versus 'unsatisfied and no opinion').

What does seem fairly clear from the analyses performed so far is that the data are fairly robust, and no matter how we modify them, we obtain largely the same result. That should give us cause for some degree of confidence in the results. The moral of the story, then, is to take your data and analyse them in a number of ways and see if the conclusions are broadly the same. If they are not, then it will be clear that the conclusions are to some degree at least dependent on the method of analysis and will need to be treated with caution.

One technique that is frequently applied to the analysis of summated ratings is factor analysis. This technique was considered earlier on pp. 129–31. There, it explains that factor analysis reviews the inter-correlations between a number of variables, and then groups together those that are highly inter-correlated with one another and not correlated with variables in another group. These groupings are the factors that represent higher order or more abstract concepts. It is a technique that may be used where there is a large number of attitude statements recorded on rating scales that can reasonably be assumed to have achieved the interval level. The results may enable the researcher to detect underlying dimensions that were not apparent from looking at a series of bivariate or even multivariate correlations. Some researchers then go on to use these factors in further analysis, for example in structural equation modelling (see Hair *et al.*, 1998, Chapter 11).

The reliability and validity of summated ratings

Where measurement is derived from a multi-item scale, new sources of measurement error potentially emerge. Evidence of this may come from a number of sources.

1 Repeated measures of apparently the same variable do not produce similar results

The extent to which repeat measurements produce similar results is generally referred to as scale reliability. There are two approaches to its assessment. The first measures scale *stability* over time and depends on one or more retests at a later date. There are, however, fairly key problems with this measure, for example:

■ how long to wait between tests,
■ what size of differences between measures count as evidence of instability,
■ to what extent differences discovered reflect scale instability as opposed to genuine changes in the characteristics being measured.

The length of time between tests will affect all of these. Wait too long and the probability of changing characteristics like attitudes is quite high; too soon and there will be test bias – people may remember how they responded the first time and be more 'consistent' in their responses than is warranted by their attitudes.

The second measure of reliability measures scale *equivalence*, showing how two equivalent indexes given at virtually the same time are in agreement. This is sometimes called the 'split-half' technique as the total set of items is divided into two equivalent halves. This may be done on a random or systematic basis. The total scores of the two halves is then correlated. There are two key problems with this approach:

- what degree of correlation indicates reliability,
- the split between the scales may be carried out in many different ways, each way producing different results.

2 The items in the scale are not internally consistent

Internal consistency is a matter of the extent to which the items used to measure a concept 'hang' together. Ideally, all the items used in the scale should reflect some single underlying dimension; statistically that means that they should correlate one with another. An increasingly popular measure for establishing internal consistency is a coefficient developed by Cronbach in 1951 that he called *alpha*. This takes the average correlation among items in a summated rating scale and adjusts for the number of items. This measure is in fact the equivalent of taking every possible split-half combination and is often taken as a measure of scale reliability. Reliable scales are ones with high average correlation and a relatively large number of items. The coefficient varies between zero for no reliability to unity for maximum reliability.

Alpha has effectively become *the* measure of choice for establishing the reliability of multi-item scales. According to the Social Sciences Citation Index it has been referenced in over 2200 articles in 278 different journals in the last 20 years (Peterson, 1994). Its availability at the click of a mouse button in survey analysis programs like SPSS has almost certainly meant that it is commonly reported by researchers, but often with little understanding of what it means and what its limitations are. How to obtain Cronbach's alpha on SPSS is explained at the end of this chapter. There is also a background discussion on the interpretation of the coefficient on pp. 221–2.

3 The items in the scale do not adequately sample the domain of features that should be included

What is commonly referred to as 'content validity' focuses on the adequacy with which the domain of the characteristic is adequately sampled by the measure. Thus measuring customer satisfaction with a new car by asking a series of questions about speed and acceleration would not adequately sample the domain of characteristics or features that determine customer satisfaction. It would, in other words, lack content validity. Content validity is sometimes known as 'face' validity because the measure is reviewed on the basis of whether or not it seems to be reasonable 'on the face of it'. The key to content validity lies in the procedures that we use to develop the instrument. Such a procedure would begin with a clear definition of the concept, perhaps relating this to how the concept has been defined in the past. The next step is to formulate a large number of items that broadly represent the concept as defined. In the last stage the items will be pruned and refined so that items that do not discriminate between respondents or cases are excluded, and any items that overlap to too great an extent with other items are avoided.

4 The scale fails to predict what it was designed to predict

The usefulness of the measuring instrument as a predictor of some other characteristic or behaviour is sometimes referred to as 'pragmatic', 'predictive' or 'criterion' validity. If, for example, a particular measure of customer satisfaction enables us to predict with some accuracy whether or not a consumer will repeat purchase then we could say that it has pragmatic validity. The focus is purely on the size of the correlation between the measure and what it is predicting. It does not really address the issue of what in fact is being measured.

5 The scale does not relate to other constructs to which it is theoretically related

Scales, ideally, should relate to other concepts to which theoretically they are meant to be related. Some authors refer to this as 'construct' or 'convergent' validity. Thus a good measure of social class should, ideally, relate to characteristics like lifestyle, leisure pursuits, holiday-making, purchasing behaviour and so on.

6 The scale does relate to other constructs to which it is meant to be theoretically different

Scales should, again ideally, *not* correlate with other measures from which they are meant to be theoretically different. This is often called 'discriminant' validity.

Warning

Most statistics texts only refer to the concepts of validity and reliability when talking about error. However, bear in mind that these concepts are relevant only to the measurement process and to measurement error. A 'valid' and 'reliable' measure does not mean that there are no errors; it only means that the process of measurement appears to be unproblematic.

Suggestion

From the point of view of survey data construction, the conventional definition of 'validity' in measurement – that a measure is valid if it measures what it is intended to measure – needs to be amended. Researchers act as though the 'value' which is recorded for a respondent is defined both by the aims or intentions of the researcher, as implemented in the acts of measurement and scaling, and by the nature, reality, life-world of the respondent. Validity, in short, contains two distinct components: the intention of the researcher and the nature of the respondent. A survey datum may reflect both, neither or just one of these. If it conveys the researcher's intention, but fails to represent adequately the respondent's reality, the measure is relevant, but inaccurate. If it represents the respondent's reality adequately, but in a way that does not satisfy the needs of the researcher or the objectives of the research, it is irrelevant, though accurate. Survey data must fulfil both conditions to be 'valid'.

WHAT DO YOU DO WITH 'DON'T KNOW'S?

'Don't know' answers are one type of non-committal reply that a respondent may give along with undecided, no opinion or neutral responses in a balanced rating scales with a middle point. These responses may be built into the design of the questionnaire with explicit options for a non-committal response. With explicit 'don't know' options available, the proportion of such responses may be anything up to 90 per cent and rates of over 10 per cent are common (see Durand and Lambert, 1988). Even without such options on the questionnaire, up to 60 per cent of respondents in some studies have still given 'don't know' replies. An understanding of the pattern of such replies is important for:

▥ formulating research methodology, particularly questionnaire design, item phrasing or sampling plan,
▥ interpreting the results when there are many 'don't know' responses.

Non-committal replies have been very differently interpreted by researchers. These interpretations fit into two broad patterns:

▥ 'don't know' responses are a valid indicator of the absence of attitudes, beliefs, opinions or knowledge,
▥ 'don't know' replies are inaccurate reflections of existing cognitive states.

The first interpretation provides a rationale for including explicit non-committal response categories in the questionnaire. It also implies that such responses should be excluded from the analysis, even if this means that the number of cases on which the analysis is based is thereby reduced. If there are a lot of respondents in this category, then it is possible that the question to which people are being asked to respond is not well thought through and there may be an argument for excluding the question from the analysis altogether.

The second interpretation has been used to set in motion various efforts to minimise 'don't know' responses on the basis that only committed responses will reflect a respondent's true mental state. Such efforts will include providing scales that have no middle position or non-committal option, or have interviewers probe each non-committal reply until a committal response has been obtained.

If there are relatively few 'don't know's then leaving them out of the analysis may well be the best course of action to take, particularly if the number of remaining cases is still adequate for the statistical analyses being proposed. There will usually be a case for including the 'don't know's in the preliminary univariate analysis. A decision can then be taken about whether they are to be excluded from subsequent bivariate and multivariate analyses. If they are to be excluded, then the researcher, in SPSS, can define such a category as a user-defined missing value. The topic of missing values is taken up in the next section.

Survey research findings are certainly not invariant to decisions about what to do with non-committal responses. Treating such responses as randomly distributed missing data points when, in fact, some responses are a genuine result of ambivalence or uncertainty may introduce bias into the data. The same would be true if responses are included as neutral positions when they are in fact an indicator of no opinion or refusal to answer. A first step in any analysis would be to investigate the extent to which non-committal responses are a function of demographic, behavioural or other cognitive variables. Some studies, for example, have reported an inverse relation between education and 'don't know' responses (the better educated are less prone to give them), but it has to be said that other research has found exactly the reverse. Durand and Lambert (1988) found that 'don't know' responses vary systematically with sociodemographic characteristics and with involvement with the topic area.

MISSING VALUES

In any survey, not all respondents will answer all the questions. This is less likely to be the result of individual refusal to answer some of the questions (although this does happen) or people accidentally omitting to consider some of the questions, than a result of questionnaire design whereby not all the questions are relevant to all the respondents. Approaches to the treatment of missing values vary. At one extreme is what is sometimes called listwise deletion. *All* questionnaires that contain missing values for reasons other than non-applicability are excluded from the analysis – in fact the data from such questionnaires will not even be entered into the data matrix. This means that each questionnaire included is fully complete. This procedure is fine and appropriate where there are relatively few exclusions as a result, and where the number of questionnaires returned is large enough for the analyses that will be performed. Where the number of resulting exclusions is considerable, however, or the number of cases is critical, then listwise deletion may not be a wise course of action.

A little less extreme is to enter all the questionnaires into the data matrix, but to exclude from the particular calculation or table involved cases for which values are missing, for whatever reason. This is fine when the number of cases entered into the data matrix is large or at least sufficient for the kinds of analyses that are required. However, there is always the danger that this approach may reduce the number of cases used in a particular analysis to such an extent that meaningful analysis is not possible.

Where values are missing because the question item does not apply to a particular respondent, there is little the researcher can do except maybe increase the size of the sample or impose quotas that will ensure a minimum number of applicable responses. Where a question *would* be appropriate to a given respondent, but an answer is not recorded, then such missing values may be referred to as 'item non-response'. Most researchers are inclined to just accept that there will be some item non-response for some or even many of the variables and will simply exclude them from the analysis. There is, however, a bewildering array of techniques that have been suggested in the literature for other ways of dealing with item non-response. Most of these involve filling the gaps caused by missing values by finding an actual replacement value. The process is sometimes called 'explicit imputation' and the idea is to select a replacement value that is as similar as possible to the missing value.

Where variables are interval, one remedial technique, for example, is to substitute the mean value for the missing value. More sophisticated approaches involve regression analysis or factor analysis. For categorical variables one technique that is sometimes used is to give the questionnaire with the missing value the same value as the questionnaire immediately preceding it.

Most of the techniques assume, however, that question items not responded to are not responded to at random. This can be quite difficult to determine. Furthermore, when the amount of item non-response is small – less than about 5 per cent – then applying any of the methods is unlikely to make any significant difference to the interpretation of the data. Ideally, of course, researchers should, in reporting their findings, communicate the nature and amount of item non-response in the dataset and describe the procedures used to remedy or cope with it.

SPSS makes a distinction between two kinds of missing value: system missing values and user defined missing values. The former result when the person entering the data has no value to enter for a particular variable (for whatever reason) for a particular case. In this situation the person will skip the cell and SPSS will enter a period in that cell to indicate that no value has been recorded. For univariate output, SPSS will produce a Statistics table that gives you the number of valid and the number of missing cases, and a Frequencies table that lists the valid (non-missing) values and the system missing values (see Table 12.8). Percentages are then calculated both for the total number of cases entered into the data matrix and for the total of non-missing or valid cases – what it calls the 'valid' per cent. For crosstabulations, SPSS will give you a Case Processing Summary giving the valid, missing and total number of cases and the percentages of each (see Table 12.9). Any case that has a missing value for *either* variable will be deemed as missing. The crosstabulation itself will include only the valid cases (see Table 12.9). The treatment of missing values on Graphs varies from graph to graph. Bar Charts, for example, has a default of including a bar for missing values, but this can be omitted by selecting the Options button on the Define Bar dialog box.

Table 12.8   *Analysis of missing values: univariate*

Statistics

Who encouraged you?

N	Valid	85
	Missing	35

Who encouraged you?

		Frequency	Percent	Valid Percent	Cumulative Percent
Valid	Friend	33	27.5	38.8	38.8
	Parent	30	25.0	35.3	74.1
	Other relative	4	3.3	4.7	78.8
	Teacher	2	1.7	2.4	81.2
	Club leader	15	12.5	17.6	98.8
	Other	1	.8	1.2	100.0
	Total	85	70.8	100.0	
Missing	System	35	29.2		
Total		120	100.0		

Table 12.9   *Analysis of missing values: bivariate*

Case Processing Summary

	Cases					
	Valid		Missing		Total	
	N	Percent	N	Percent	N	Percent
Who encouraged you? * What sex are you?	85	70.8	35	29.2	120	100.0

Who encouraged you? * What sex are you? Crosstabulation

Count

		What sex are you?		Total
		Male	Female	
Who encouraged you?	Friend	31	2	33
	Parent	22	8	30
	Other relative	2	2	4
	Teacher	1	1	2
	Club leader	13	2	15
	Other	1		1
Total		70	15	85

User defined missing values are ones that have been entered into the data matrix, but the researcher decides to exclude them from the analysis, as was the situation in the previous section when respondents giving a 'neither' response were excluded from Table 12.7. The same procedure might be applied to those respondents giving a 'don't know' reply. This is achieved in SPSS by using the Define Variable/Missing Values procedure, which is explained at the end of the chapter. All values defined in this way will be excluded from all the analyses.

It would be a sensible policy to reserve system missing values in effect for questions that are not applicable to the respondent in question and to give another code for those where responses are missing for other reasons, so we might enter a code of zero for item non-response. The combination of system defined and user defined missing values can mean that, for some tables or calculations, the number of cases used is considerably less than the number of cases entered into the data matrix. Furthermore, it will mean that the number of cases included will vary from table to table or statistical analysis. If the number of cases in the data matrix is quite small to begin with, this can have serious implications for the analysis – see the previous section on what to do when there are few cases.

HANDLING MULTIPLE RESPONSE ITEMS

There are often questions in a survey that allow respondents to pick more than one answer. Question 19 on the table tennis questionnaire, for example, asks respondents to tick whether or not they play one or more of four other sports. In

Table 12.10   *A multiple response question*

```
Group $SPORT  Play other sport
      (Value tabulated = 1)
```

Dichotomy label	Name	Count	Pct of Responses	Pct of Cases
Play badminton	BADMIN	12	8.6	10.8
Play football	FOOT	82	58.6	73.9
Play squash	SQUASH	17	12.1	15.3
Play tennis	TENNIS	29	20.7	26.1
		-------	-----	-----
Total responses		140	100.0	126.1

```
9 missing cases;   111 valid cases
```

principle a respondent could tick all of them (although how he or she could fit them all in is another matter!). For the purpose of analysis, each sport will need to be treated as a separate variable, each one of which is ticked or not ticked. In other words each is binary. SPSS, using the Analyze/Multiple Response procedure, can then be instructed to treat the set of sports as one question. The result is shown in Table 12.10. This shows that in total there were 140 ticks over the four items in the question. 58.6 per cent of these responses indicated football, 20.7 per cent tennis and so on. There are 111 'valid' cases in the table and nine are missing. This means, in effect, that there were nine respondents who did not play

Table 12.11   *Crosstabulating a multiple response by another variable*

```
                          SEX
             Count  Imale      female
                    I                     Row
                    I                     Total
                    I     1 I     2 I
$SPORT       --------+--------+--------+
      BADMIN    I     9 I     3 I    12
Play badminton   I       I       I  10.8
                 +--------+--------+
        FOOT     I    82 I     0 I    82
Play football    I       I       I  73.9
                 +--------+--------+
      SQUASH     I     9 I     8 I    17
Play squash      I       I       I  15.3
                 +--------+--------+
      TENNIS     I    16 I    13 I    29
Play tennis      I       I       I  26.1
                 +--------+--------+
         Column        97      14     111
         Total       87.4    12.6   100.0


111 valid cases;   9 missing cases
```

any of the four sports indicated, and so are excluded from the table. Of the 111 valid cases, 73.9 per cent indicated football, 26.1 per cent tennis and so on. It would, however, probably have been more useful to have these percentages relating to all 120 cases. If we had another item on the question for 'none of these' and included this in the multiple response set, then all 120 cases would have been covered.

In this situation, the per cent of cases would give the same result as a frequency table for each item, but put into the same table, while the per cent of responses takes the four items together. If we wanted to look at the relative popularity of these sports comparing the males with the females, then the multiple response item can be crosstabulated against sex of respondent. The result is shown in Table 12.11. This uses the 111 valid responses and splits them into males and females. None of the females plays football – they are more likely to play tennis as another sport. Notice, however, that the column totals are giving you the numbers of cases (males and females), but entered into the cells are the numbers of responses, which total more than the numbers of cases. Thus the number of responses given by males totals more than the 97 males. Be clear that the total number of responses can be either greater or less than the number of cases.

CAN YOU USE STATISTICAL INFERENCE ON NON-RANDOM SAMPLES?

In Chapters 9 and 10 it was made clear that statistical inference should be applied only when random sampling is involved. Furthermore, the particular calculations illustrated assume that the random samples are simple random samples. This means that each case selected has both a known and an equal chance of being selected. So, if we pick 100 names from a list of 1000 names at random, then each case has a one-in-ten chance of being selected. In practice, samples are seldom taken in this way. The selection may be subjected to some degree and some combination of stratification, clustering or the imposition of quotas. (These concepts were explained in Chapter 8.) Stratification is the random selection of cases, but within strata, for example selecting a certain number of males at random and a certain number of females at random. This would be stratification by sex of respondent. The effect of stratification is to decrease the sampling error because it removes some of the variation that might otherwise arise from under- or over-representation of cases reflecting the stratification factor, for example having too many females or too many males. By contrast, clustering is the random selection of cases within defined geographical areas and has the effect if increasing sampling error.

Statisticians have suggested various ways in which the standard error can, indeed should, be adjusted when these techniques are used. (See Kish, 1965 for a detailed explanation of the calculations involved.) However, the calculations are complex, while stratification and clustering are often in practice combined so the overall effect may be difficult to determine. Researchers typically ignore all the complexities and apply the formulae that relate to simple random samples without making any adjustment. An alternative that is not commonly considered is to apply an overall adjustment to the standard error based on approximate rules of thumb. This overall adjustment is called a 'design factor'. Koerner (1980) suggests, for example, that simple stratified random samples should have a design factor of 0.8–0.9 (so the standard error is, in fact, decreased slightly), but if used in a multistage design should be between 1.05 and 1.9. Clustering increases error depending on the number of cases or sampling units in the cluster and should be between 1.02 and 1.26.

Quota sampling is a non-random form of sampling because it is the interviewer who actually makes the selection of who to approach. Different approaches, however, are taken about the applicability of statistical inference to quota samples. One approach argues that quota sampling, if done carefully, is a good approximation of a random sample and the application of statistical tests tells us something that we would not otherwise know. However, a design factor should be applied. According to Koerner (1980) unsophisticated quota samples should have a design factor of about 2.0, but complex interlocking quotas are less prone to error and should be between 1.22 and 1.4. Other sources, for example, Wolfe (1987) suggest that quota samples should have higher factors – at least 2.5. A more purist approach is to argue that, since quota sampling is non-probability sampling and statistical inference relies on probability theory, then statistical inference should not be applied at all.

At the same time it must be remembered that even random samples seldom obtain 100 per cent response. In fact the response rate is often below 30 per cent. The effects of this non-response may well be a considerable degree of bias, which is ignored in estimation and testing the null hypothesis. We also saw in Chapter 10 that where samples are quite large – over 100 or so, which they usually are – then even very small differences or very low coefficients of association turn out to be 'statistically significant'. Furthermore, confidence intervals can be more like confidence tricks if bias or other sources of non-sampling error are present. The application of statistical inference to survey data must thus be approached with extreme caution and worrying about whether or not your sample counts as 'random' may not be necessary. More important is the response rate and whether or not there is any evidence that responders are in any way systematically different from those who do not respond.

Where a researcher is looking at a lot of crosstabulations, then statistical inference can be deployed to determine which tables can be safely ignored in the analysis because they have an unacceptably high likelihood they might simply result from random sampling fluctuations. However, even amongst the surviving tables there may well be some very low degrees of association, particularly if, for example, the sample size is over 500 or so. To describe these as 'results' or 'findings' will be to overstate the case. What is important is to use descriptive statistics to analyse what patterns are actually there in the data.

Sampling in practice is largely a matter of trade-offs between a number of competing factors. Samples that are as random as possible are useful if the data are to be used for a wide variety of purposes and the data should be as representative as possible in all respects. Where the purpose of the research is very focused, then quota samples may well be adequate. On the whole, larger samples are better than smaller ones and if, for example, using quota sampling enables the researcher to select a bigger sample then he or she would have been able to obtain using random methods, then this may well be advantageous.

This section has outlined a number of possibilities and introduced a number of issues, but what is to be recommended? If you have a random sample, but the response rate is poor, then it is important to check for bias, particularly if you want to use the sample result for estimation. Chapter 3, p. 58, covered the different sources of bias and indicated how researchers sometimes check for it. Using statistical inference for testing null hypotheses is usually of limited value unless the sample is quite small, checks have been made for bias and show that bias is very limited, and the hypotheses have been genuinely set up in advance of the data analysis. So, what if your supervisor, tutor or reviewer of your article nevertheless insists that you conduct tests of significance? By all means deploy them; they will not be so much 'wrong' as adding very little to your analysis. What is important is that you do not *stop* at finding 'significant' results. A significant result should be the *beginning* of a further analysis of the results. For example, if a significant association is found between two variables then an analysis of the degree of association would be appropriate, followed by the checking of that relationship against other key variables.

If your sample is non-random, for example you have used quota sampling, can you still use statistical inference? There are two main possibilities here. One is to argue, quite clearly, that since the sample is non-random, tests of significance are not appropriate. Alternatively, they may be calculated, but either a design factor may be applied or the results should be treated with extreme caution, so that a 'significant' result is only an indication of a possible relationship – it will require further research to establish this with any degree of reliability.

USING SPSS

Some of the SPSS procedures used in this chapter have been explained earlier in the book. Thus **Recode** was considered on pp. 92–4, and **Compare Means** on p. 181.

It remains to explain, however, five more SPSS procedures:

- Compute,
- Basic Tables,
- Define Variable/Missing Values,
- Multiple Response,
- Scale reliability.

Using Compute

Imagine that you want to create a total satisfaction score from the five items in Question 9 in the *tabten* data. This means we need to add up all the scores *for each case* to give a total, which will have a maximum of 25 and a minimum of 5. It will be a new variable – let us call it 'totalsat'. Select Transform, then Compute. You will obtain the Compute Variable dialog box (Figure 12.3). Notice that there are lots of functions that we could perform on the variables – but all we want to do is add the five variable together, so highlight 'practice' and put into the Numeric Expression box by clicking on >. Now click on the + button and bring over the variable 'compfac', then on + again and so on until you have the five variables added together as in Figure 12.3. Enter the new variable name 'totalsat' in the Target Variable box and click on OK. A new variable will appear on your data matrix, giving the total scores for each case. From this point you can either use Compute to give you an average score by putting the variables between brackets

Figure 12.3   The 'Compute Variable' dialog box

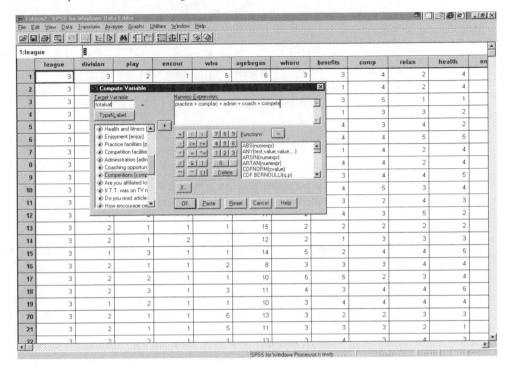

and dividing by 5 (remember that you should change the number of decimal places to 1 or 2 for the variable) or you can use Recode to group the responses into, say, high, medium and low score categories.

Using Basic Tables

To reproduce Table 12.2, which shows the count and column percent for each level of satisfaction with each of the five elements of playing table tennis, but in a single table, select Analyze/Custom Tables/Basic Tables. This gives you the Basic Tables dialog box. Put the five variables 'practice', 'compfac', 'admin', 'coach' and 'comp' into the Subgroups/Down box. Change the radio button to Each separately (stacked) and click on the Statistics button. Bring 'Count' and 'Col%' across to the Cell Statistics box. Click on Continue. If you want Group Totals as in Table 12.2 then click on Totals and on Totals over each group variable in the Basic Tables:Totals box. Now click on Continue, then OK.

Using Define Variable/Missing Values

To create user defined missing values for any particular variable, select Define Variable by double-clicking on the grey area at the top of the data matrix that contains the variable name, then select Missing Values. This gives you the Define Missing Values dialog box. This enables you either to pick out particular codes to be treated as missing values by clicking on the Discrete missing values radio button and entering up to three codes, or selecting a range of missing values. To exclude the 'neither' category in the satisfaction ratings of specified practice facilities for table tennis, as was done to create Table 12.7, double click on the grey area that contains the variable 'practice', click on Missing Values, click on the radio button for Discrete missing values and enter the code '3' in the box. Now click on Continue then on OK. You can now, for example, use Analyze/Descriptive Statistics/ Frequencies, putting 'practice' into the Variable(s): box to see the result. There are now 43 missing values arising from those who checked the 'neither unsatisfied or satisfied' option.

Using Multiple Response

To treat the four variables 'badminton', 'football', 'squash' and 'tennis' as a multiple response question, as was done to produce Table 12.10, select Analyze/ Multiple Response/Define Sets. Bring these variables across to the Variables in Set box. Since the code value of 1 was entered for those who ticked 'Yes', enter the value '1' in the Dichotomies Counted value: box under Variables Are Coded As. You will also need to give the new variable a name. Give it a name like 'sport' (for other sports). Click on the Add button in the Mult Response Sets: box, then on Close. The new variable, however, does not appear in the data matrix. To access it, click on Analyze/Multiple Response and either Frequencies or Crosstabs depending on whether you want univariate or bivariate analysis. To produce Table 12.10 select Frequencies. Move 'sports' from the Multiple Response Sets: box across to the Table(s) for: box and click on OK.

If you use the Crosstabs procedure, you will need to define the range of the minimum and maximum values to be included in the other variable. So to crosstabulate 'sport' by 'sex', you will need to click on Define Ranges and enter '1' and '2'. Click on OK.

Using Reliability Analysis

SPSS offers a number of measures of scale reliability, including Cronbach's alpha that was explained earlier. These measures are to be found under Analyze/Scale/ Reliability Analysis. This will give you the Reliability Analysis dialog box. Cronbach's alpa is the default model, but split half techniques are available, along with Guttman and Parallel models. To obtain Cronbach's alpha for the five items that make up the 'totalsat' variable and which was used in Table 12.4, move the five variables 'practice', 'compfac', 'admin', 'coach' and 'compete' into the items: box. Click on OK and SPSS gives you a Cronbach's alpha of 0.7303. By the Nunnally criterion (which is explained in the discussion section below) this is a sufficiently large value to establish reliability provided the research is preliminary, basic or exploratory, but not if it is to be applied to important decisions.

To check whether any of the items making up the scale are restricting the value of alpha, click on Statistics in the Reliability Analysis dialog box, then on the Scale if item deleted box under descriptives for. Click on Continue then on OK. The output shows what happens to the value of alpha if each item in turn is deleted. The results indicate that, in this case, it is best to keep all four items since omitting any item will give a lower value for alpha.

To obtain Table 12.3, use Analyze/ Descriptive Statistics/Descriptives. In the Descriptives box, bring over the five variables and click on Options and put a tick in the Mean box, then Continue and OK. To create Table 12.4 you will need the Transform/Compute facility followed by the Analyze/Compare Means/Means procedure.

BACKGROUND DISCUSSION: THE INTERPRETATION OF CRONBACH'S COEFFICIENT ALPHA

Cronbach's alpha is a measure of internal reliability for multi-item summated rating scales. It takes the average correlation among items in a scale and adjusts for the number of items. Reliable scales are ones with high average correlation and a relatively large number of items. The coefficient varies between zero for no reliability to unity for maximum reliability. The formula subtracts from unity the sum of the variance for each item (σ_i^2) divided by the variance of the scale (σ_s^2) and multiplies by the number of items divided by the number of items minus one.

$$\alpha = \left(1 - \sum \frac{\sigma_i^2}{\sigma_s^2}\right)\left(\frac{k}{k-1}\right)$$

The latter value, of course, approaches unity as the number of items increases. If the variance for each item is identical, or the variances are converted to Z scores, the formula reduces to the inter-item correlation, r, multiplied by the number of items, k, divided by one plus the inter-item correlation multiplied by the number of items minus one.

$$\frac{kr}{1 + r(k-1)}$$

Strictly-speaking, Cronbach's alpha is the first of these procedures; the 'standardised' alpha may give a slightly different result (Cortina, 1993).

Despite its wide use, there is little guidance in the literature (and none from Cronbach himself) as to what constitutes an 'acceptable' or 'sufficient' value for alpha to achieve. Most users of the statistic cite Nunnally's (1978) recommendation that a value of 0.7 should be achieved. It is assumed that if alpha for any scale is greater than 0.7 then it is acceptable. However, all those authors making recommendations about acceptable levels of alpha, including Nunnally, indicate that the desired degree of reliability is a function of the purpose of the research, for example whether it is exploratory or applied. Nunnnally himself in 1978 suggested that for preliminary research 'reliabilities of 0.70 or higher will suffice'. For 'basic' research, he suggests that 'increasing reliabilities much beyond 0.80 is often wasteful of time and funds' (Nunnally, 1978, p. 245). In contrast, for applied research, 0.80 'is not nearly high enough'. Where important decisions depend on the outcome of the measurement process a reliability of 0.90 'is the minimum that should be tolerated'.

None of Nunnally's recommendations, however, have an empirical basis, a theoretical justification, or an analytical rationale. Rather they seem to reflect either experience or intuition. Interestingly, Nunnally had changed his own recommendations from his 1967 edition of *Psychometric Theory*, which recommended that the minimally acceptable reliability for preliminary research should be in the range of 0.5 to 0.6.

Peterson (1994) reports the results of a study to ascertain the values of alpha actually obtained in articles and papers based on empirical work. From a sample of over 800 marketing and psychology related journals, conference proceedings and some unpublished manuscripts, he reviewed all alpha coefficients found in each study, resulting in 4286 coefficients covering a 33-year period. Reported coefficients ranged from 0.6 to 0.99 with a mean of 0.77. About 75 per cent were 0.7 or greater and 50 per cent were 0.8 or greater. Peterson found that reported alphas were not greatly affected by research design characteristics, such as sample size, type of sample, number of scale categories, type of scale, mode of administration, or type of research. One exception to this is that during scale development items are often eliminated if their presence restricts the value of alpha. Not surprisingly, the alpha coefficients reported were significantly related to the number of items eliminated.

It is important to remember that Alpha measures only internal consistency; if error factors associated with the passage of time are of concern to the researcher, then it will not be the most appropriate statistic. However, since alpha approximates the mean of all possible split-half reliabilities, it can be seen as a superior measure of scale equivalence. It is not, however, as is commonly supposed, an indication of unidimensionality. Alpha can, in fact, be quite high despite the presence of several different dimensions (Cortina, 1993).

When interpreting alpha coefficients, it is often forgotten, furthermore, that the values achieved are in part a function of the number of items. Thus for a three-item scale with alpha = 0.80, the average inter-item correlation is 0.57. For a ten-item scale with alpha = 0.80 it is only 0.28. What needs to be kept in mind is that in evaluating, say, a 40-item scale, alpha will be relatively large simply because of the number of items, and the number of items is not exactly a great measure of scale quality. When many items are pooled, internal consistency estimates are inevitably large and invariant, and therefore of limited value.

Alpha, in short, should be used with some caution. It is appropriate only when the researcher requires a measure of internal consistency, and is helpful only then if the number of items used is fairly limited. The value of alpha to be taken as 'acceptable' must be related to the purpose of the research, and even then only used as an indication rather than a 'test' to be passed with a fixed value. Furthermore, if researchers are concerned about dimensionality, then procedures like factor analysis are probably more appropriate.

SUMMARY

Scales can sometimes be upgraded in ways that make assumptions about the data that seem reasonable or can be justified. The most common situation is for ordinal scales to be upgraded to interval scales by adding a scoring system. To treat nominal scales in this way, however, would not be appropriate. Treating ranked scales as interval (or interval scales as ranked) seems to make very little difference to the results of the analysis. Downgrading scales is always a legitimate operation because the 'higher' scales possess all the characteristics of lower ones, but it means discarding information. However, it can be usefully

Summary continued

undertaken for variables that are to be associated with another variable that is on a lower level of measurement.

When approaching the analysis of a data matrix, it helps if you have set up formally written hypotheses before you begin. This was discussed on pp. 186–8. Doing so will focus your attention on key variables and on what relationships between variables to investigate. However, in practice, this is not always feasible and there is, furthermore, always the danger that formal hypotheses may divert the researcher's attention away from finding other interesting things in the data. Some researchers will even argue that they do not wish to prejudge what they expect to see in the data and will engage in data dredging. Many researchers, however, will combine the two approaches, moving backwards and forwards between ideas and data. This avoids the data overload from producing large numbers of tables or calculations, while also allowing for the possibility of serendipity.

The number of cases in a data matrix reflects the number of usable returns. A minimum of 100 cases will be needed simply for univariate percentage calculations. Where variables are to be crosstabulated, ideally, there should be 100 cases for each subgroup that will be used in calculations. Thus a five by five table should be based on at least 500 cases in the matrix, otherwise the frequencies in the cells become too small for accurate interpretation. Where a whole range of different analyses and breakdowns will be needed, then there should be 1000 or more cases.

Where the desirable number of cases cannot be, or has not been, achieved, then either caution is required in the interpretation of the data or alternative strategies need to be adopted. These strategies will include recoding variables so as to create fewer categories or, more extreme, changing or modifying the style or research to one that requires fewer cases.

There is a wide range of strategies for analysing the data that emerge from summated rating scales. These include:

- reviewing the frequencies and percentages of each response category for each of the items making up the scale,
- calculating average scores for each item by treating response categories for each item as if they were metric by allocating scores as values,
- adding items together to create a total for each respondent and dividing by the number of items to give an overall average score,
- these average scores can themselves be averaged and compared for sub-groups of cases,
- using the (assumed) interval properties of the total scores, summated rating scales can be used for correlation with other interval variables,
- crosstabulating each of the items making up the scale separately against other categorical variables,
- the scale values for each item can be regrouped in various ways, for example, collapsing 5-point scales into 3-point scales, treating the neutral responses as missing values and excluding them from the analysis, or adding the neutral responses into either the positive or the negative end of the scale.

Summary continued

In practice, it is sensible to try all of these procedures and see whether they produce broadly the same or similar conclusions. Scale reliability can be simply checked by getting SPSS to calculate Cronbach's coefficient alpha, but it is important to remember that there is no 'magic' value that can be used as a 'test'. Rather the result is an indication which needs to be interpreted in the light of the purposes for which the scale is to be used.

A further decision needs to be taken as to whether or not those respondents who indicate that they 'don't know' as an answer should be included in the analysis. A common-sense strategy will be to include them in the preliminary univariate analysis since the researcher can see what role such responses play in each question where they occur, but to exclude them from bivariate and multivariate procedures.

In any survey there will be missing values – not all the respondents will answer all the questions. Where values are missing because respondents have refused to answer the question or omitted to answer by accident or through confusion, they may be treated as 'item non-response'. Some researchers will try to fill the gaps left by such items by substituting a replacement value as similar as possible to the missing value. Other researchers will just accept that there will be some item non-response. Where values are missing because those questions are not applicable to the respondent, then SPSS gives the researcher various options for ways of treating them. They can be treated as system missing values and left blank in the data matrix, or a specific code can be entered to indicate a missing value. To exclude these from an analysis they will need to be defined as user-defined missing values from the **Define Variable** dialog box.

For questions where the respondent may pick more than one response it is necessary to treat each response category as a separate variable that is either ticked or not ticked. SPSS can then be instructed to treat the set of responses as a single Multiple Response item.

Strictly-speaking, statistical inference should be used only where random samples have been taken. Even then, they may be of limited value because:

■ except for small samples, even very small degrees of association, differences or correlations will turn out to be 'significant',
■ they take into account only error arising from random sampling fluctuations,
■ there will be considerable non-response error plus other sources of non-random error which together account for between 90 per cent and 95 per cent of total survey error, so tests of significance relate to only 5 per cent to 10 per cent of total survey error.

Some researchers will still deploy statistical inference even on non-random samples (or even on total populations). The value of doing this is even more limited than for random samples. At the very least a design factor should be applied to the standard error calculation, but this is often not done. If your samples are non-random, then either argue quite clearly that they are inappropriate, or use them with extreme caution and rely not on statistical inference but on descriptive statistics to analyse the data.

Exercises

1. Pick a variable from the *tabten* survey like 'else' and crosstabulate it against every other variable in the set. Are any of the tables you have created meaningless or just pure nonsense? Have any of the tables produced interesting or surprising results?
2. Select two or three books on social research or marketing research and look up 'sample size' in the index. Read the pages indicated. How does what is suggested there compare with the suggestions in this text?
3. Crosstabulate the variables 'agenow' and 'where'. The first variable has seven categories and the second variable has eight, giving a crosstabulation with 56 cells – far too many. Using **Recode** try various ways of reducing the table to a two-by-two or a two-by-three.
4. Using the responses from Question 8 (which includes the variables 'benefits', 'comp', 'relax', 'health' and 'enjoy'), try each of the procedures suggested for analysing summated rating scales.
5. Using the **Define Variable/Missing Values** procedure, check out what would happen to your analysis in Exercise 4 if the middle category (value 3) was excluded from the analysis.
6. Create Table 12.3 using the **Transform/Compute** facility followed by the **Statistics/Compare Means** procedure.

Points for discussion

1. In the *tabten* dataset, Questions 8 and 9 use rating sales, although they are not of the Likert type. Would upgrading these scales to interval scales by using the codes 1–5 as metric quantities be sensible or legitimate?
2. Is data dredging something you should try to avoid?
3. A researcher, for a variety of reasons, has ended up with 35 usable responses in a survey. What would you advise him or her to do?
4. If you try a number of different ways of analysing summated rating scales and only one of these procedures produces the result you want, is it 'cheating' to report that one procedure as establishing your 'findings'?
5. Look again at Table 9.2. If the 120 cases had *not* been a random sample, but a quota sample, what are the various ways in which you could approach the problem?

Further reading

Alt, M. and Brighton, M. (1981) 'Analysing Data: Or Telling Stories?', *Journal of the Market Research Society*, Vol. 23, No. 4, pp. 209–19.

Read this one after Selvin and Stuart, since it gives another perspective on data dredging.

Bourque, L. and Clark, V. (1992) *Processing Data: The Survey Example*, California, USA, Sage.

A short and very practical booklet that takes you through from data collection strategy to data transformations. Data processing is likened to the backstage of a theatre: rarely seen and frequently ignored.

Durand, R. and Lambert, Z. (1988) 'Don't Know Responses in Surveys: Analysis and Interpretational Consequences', *Journal of Business Research*, Vol. 16, No. 2, pp. 169–88.

An accessible article that looks at the correlates of the tendency to give 'don't know' responses.

Selvin, H. and Stuart, A. (1966) 'Data-Dredging Procedures in Survey Analysis', *The American Statistician*, June, pp. 20–3.

This is the seminal article on data dredging. The authors describe three kinds of data dredging that they call 'snooping', 'fishing' and 'hunting'. The limitations and statistical consequences of using data dredging are clearly explained.

Stewart, D. (1982) 'Filling the Gap: A Review of the Missing Data Problem', *An Assessment of Marketing Thought and Practice*, American Marketing Association, Chicago, USA.

Lists all the techniques for handling missing data all in one table.

References

Cortina, J. (1993) 'What is Coefficient Alpha? An Examination of Theory and Applications, *Journal of Applied Psychology*, Vol. 78, No. 1, pp. 98–104.

Kish, L. (1965) *Survey Sampling*, New York, John Wiley.

Koerner, R (1980) 'The design factor – an underutilised concept?', *European Research*, November, pp. 266–71.

Nunnally, J. (1978) *Psychometric Theory*, 2nd edn, New York, McGraw-Hill.

Peterson, R. (1994) 'A Meta-analysis of Cronbach's Coefficient Alpha, *Journal of Consumer Research*, Vol. 221, September, pp. 381–91.

Wolfe, A (1987) *Sampling Error and Significance Tables for Research Executives*, Industrial Marketing Research Association, Lichfield, Staffs.

chapter 13

Analysing Open-ended Questions

Learning objectives

This chapter will help you to analyse answers to open-ended questions in a survey. In particular, it will help you to understand:

■ when open-ended questions are appropriate,

■ why treating recorded verbatim responses as qualitative data can be very helpful,

■ how to convert open responses into quantitative data by developing a coding frame.

INTRODUCTION

In designing a survey questionnaire it is often felt by the researcher that it is undesirable or impossible to 'close' some of the questions by specifying the eligible responses to the respondent. Open-ended questions leave respondents free to formulate replies in their own words. The interviewer (or the respondent in a self-completed questionnaire) writes in the answer, usually word-for-word. Normally there will be one or more blank lines for this purpose. Open-ended questions tend to be used in the following situations.

■ The researcher is unsure about what the responses might be, for example, 'Why did you decide to select Brand X?'

■ The possible responses are too many to list, for example, 'How old are you?' or, 'What is the name of the shop where you last purchased toothpaste?'

■ The researcher wants to discover responses that individuals give spontaneously or to introduce a topic by getting the respondents to formulate their thoughts in their own words.

■ The researcher wants to avoid pre-judging responses or to avoid bias that might result from suggesting responses to individuals in a way that might happen with closed questions.

■ The researcher wants to 'mop up' any views that may not have been elicited from closed questions.

■ The researcher wants to be able to enliven the final report with quotes from respondents.

This chapter considers how researchers can analyse such questions and what are some of the problems in doing so. There are, in fact, two main approaches the researcher can adopt:

■ Treat the responses as qualitative data and use them to summarise in words the range of views being expressed or as a source of quotes with which to illustrate points that are being made,
■ Transform the responses into quantitative data by coding them.

TREATING RESPONSES AS QUALITATIVE DATA

Qualitative data as text or narrative are a source of well-grounded, rich descriptions and explanations of processes in identifiable local contexts (Miles and Huberman, 1994). It is often possible to perceive chronological flow, to see what events resulted in which consequences, and to derive explanations. Such data may result in unanticipated findings and may help researchers to go beyond their initial ideas and to generate or revise conceptual frameworks. Qualitative data, however, have their drawbacks:

■ they are labour-intensive and often slow to collect,
■ they tend to reflect researcher bias,
■ they are slow and often difficult to analyse,
■ they are a poor basis on which to generalise,
■ it is usually difficult to establish validity and reliability.

Above all, no bank of explicit methods and techniques that the qualitative researcher can use has been developed. Explanations of how qualitative data were collected and analysed tend to be a reflection of personal experience. Individual researchers just give an account of how they did it, making no reference to any agreed principles or standards of practice as there are for handling quantitative data. Some researchers argue against even *looking* for such methods; that qualitative research is an art form and that approaches need to be intuitive. Some argue that there is no reality 'out there' that the researcher should be trying validly to identify. Social processes are ephemeral, fluid and transient. A contrasting view, such as that adopted by Miles and Huberman (1994), is that the analysis of qualitative data mirrors that of quantitative and entails the processes of data reduction, data display and drawing conclusions.

Qualitative data, it was explained in Chapter 1, are non-numerical records and arise as isolated words, phrases, statements, commentary or detailed description. Such data possess an immediacy, an appeal to intuitive understanding that does not necessarily require any further 'interpretation' or processing. Respondents sometimes say things in a way that encapsulates a particular viewpoint or provides a pithy comment on a situation. Such comments can be used in two main ways. First, they can be used as a basis for reviewing, summarising or elaborating the range or type of view, opinion or attitude being expressed by respondents. Comments may be paraphrased or put into broad categories so that a report of the results might read something like: 'A number of respondents were broadly in favour of a complete ban of all forms of advertising of cigarettes. Others had reservations about further impositions on the freedom of individuals to make up their own minds'.

Second, recorded verbatim responses are a potent source of quotations with which to enliven a report that might otherwise be a somewhat dry review of statistical findings. Qualitative responses, or a selection or sample of them, might, furthermore, be collected together in an appendix to a report in order to allow the reader to get a feel for the kinds of things respondents have been saying.

Data handled in this way should be treated independently of SPSS. The best way is a two-stage procedure whereby the researcher first runs through all the comments that have been written against a particular open-ended question directly from the questionnaire. This will enable the researcher to see the potential for quotes and whether it would be sensible to proceed to the second stage at which all the comments are gathered together and written down.

Treating responses to open-ended questions as qualitative data can lead to insights in a way that other approaches may not. These other approaches involve the application of coding to transform the data into quantitative data.

CODING THE DATA

Coding is the process of converting verbatim answers into numerical code. The process might be called 'postcoding' or may even be referred to as 'content analysis', although the latter term tends to be restricted to the processes that are used to analyse the content of printed or broadcast communication, particularly advertising copy. See Kolbe and Burnett (1991) for an excellent summary of content analysis.

The approach to coding can be split into two situations. In the first situation, the open-ended question is being used to capture factual information, since listing all the options for responses in a closed question would take up too much space. Where respondents can give their answer in numerical form, for example putting in their age, then no additional coding is necessary. The actual age can simply be put into the data matrix. This might be called 'empirical coding' in which the numerical value of the code corresponds with the specific magnitude of the quantity being measured. Where responses are in words, then coding will involve creating a list of the answers given, assigning number codes to the list, and recording codes for each respondent's answers. It may be necessary to develop coding rules which specify codes to be allocated when the answer does not fit any of the obvious categories. For example, if respondents are asked, 'Not counting yourself, how many other people were you with?' then most will give a clear number, but some may say '30–40' or 'a lot'. In this situation, one rule might be to give the mid-point of a range of values, so the answer '30–40' will be coded as 35.

One of the most problematic codings of factual information is for occupation. These may be coded into social grade, social class or socio-economic status. Market researchers will tend to use a system of social grading developed by the National Readership Survey, as illustrated in Table 13.1, Column A. Social scientists, on the other hand, will more likely use the Government's official classification based on social class. This system, however, has been in use since the Census of 1911 and will be replaced in the Census of 2001 by a new National Statistics Socio-economic Classification (SEC), as illustrated in Table 13.1, Column B. The market researcher's social grading system is household based

Table 13.1　*Social grade and socio-economic classification*

Column A		Column B	
Social Grade		**SEC**	
A	Higher managerial, administrative and professional	1.	Higher managerial and professional
B	Intermediate managerial, administrative and professional	2.	Intermediate managerial, administrative and professional
C1	Supervisory or clerical and junior managerial administrative and professional	3.	Intermediate
C2	Skilled manual	4.	Small employers and own account workers
D	Semi-skilled and unskilled manual	5.	Supervisors/craft and related
E	State dependants, casual and lowest grade workers	6.	Semi-routine occupations
		7.	Routine occupations
		8.	Never worker/longer-term unemployed

so that the chief income earner's current or previous occupation determines the social grade of all household members. In the Government's current social class system only individuals who are working are classified. The new system will group occupations on the basis of employment conditions and relations rather than, as in the older system, on skills.

Social grade is a strictly hierarchical ordinal scale, with A being the top group of the most senior managers and the professional elite, and E being the bottom group depending solely on the state. The new SEC is less clearly an ordinal scale. Classes 4 and 8, for example, are clearly outside an occupational status order. Even the occupations are less hierarchical – a teacher, for example, may be classified as A, B or C1 with social grade depending on the seniority of the position and the type and size of school. With SEC a teacher is Class 1 in all cases. See Meier and Moy (1999) for an explanation of the new system.

Where open-ended questions are being used not to capture factual information, but to record respondent opinions, attitudes, views, knowledge and so on, then creating a sensible code frame is the most important part of the analysis. By definition this is likely to get quite complex – if it were easy then the question could no doubt be precoded! The aim is to formulate a set of categories that accurately represents the answers and where each category includes an appreciable number of responses. Ideally, the set of categories should be exhaustive, mutually exclusive and minimise the loss of information. Furthermore, they should be meaningful, consistent and relatively straightforward to apply. There may also need to be codes for 'no response', 'not applicable' and 'don't know'. Where the information is very detailed there may need to be many codes and two or even three-digit codes may be developed.

Developing a frame may require several 'passes' over the data. It is probably a good idea to have all the comments collected and typed out, but this may not be possible. A method of constant comparison is probably best. Begin by looking at a few of the comments and see whether they should be put into separate categories. Then look at a few more and see if some can be put into the same

Table 13.2   *Analysis of an open-ended question*

How are people encouraged to take up table tennis?

		Frequency	Percent
Valid	Facilities/beginner-oriented clubs	23	19.2
	Coaching	17	14.2
	School/youth club involvement	24	20.0
	Advertising/promotion/exhibitions	21	17.5
	TV/media/publicity	28	23.3
	Improved image	6	5.0
	Money in the sport	1	.8
Total		120	100.0

category or whether more categories will need to be developed. When too many categories begin to emerge, look for similarities so that some categories can be brought together. If there are a large number of responses then it may not be sensible to look through all of them to develop the frame, but take a sample. Thus if there are 500 cases, a sample of 50–100 should enable the frame to be finalised. It also helps if more than one person develops a code frame separately; they should then work together on a final code. This maximises the objectivity, validity and reliability of the process.

Question 13 in the *tabten* data is open-ended. This asks respondents what they think could be done to encourage people to take up table tennis on a regular basis. The responses were coded into the categories shown in Table 13.2, which also shows the results of the analysis.

It helps if the researcher sets up the objectives for which the code frame is to be used before beginning the process. Thus if the objective is to look for positive and negative statements about a situation or a product then answers will be coded along this dimension, perhaps with categories of very positive, vaguely positive, mixed, vaguely negative and very negative. Sometimes answers to open-ended questions can be coded in several ways according to different dimensions. Thus a study of injuries following an earthquake could look at the way injuries occurred, the parts of the body affected, where the injury occurred, what the person was doing at the time and so on. Each of these aspects may need to be recorded separately in a different variable.

At one time researches had to code all open-ended questions before data entry could begin. With modern survey analysis packages like SPSS, however, this may be done after all the precoded questions have been entered. This is a big advantage because researchers are not always sure how responses to open-ended questions should be coded until they have started analysis of the data. In short, it is sometimes better to delay coding of open-ended responses until they are needed for analysis.

OPEN VERSUS CLOSED QUESTIONS

Conventional wisdom has it that open questions are better than closed questions for gathering information about complex issues, that they avoid the bias that may result from suggesting responses to individuals, but that the main problem compared with closed questions is the extra time and cost involved in their analysis. Schuman and Presser (1979) argue that the controversy over open versus closed modes of inquiry in surveys has been largely resolved in practice by the victory of the closed form. No doubt this is largely because of the efficiency and convenience of such questions for interviewing, coding and analysis. However, the potential failure of closed questions to provide an appropriate set of alternatives meaningful in substance and wording to respondents can be avoided, according to the authors, by beginning a survey in an exploratory, pilot or pretesting phase with open questions, then using the resulting responses as a basis for developing closed responses. If this is done, differences discovered by Schuman and Presser in univariate distributions and in bivariate relations between open and closed forms are probably due more to interviewing and coding problems arising from open questions than to bias from closed questions.

Evidence presented by Collins (1980) suggests that some interviewers are more able than others to elicit (or faithfully record) responses to open questions. Furthermore, there is doubt over the reliability of coders to correctly classify responses to open questions. SPSS, in fact, offers a measure of inter-coder reliability called *Kappa*, which is available on the Analyze/Descriptive Statistics/ Crosstabs/Statistics procedure. This computes a simple index of reliability by considering all possible pairings of coders and seeing on what proportion they agree. This figure is then corrected for the amount of agreement that would be expected by chance.

Open questions are still, nevertheless, used in many surveys. Particularly where the number of respondents is likely to be perilously small for quantitative analysis, then having a larger than usual number of open questions will potentially provide the researcher with a more flexible and detailed basis for reporting the results. However, where the information required is relatively straightforward or the number of cases to be used is large, then as many as possible of the questions should be closed. Some questions may combine closed and open elements, for example there may be an 'Other, please specify' space for respondents to write in other items or comments at the bottom of a set of closed items.

SUMMARY

Open-ended questions leave respondents free to formulate their replies in their own words, which are then captured in a questionnaire or on tape. There are a number of reasons why researchers will do this rather than try to generate a set of closed response categories. As qualitative data, open responses may be collected together, summarised and used as a source of quotes. Coding, on the other hand, converts open responses into numerical codes that can be entered into SPSS and used in the same way as other quantitative variables. The coding of factual information is usually relatively straightforward. The coding of views, opinions, attitudes and so on is likely to be rather more complex and will be a subjective process undertaken either by the researcher or trained coders.

Summary continued

While closed questions should be used wherever possible, it is often a good idea to include a limited number anyway, even if only to alleviate the tedium of responding to long lists of closed items. Factual open-ended questions can, in fact, be more efficient in terms of space and detail than precoded ones.

Exercises

Below is a set of responses that have been collected from a question about why respondents drink a particular brand of beer. Generate a coding frame of about six or seven categories, giving each category a numeric code and indicate which items fit into which category.

1. Because it tastes better
2. I buy whatever beer is on sale
3. It has always been my brand
4. It's the brand my wife buys in the supermarket
5. It's my husband's favourite brand
6. Don't know
7. It has the best taste
8. It is the cheapest
9. I like the way it tastes
10. It doesn't upset my stomach in the way other brands do
11. I've been drinking it for over 20 years
12. All my friends drink it
13. I have no idea
14. I don't like the heavy taste of other beers
15. It is the brand that most of the blokes at work drink
16. Other brands give me headaches
17. No particular reason

Points for discussion

1. Should researchers always include at least one or two open-ended questions in a questionnaire?
2. Since the process of coding open answers is subjective, are the results necessarily less reliable than for closed questions?

Further reading

Collins, M. (1980) 'Interviewer Variability: A Review of the Problem', *Journal of the Market Research Society*, Vol. 22, No. 2, pp. 77–95.

Kolbe, R and Burnett, M (1991) 'Content-Analysis: An Examination of Applications with Directives for Improving Research Reliability and Objectivity', *Journal of Consumer Research*, September, pp. 243–50.

Meier, E. and Moy, C. (1991) 'Social classifications – a new beginning or less of the same?', *Journal of the Market Research Society*, Vol. 41, No. 2, pp. 135–51.

Miles, M. and Huberman, A. (1994) *Qualitative Data Analysis*, 2nd edn, London, Sage.

Schuman, H. and Presser, S. (1979) 'The Open and Closed Question', *American Sociological Review*, Vol. 44 October, pp. 692–712.

This article, although a little dated and rather more detailed than is really required in this context, nevertheless is one of the few systematic attempts to compare the results of complex open and closed questions within a framework of the standard large-scale attitude survey.

The Table Tennis Questionnaire

Thank you for agreeing to complete this questionnaire. It will only take you a few minutes. Please reply by putting a tick in the box or boxes that correspond with your answer.

All responses will be treated in strict confidence – no individual will be identifiable from the results of the survey.

When you have finished, please put the questionnaire in the envelope provided. No stamp is required.

1. In which league do you compete?

Bangor and District ☐ 1
Belfast ☐ 2
Greystone ☐ 3
Antrim ☐ 4

2. In which division do you compete?

First ☐ 1
Second ☐ 2
Third ☐ 3
Fourth ☐ 4

3. How many times on average do you play per week?

Once ☐ 1
Twice ☐ 2
Three times ☐ 3
Four times or more ☐ 4

4. Were you encouraged by anybody to take up the sport?

Yes ☐ 1
No ☐ 2 Go to Q6

5. If yes, was it:

A friend ☐ 1
Parent ☐ 2
Other relative ☐ 3
Teacher ☐ 4
Club leader ☐ 5
Other ☐ 6

6. At what age did you take up table tennis? _____

7. Where did you first play the sport? (Tick one only)

Primary school	☐ 1
Secondary school	☐ 2
Youth club	☐ 3
Youth organisation, e.g. scouts/guides	☐ 4
Table-tennis club	☐ 5
Coaching scheme	☐ 6
Leisure centre	☐ 7
Other	☐ 8

8. Would you please rate the importance you attach to the various aspects of playing table tennis listed below.

	Unimportant	Fairly unimportant	Neither	Fairly important	Very important
	1	2	3	4	5
Social benefits	☐	☐	☐	☐	☐
Competition	☐	☐	☐	☐	☐
Relaxation	☐	☐	☐	☐	☐
Health & fitness	☐	☐	☐	☐	☐
Enjoyment	☐	☐	☐	☐	☐

9. How satisfied are you with the following elements of table tennis in N. Ireland?

	Unsatisfied	Fairly unsatisfied	Neither	Fairly satisfied	Very satisfied
	1	2	3	4	5
Practice facilities	☐	☐	☐	☐	☐
Competition facilities	☐	☐	☐	☐	☐
Administration by ITTA	☐	☐	☐	☐	☐
Coaching opportunities	☐	☐	☐	☐	☐
Competitions	☐	☐	☐	☐	☐

10. Are you affiliated to the ITTA?   Yes ☐ 1   No ☐ 2

11. If table tennis was on TV more often, would you watch it?   Yes ☐ 1   No ☐ 2

12. Do you read articles on table tennis in the local papers?   Yes ☐ 1   No ☐ 2

13. What do you think could be done to encourage people to take up table tennis on a regular basis?

_____

_____

_____

14. What age are you?

Under 15 ☐ 1
15–24 ☐ 2
25–34 ☐ 3
35–44 ☐ 4
45–54 ☐ 5
55–64 ☐ 6
Over 65 ☐ 7

15. What sex are you?

Male ☐ 1
Female ☐ 2

16. What is your current occupation?

Manual ☐ 1
Non-manual ☐ 2
Self-employed ☐ 3
Retired ☐ 4
Student ☐ 5
Unemployed ☐ 6

17. Does anybody else in your household play table tennis?

Yes ☐ 1
No ☐ 2

18. Approximately how much have you spent on table tennis in the last 6 months?

_____

19. Which of the following sports do you play in addition to table tennis?
(Tick as many as apply)

Football ☐ 1
Tennis ☐ 2
Squash ☐ 3
Badminton ☐ 4

Thank you for completing this questionnaire. Please return in the envelope provided.

appendix 2

Using Pinpoint

> Pinpoint is a survey analysis package that allows the researcher to:
>
> - design questionnaires or data collection sheets,
> - enter data,
> - analyse the data.
>
> There are three main areas in which you will work on a PinPoint 'project'.
>
> - form design and editing,
> - form filling,
> - data analysis.

FORM DESIGN AND EDITING

Every new PinPoint project begins with the design of its 'form', or data collection sheet. When you work with a form in PinPoint you work with the Form Editor. The Editor can be thought of as a 'window' onto a form in which you can do several things.

- Format the page attributes of your form.
- Set up a multi-page form.
- Write and edit questions.
- Prepare your form for printing.
- Import answer data from other PinPoint projects or other applications.
- Edit an existing project's form and update the completed answer sheets in its stack.
- 'Send' a new form to the sheet editor for completion as the first answer sheet in a new stack.

The Form Editor allows you to describe the data to be collected (write questions), modify them, move them around the paper so they are presented in the required order, and add explanatory text and/or pictures, until you are satisfied.

Using PinPoint, there is no need to sketch out a design for your form and the questions to be asked before beginning in PinPoint, since PinPoint itself provides you with all the tools for sketching. As you are working on the form you can continually refine it by moving, adding and removing work – in many ways it is easier to work in PinPoint than it is to use pencil and paper.

From the File menu, choose New Project. A new form will be created as a single page of the size and orientation as described by the active printer.

Try the following exercise.

1. Click on the Pinpoint icon.
2. Click on File/New project.
3. Click on the Question tool (far left on the tool bar – descriptions of the buttons appear on the bottom of the screen as you move the mouse over them).
4. Hold down the mouse button and drag down and across to mark out the area into which the question will be placed. (Note that the precise sizing and placement is not important at this stage.) These can be changed later.
5. As you release the mouse button the Question Details dialog box will appear.
6. Type in 'Have you purchased a newspaper in the last week?' in the question area box (you can pick any other font by clicking on the Font button).
7. Click on the Reference name box. Delete what is already entered and type 'Newspaper'.
8. Click on the Yes/No radio button in the answer box.
9. Click on OK.
10. Double-click in the area of the question to return to the Question Details dialog box and try changing some of the style options.
11. Drag out the area for a new question. Type 'In which of the following age groups are you?'.
12. Put 'Age' into the Reference name box.
13. Click on Multiple choice.
14. Click on Add and type 'Under 20'. Click on OK.
15. Click on Add and type '20–39'. Click on OK.
16. Click on Add and type '40 plus'. Click on OK.
17. You can edit or delete any of these items.
18. Delete Left of text and click on Justify text to box. Click on OK.
19. Click on the pointer. Click on a question and try dragging it about the screen. Try moving the answer boxes.
20. Text may be added anywhere by clicking on A and using 'I' to indicate where the text is to go.
21. Add a couple of questions of your own.
22. Click on File, then Print Form.

FORM FILLING

A completed or 'filled in' copy of a form is known in PinPoint as an 'Answer sheet'. During answer sheet compilation a copy of the form is always displayed on screen. Answers can be entered directly onto the screen by your respondents, or else answer data can be 'copied in' from a collection of completed paper forms.

Because PinPoint's forms can contain many question 'formats' together with free-form text notes and built-in data entry checks, precise information can entered quickly and accurately.

1. Click on File then Save Form
2. You will obtain the Save As screen.
3. Give the file a name, change to H drive and save in your own directory It will be a '.ppf' file
4. Click on View, then *Answer sheets.*

5. Complete about 15 forms with fictional data by clicking on a range of different answers. At the end of each sheet click on Sheet then New, then Yes.
6. Now imagine you have 150 forms with 70 questions on each!

DATA ANALYSIS

A completed set of answer sheets is known as a 'stack'. When a stack of answer sheets has been compiled the sheets are placed into a 'worksheet' for analysis.
PinPoint's worksheets provide the tools for:

■ Displaying completed answer sheets in tabular form;
■ Sorting and selecting the sheets;
■ Performing statistical analyses on interval variables;
■ The production of graphs, charts and tables.
■ Under Save As one option is to save the worksheet as an SPSS file.

You can add new answer sheets to a stack, and edit or 'update' a project's form and any existing answer sheet(s) at any time:

1. Click on View/Worksheet.
2. Click on Quick Analysis – you will get the Quick Graphs dialog box.
3. Click on All.
4. Choose Counts or Percentages from the Analysis box.
5. Select a style from the Style Gallery – the one far left produces tables rather than graphs. Try it.
6. Click on OK – you will obtain the Table Properties dialog box.
7. Choose the calculations you want – I suggest On columns and Total. Click on OK.
8. You will obtain a univariate table for each variable.
9. To create a crosstabulation click on the Create a cross tab table icon.
10. You will then be invited to put in the variables you wish as the rows – highlight each variable and click on Add then OK.
11. Do the same for columns. Click on OK.
12. In the Crosstab Options box the Counts and Percentages by columns will be pre-selected. Choose the statistics you want. Click on &sans;Print – it will not show the table on screen, but will go straight to the printer.

THE PROJECT

PinPoint stores all project information – the form, the completed answer sheets, the worksheet and all its attributes and any associated graphical presentations – in a single '.ppf' project file.
Copying a project from one machine to another, therefore, is just a matter of copying a single project file into an existing PinPoint installation.

SPSS Release 10.0

SPSS Release 10.0 has an entirely new way of defining and labelling variables and values using a new *Variable View* screen, as shown on Figure A3.1. To obtain it, click on the Variable View tab at the bottom left of the Data Editor Window. Each variable now occupies a row rather than a column as in the Data Editor window. Enter the name of the first variable in the top left box. As soon as you hit Enter or down arrow or right arrow, the remaining boxes will be filled with default settings, except for Label. It is always better to enter labels, since these are what are printed out in your tables and graphs. For categorical variables, you will also need to put in Values and Value Labels. Click on the appropriate cell under Values and click again on the little grey box to the right of the cell. This will produce the Value Labels dialog box. Enter an appropriate value, for example, '1' and Value Label, for example, 'Male', and click on Add. Repeat for each value. The completed *Variable View* screen for the data used in Chapter 3 for SPSS Release 9.0 and illustrated in Figure 3.3 is shown in *Variable View* format in Figure A3.2.

Figure A3.1   **SPSS Release 10.0 'Variable View'**

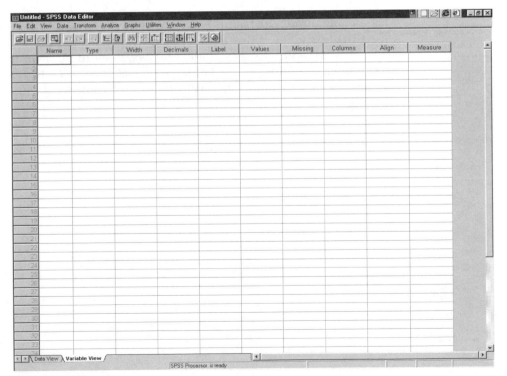

Figure A3.2 ***Completed 'Variable View' for Figure 3.3***

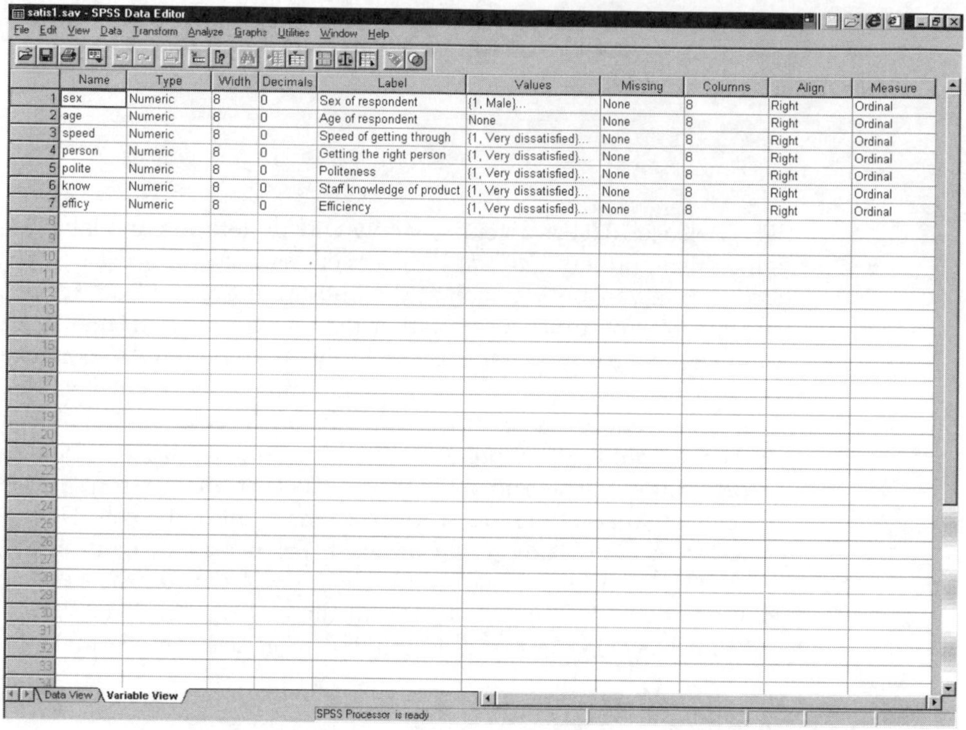

	Name	Type	Width	Decimals	Label	Values	Missing	Columns	Align	Measure
1	sex	Numeric	8	0	Sex of respondent	{1, Male}...	None	8	Right	Ordinal
2	age	Numeric	8	0	Age of respondent	None	None	8	Right	Ordinal
3	speed	Numeric	8	0	Speed of getting through	{1, Very dissatisfied}...	None	8	Right	Ordinal
4	person	Numeric	8	0	Getting the right person	{1, Very dissatisfied}...	None	8	Right	Ordinal
5	polite	Numeric	8	0	Politeness	{1, Very dissatisfied}...	None	8	Right	Ordinal
6	know	Numeric	8	0	Staff knowledge of product	{1, Very dissatisfied}...	None	8	Right	Ordinal
7	efficy	Numeric	8	0	Efficiency	{1, Very dissatisfied}...	None	8	Right	Ordinal

The default under Decimals is usually 2. If all the variables are integers, then it is worthwhile changing this to zero. Simply click on the cell and use the little down arrow to reduce to zero. Under Measure, you can put in the correct level of measurement – nominal, ordinal or scale (that is, interval/ratio/metric). To copy any variable information to another variable, like value labels, just use Edit/Copy and Paste.

Glossary

Ad hoc survey A 'one-off' piece of research that has a beginning point and an end point.

Analysis of variance A procedure for testing the statistical significance of differences in scores in an interval-scaled variable between categorical groups, samples or treatments.

Bar chart A graphical display in which each category of a categorical variable is depicted by a bar whose height or length represents the frequency or proportion of observations falling into each category.

Binary scale A scale that has two categories, one for cases that possess a characteristic and one for those that do not.

Bivariate analysis The display, summary or drawing of conclusions from the way in which two variables are related together.

Case Any member of the survey population whether or not they have responded by providing usable questionnaire returns.

Categorical scale A scale that consists at a minimum of sets of categories that are exhaustive, mutually exclusive and refer to a single dimension, but which may, in addition, possess order.

Causal analysis A study of the way in which some events or circumstances can produce or bring about other events or circumstances.

Causal research Research that analyses the degree of influence of one or more independent variables upon one or more dependent variables.

Census An attempt by a researcher to contact or to study every case or unit in the population.

Chi-square A statistic that measures the overall departure of a set of observations from some theoretical proposition. It adds up the squared differences between observed values and the values expected from the theoretical proposition taken as a proportion of the expected differences.

Clustering The random selection of cases or units in geographically concentrated areas.

Coding The transformation of edited questionnaires into machine-readable form.

Continuous research Measurements are taken on a periodic basis with no envisaged end or completion of the research process.

Continuous variable A scale whose values consist of calibrations that might generate potentially an unlimited number of scale values.

Correlation A measure of the extent to which the values of two interval variables covary and approximate a rising or a falling straight line in a scattergram.

Critical values Values that lie exactly on the boundary between accepting and rejecting the null hypothesis.

Chart Any form of graphical display of numerical information.

Cramer's V A statistical measure of association for two categorical variables that have been crosstabulated and based on the notion of departure from independence.

Cronbach's alpha A measure of scale reliability. It takes the average correlation among items in a summated rating scale and adjusts for the number of items.

Crosstabulation The frequencies of cases that combine a value on one categorical variable with values on another laid out in rows and columns.

Data Systematic records made by individuals

Data display The presentation of data in tables, charts or graphs.

Data dredging Data are explored in every conceivable way to see if any patterns emerge.

Data summary   Reducing the data in a univariate distribution or the relationship between two or more variables to a single statistic that acts as a summary.

Data matrix   A record of all the values for all the variables for al the cases laid out in rows and columns.

Dependent variable   A variable that is seen as an outcome or effect of an independent variable. A variable that the researcher is trying to predict, understand or explain.

Derived measurement   The use of two or more measures in some combination to generate a total or single score.

Descriptors   Variables used to describe a set of cases and not being studied for their relationships to other variables.

Descriptive research   Research that is concerned with measuring or estimating the sizes, quantities or frequencies of characteristics.

Dimension   A continuum that is a construct derived from combining two or more variables.

Direct measurement   A one-to-one correspondence between the concept and the variable used to measure. This is made possible either because the characteristic is concretely observable or because the researcher defines the concept in terms of the variable.

Discrete variable   A scale generated by counting the number of units contained in an entity as a measure of size.

Editing   The scrutiny of returned questionnaires to ensure that as far as possible they are complete, accurate and consistent.

Eta   A statistical measure of association where the independent variable is binary or nominal and the dependent variable is interval.

Estimation   Using the value of a statistic derived from a sample to estimate the value of the corresponding population parameter.

Explanation   A range of devices that may be used to clarify and make comprehensible to an audience.

Exploratory research   Research aimed at generating ideas, insights or hypotheses.

Frame errors   Errors arising from the use of lists of the population to be studied that have various shortcomings.

Frequency   The number of times a scale value occurs in a given distribution for a particular variable.

Frequency table   Frequencies of scale values, usually either categorical or grouped interval, laid out in a column.

Histogram   A graphical display for interval-scales variables in which the width of the bars represents class intervals and the length or height represents the frequency or proportion with which each interval occurs.

Hypothesis   A formal statement that the researcher makes about one or more variables that are the focus of the research, but which is as yet untested.

Independent variable   A variable that is treated as a cause or influence.

Indirect measurement   Taking an indicator of a concept as a variable measure of that concept.

Interval scale   A scale that arises from the processes of either calibration or counting.

Investigative research   Research that focuses on the extent of association or correlation between two or more variables.

Kurtosis   A measure of the distribution shape based on the extent to which values cluster about the mean compared with a normal distribution.

Labelling scale   A set of values in which each value identifies and labels only one case.

Likert scale   A summated rating scale derived from the summation of 5- or 7-point ratings of agreement or disagreement with a number of statements relating to an attitude object.

Mean   A measure of central tendency for interval-scaled variables calculated by totalling all the scale values in a distribution and dividing by the number of observations made.

Measurement   A process by which the characteristics or properties of respondents that are to be used as variables are specified.

Median   A measure of central tendency calculated by taking the value that splits all the observations for a variable into two halves arranged in an ascending or descending series.

Metric table   A table used to display metric quantities.

Mode   A measure of central tendency established by taking the most commonly occurring value in a distribution.

Multidimensional measurement   A concept that consists of two or more dimensions that are not totalled but either kept separate as a profile or as a point in multidimensional space.

Multivariate analysis   The display, summary or drawing of conclusions from variables taken three or more at a time.

Nominal scale   A set of scale values having three or more categories that are mutually exclusive, exhaustive and refer to a single dimension.

Non-parametric statistics   Statistics that do not assume that data are interval or that the mean or standard deviation can be calculated.

Normal distribution   A symmetrical bell-shaped distribution that describes the expected probability distribution for random events.

Null hypothesis   A statement made about a population of cases in advance of testing it on data.

Ordinal scale   A scale possessing all the characteristics of a nominal scale plus an implied order of the categories.

Parametric statistics   Statistics that assume interval data, and that the calculation of a mean or standard deviation is a legitimate operation.

Pie chart   A graphic in which the frequencies or proportion of each category of a categorical variable is represented by a slice of a circle.

Population   A total set of cases or other units that are the focus of the researcher's attention.

Population parameter   A variable relating to a total population of cases or units.

Purposive sample   A non-probability sample in which the selection of sampling units is made by the researcher using his or her own judgement or experience.

p-value   The probability in random sample of obtaining a value as extreme or more extreme than the one actually obtained if the null hypothesis were true.

Qualitative data   Systematic records that consist of words, text or images.

Quantitative data   Systematic records that consist of numbers constructed by utilising the dual processes of measurement and scaling.

Quota sample   A representative but non-probability sampling procedure that ensures that various subgroups of a population will be represented to an extent chosen by the researcher.

Random error   Error arising from a random sampling procedure in which there will be chance fluctuations.

Random sample   A probability sample in which the selection of sampling units is made by methods independent of human judgement. Each unit will have a known and non-zero probability of selection.

Randomisation   The selection of sampling units by chance.

Ranking scale   A set of scale values in which each case has its own rank. There are as many rankings as cases.

Regression   The use of a formula describing a straight line that represents the 'best fit' in a scattergram to predict the values of one interval-scaled variable from another.

Representative sample   The selection of sampling units in such a way that they attempt to reproduce the structure and features of a population of units.

Respondent   An individual to whom questions have been successfully addressed or who has completed specified information-giving tasks.

Sample   A subset of cases or other units from a total population.

Sample design   The particular mix of procedures used for the selection of sampling units in a particular piece of research.

Sampling error   The difference between the result of a sample and the result that would have been obtained from a census using identical procedures.

Sampling distribution   A theoretical distribution of a statistic for all possible samples of a given size that could be drawn from a particular population.

Sampling frame　A complete lists of the population of units or cases from which a sample is to be taken.

Sampling point　A designated geographical area within which an interviewer conducts his or her selection of cases or units.

Sampling unit　Whatever entity is being sampled.

Scale　A set of values that meet certain formal logical requirements.

Scaling　A process by which researchers select a value from a scale of values to enter into a data matrix.

Scattergram　A graphical display of the relationship between two interval-scaled variables in which each case is represented by a dot that reflects the position of two combined measurements.

Semantic differential scale　A multidimensional scale that represents a profile of characteristics expressed as bipolar opposites like 'sweet-sour' that constitutes a 7-point rating scale.

Simple random sample　Each sampling unit has an equal chance of being selected from a list.

Skewness　A measure of distribution shape based on the difference between the mean and median values in a distribution.

Social surveys　The systematic collection of data based on addressing questions to respondents in a formal manner and making a record of their replies.

Spearman's rho　A measure of correlation between two fully ranked scales.

Standard deviation　An average of deviations of values about the mean for a given statistic.

Standard error　The standard deviation of a sampling distribution.

Statistical inference　A process by which sample statistics are used to estimate population parameters or to test statements about a population with a known degree of confidence.

Stratification　A random sampling technique in which simple random sub-samples are drawn from separate groups or strata.

Summated rating scale　A measure derived from summing together two or more separate rating scales.

Survey population　The total set of cases in which the researcher is interested for the purpose of the research.

Systematic error　Error arising from sampling procedures that result in the over- or under-representation of particular kinds of sampling unit mostly in the same direction.

Systematic selection　The selection of sampling units using a rules that remove human judgement from the selection process.

Total survey error　The sum of all sources of error, both those arising from the sampling process plus non-sampling errors.

Unit　See sampling unit.

Univariate analysis　The display, summary or drawing of conclusions from a single variable or set of variables treated one at a time.

Value　The actual number or category recorded by the researcher, having made a selection from a scale of values.

Variable　A characteristic that varies at a minimum between two scale values. In a survey it is a dimension that respondents are responding about.

Z-test　A test against the null hypothesis carried out on a univariate hypothesis by comparing the result from a sample with a standardised normal distribution.

References

Albaum, A. (1997) 'The Likert scale revisited: an alternative version', *Journal of the Market Research Society*, Vol. 39, No. 2, pp. 331–48.

Alt, M. and Brighton, M. (1981) 'Analysing data: or telling stories?', *Journal of the Market Research Society*, Vol. 23, No. 4, pp. 209–19.

Armstrong, J. and Overton, T. (1977) 'Estimating Nonresponse Bias in Mail Surveys', *Journal of Marketing Research*, Vol. XIV, August, pp. 396–402.

Assael, H. and Keon, J. (1982) 'Nonsampling versus sampling errors in survey research', *Journal of Marketing*, Vol. 46, Spring, pp. 114–23.

Babbie, E. and Halley, F. (1998) *Adventures in Social Research: Data Analysis Using SPSS for Windows 95*, Thousand Oaks, California, Pine Forge Press.

Blalock, H. (1961, 1964) *Causal Inferences in Nonexperimental Research*, The University of North Carolina Press, USA.

Bond, R. and Saunders, P. (1999) 'Routes of success: influences on the occupational attainment of young British males', *British Journal of Sociology*, Vol. 50, No. 2, pp. 217–49.

Bourque, L. B. and Clark, V. A. (1992) *Processing Data: The Survey Example*, London, Sage.

Bowers, D. (1996) *Statistics from Scratch: An Introduction for Health Care Professionals*, Chichester, John Wiley and Sons.

Bowers, D. (1997) *Statistics Further from Scratch: An Introduction for Health Care Professionals*, Chichester, John Wiley and Sons.

Bowles, T. and Blyth, B. (1997) 'How do you like your data: raw, al dente or stewed?', *Journal of the Market Research Society*, Vol. 3, No. 1, pp. 163–74.

Brown, M. (1994) 'Estimating newspaper and magazine readership', in R. Kent (ed.), *Measuring Media Audiences*, London, Routledge.

Bryman, A. and Cramer, D. (1999) *Quantitative Data Analysis with SPSS Release 8 for Windows*, London, Routledge.

Churchill, G. (1979) 'A Paradigm for Developing Better Measures of Marketing Constructs', *Journal of Marketing Research*, Vol. XVI, pp. 64–73.

Churchill, G. (1999) *Marketing Research: Methodological Foundations*, 7th edn, Fort Worth, Texas, The Dryden Press.

Churchill, G. and Peter, J. (1984) 'Research Design Effects on the Reliability of Rating Scales: a Meta-Analysis', *Journal of Marketing Research*, Vol. XXI, November, pp. 360–75.

Collins, M. (1980) 'Interviewer variability: a review of the problem', *Journal of the Market Research Society*, Vol. 22, No. 2, pp. 77–95.

Cortina, J. M. (1993) 'What is Coefficient Alpha? An Examination of Theory and Applications', *Journal of Applied Psychology*, Vol. 78, No. 1, pp. 98–104.

Cronbach, L. (1951) 'Coefficient Alpha and the Internal Structure of Tests', *Psychometrika*, Vol. 16, No. 3, pp. 297–334.

De Maio, T. (1980) 'Refusals, Who, Where, and Why', *Public Opinion Quarterly*, Summer, pp. 223–33.

DeVellis, R. (1991) *Scale Development: Theory and Applications*, London, Sage.

Diamantopoulos, A. and Schlegelmilch, B. (1997) *Taking the Fear out of Data Analysis*, London, The Dryden Press.

Dibb, S. and Farhangmehr, M. (1994) 'Loglinear Analysis in Marketing', *Journal of Targeting, Measurement and Analysis for Marketing*, Vol. 2, No. 2, pp. 153–68.

Durand, R. and Lambert, Z. (1988) 'Don't Know Responses in Surveys: Analysis and Interpretational Consequences', *Journal of Business Research*, Vol. 16, No. 2, pp. 169–88.

Engel, J. and Blackwell, R. (1982) *Consumer Behaviour*, 4th edn, Chicago, Dryden Press.

Evans, N. (1995) *Using Questionnaires and Surveys to Boost Your Business*, London, Pitman Publishing.

Fink, A. (1995) *How to Analyse Survey Data*, London, Sage.

Fink, A. and Kosecoff, J. (1998) *How to Conduct Surveys: A Step-by-Step Guide*, 2nd edn, London, Sage.

Foster, J. (2000) *Data Analysis Using SPSS for Windows, Versions 8.0-10.0 A Beginner's Guide*, 2nd edn, London, Sage.

Hague, P. (1993) *Questionnaire Design*, London, Kogan Page.

Goh, M. and Lee, H. (1996) 'Local Franchising Development in Singapore', *Franchising Research: An International Journal*, Vol. 1, No. 3, pp. 8–20.

Hair, J., Anderson, R., Tatham, R. and Black, W. (1998) *Multivariate Data Analysis*, 5th edn, London, Prentice Hall International.

Honomicl, J. (1984) *Marketing Research People: Their Behind-the-Scenes Stories*, Chicago, Crain Books.

Hughes, J. (1980) *The Philosophy of Social Research*, London, Longman.

Kent, R. (1981) *A History of British Empirical Sociology*, London, Gower.

Kent, R. (1999) *Marketing Research: Measurement, Method and Application*, London, International Thomson Business Press.

Kinnear, P. and Gray, C. (1999) *SPSS for Windows Made Simple*, 3rd edn, Hove, Psychology Press.

Kish, L. (1965) *Survey Sampling*, New York, John Wiley.

Koerner, R. (1980) 'The design factor – an underutilised concept?', *European Research*, November, pp. 266–71.

Kolbe, R. and Burnett, M. (1991) 'Content-Analysis: An Examination of Applications with Directives for Improving Research Reliability and Objectivity', *Journal of Consumer Research*, September, pp. 243–50.

Lessler, J. and Kalsbeek, W. (1992) *Nonsampling Errors in Surveys*, New York, John Wiley and Sons.

Likert, R. (1932) 'A technique for the measurement of attitudes', *Archives of Psychology*, No. 40.

McDonald, C. and King, S. (1996) *Sampling the Universe: The growth, development and influence of market research in Britain since 1945*, Henley-on-Thames, NTC Publications Ltd.

Meier, E. (1991) 'Response rate trends in Britain', *Marketing and Research Today*, Vol. 19, June, pp. 120–3.

Meier, E and Moy, C. (1999) 'Social classifications – a new beginning or less of the same?', *Journal of the Market Research Society*, Vol. 41, No. 2, pp. 135–51.

Miles, M. and Huberman, A. (1994) *Qualitative Data Analysis*, 2nd edn, London, Sage.

Nunnally, J. (1978) *Psychometric Theory*, 2nd edn, New York, McGraw-Hill.

Oppenheim, A. (1993) *Questionnaire design, interviewing and attitude measurement*, 2nd edn, London, Pinter.

Peterson, R. (1994) 'A Meta-analysis of Cronbach's Coefficient Alpha', *Journal of Consumer Research*, Vol. 221, September, pp. 381–91.

Osgood, C., Suci, G. and Tannenbaum, P. (1957) *The Measurement of Meaning*, Chicago, Univeristy of Illinois Press.

Sapsford, R. (1999) *Survey Research*, London, Sage.

Schuman, H. and Presser, S. (1979) 'The Open and Closed Question', *American Sociological Review*, Vol. 44, October, pp. 692–712.

Spector, P. (1992) *Summated Rating Scale Construction: An Introduction*, London, Sage.

Selvin, H. (1957) 'A critique of tests of significance in survey research', *American Sociological Review*, Vol. 22, pp. 519–27.

Selvin, H. and Stuart, A. (1966) 'Data-Dredging Procedures in Survey Analysis', *The American Statistician*, June, pp. 20–3.

Stewart, D. (1982) 'Filling the Gap: A Review of the Missing Data Problem' in *An assessment of Marketing Thought and Practice*, American Marketing Association, Chicago, USA.

Thomas, S. (1999) *Designing Surveys That Work. A Step-by-Step Guide*, London, Sage.

Torgerson, W. (1958) *Theory and Methods of Scaling*, London, Wiley.

Tse, D., Lee, K., Vertinsky, I. and Wehrung, D. (1998) 'Does Culture Matter? A Cross-Cultural Study of Executives' Choice, Decisiveness, and Risk Adjustment in International Marketing', *Journal of Marketing*, October, pp. 81–92.

Traylor, M. (1983) 'Ordinal and Interval Scaling', *Journal of the Market Research Society*, Vol. 25, No. 4.

Weakliem, D. and Western, M. (1999) 'Class voting, social change, and the left in Australia, 1943–96', *British Journal of Sociology*, Vol. 50, No. 4, pp. 609–30.

Williams, W. and Goodman, M. (1971) 'A Simple Method for the Construction of Empirical Confidence Limits for Economic Forecasts', *Journal of the American Statistical Association*, Vol. 66, pp. 752–4.

Wolfe, A. (1987) *Sampling Error and Significance Tables for Research Executives*, Lichfield, Staffs, Industrial Marketing Research Association.

Youden, W. (1972) 'Enduring Values', *Technometrics*, Vol. 14, No. 1, pp. 1–10.

Index